Letters Written to and for Particular Friends, on the Most Important Occasions. Directing not Only the Requisite Style and Forms to be Observed in Writing Familiar Letters, but how to Think and act Justly and Prudently, ... The Third Edition

BOOKS printed for J. OSBORN, *in* Paternoster Row;
And J. *and* J. RIVINGTON, *in* St. Paul's Church-yard.

1. *Pamela; or, Virtue Rewarded.* In a Series of familiar Letters, from a beautiful young Damsel to her Parents. And afterwards, in her Exalted Condition, between her and Persons of Figure and Quality, upon the most Important and Entertaining Subjects in Genteel Life. In Four Volumes 8vo. Published in order to cultivate the Principles of Virtue and Religion in the Minds of the Youth of both Sexes. Adorned with 29 Copper Plates, designed and engraved by Mr. *Hayman* and Mr *Gravelot*. Price bound 1 *l*. 4 *s*.

2. *Pamela*, or, *Virtue Rewarded*. In Four Volumes 12mo. Price bound 12 *s*.

3. *Pamela; ou, La Vertu Recompenseé.* Traduit de l'Angloise. En Deux Tomes. Price 6 *s*.

4. *ÆSOP*'s Fables. With instructive Morals and Reflections, abstracted from Party Considerations, adapted to all Capacities; and designed to promote Religion, Morality, and universal Benevolence. Containing 240 Fables, with a Cut ingraved in Copper to each Fable. And the Life of *Æsop* prefixed. Price 2 *s*. 6 *d*.

N. B. *This is the Æsop referred to in several Parts of* Pamela.

5. Revelation examined with Candour, or, A fair Inquiry into the Sense and Use of the several Revelations expresly declared, or sufficiently implied, to be given to Mankind from the Creation, as they are found in the Bible. By a professed Friend to an honest Freedom of Thought in religious Inquiries. In 2 Volumes.

6. An Historical Account of the Life and Reign of *David* King of *Israel*. Interspersed with various Conjectures, Digressions, and Disquisitions. In which (among other Things) Mr. *Bayle*'s Criticisms upon the Conduct and Character of that Prince are fully considered. In 2 Volumes. By the Author of Revelation examined with Candour.

7. Fifteen Sermons upon Social Duties. By the Author of the Life of *David*.

LETTERS

Written TO and FOR

PARTICULAR FRIENDS,

On the most

Important OCCASIONS.

Directing not only the Requisite

STYLE *and* FORMS

To be Observed in WRITING

Familiar Letters;

But How to

THINK and ACT *Justly* and *Prudently*,

IN THE

COMMON CONCERNS

OF

HUMAN LIFE.

CONTAINING

One Hundred and Seventy-three LETTERS.

The THIRD EDITION.

LONDON

Printed for J. OSBORN, in *Pater-noster Row*;
J and J RIVINGTON, in *St Paul's Church-yard*;
and J. LEAKE, at *Bath*. M DCC XLVI.

PREFACE.

THE following Letters are publish'd at the Solicitation of particular Friends, who are of Opinion, that they will anſwer ſeveral good Ends, as they may not only direct the *Forms* requiſite to be obſerved on the moſt importaut Occaſions, but, what is more to the Purpoſe, by the Rules and Inſtructions contained in them, contribute to *mend the Heart*, and *improve the Underſtanding*.

NATURE, PROPRIETY of CHARACTER, PLAIN SENSE, and GENERAL USE, have been the chief Objects of the Author's Attention in the Penning of theſe Letters; and as he every-where aimed to write to the *Judgment*, rather than to the *Imagination*, he would chuſe, that they ſhould generally be found more *uſeful*

than

PREFACE.

than *diverting:* Tho' where the Subjects require *Strokes of Humour,* and *innocent Raillery,* it will be seen, perhaps, that the Method he has taken, was the Effect of *Choice,* and not merely of *Necessity.*

The Writer is no Friend to long Prefaces; but it may be necessary, however, to say, what he has *aimed at* in this Performance; and to leave his *Merit* in the *Execution* of it, to proper Judges.

He has endeavour'd then, in general, throughout the great Variety of his Subjects, to inculcate the Principles of *Virtue* and *Benevolence*; to describe *properly,* and recommend *strongly,* the SOCIAL and RELATIVE DUTIES; and to place them in such *practical* Lights, that the Letters may serve for Rules to THINK and ACT by, as well as Forms to WRITE after.

Particularly, he has endeavoured to point out the Duty of a *Servant,* not a *Slave;* the Duty of a *Master,* not a *Tyrant;* that of the *Parent,* not as a Person morose and sour, and hard to be pleased; but mild, indulgent, kind, and such an one as would rather govern by *Persuasion* than *Force.*

He

PREFACE.

He has endeavour'd to direct the young Man in the Choice of his *Friends* and *Companions*; to excite him to *Diligence*; to discourage *Extravagance, Sottishness,* and *Vice* of all Kinds.

He has aimed to set forth, in a Variety of Cases, to *both Sexes,* the Inconveniencies attending *unsuitable Marriages*; to expose the Folly of a *litigious Spirit*; to console the *Unhappy*; to comfort the *Mourner:* And many of these by Arguments, tho' *easy* and *familiar,* yet *new* and *uncommon.*

With regard to the Letters of *Courtship,* the Author has aimed to point out such Methods of Address, to a young Man, as may stand the Test of the *Parents Judgment,* as well as the *Daughter's Opinion*; and, at the same time, that they should not want the proper Warmth of Expression, which Complaisance, and Passion for the beloved Object, inspire (and is so much expected in Addresses of this Nature), they should have their Foundation laid in *common Sense,* and a *manly Sincerity*; and, in a Word, be such as a *prudent Woman* need not blush to receive, nor a *discreet Man* be ashamed to look back

PREFACE.

back upon, when the *doubtful Courtship* is changed into the *matrimonial Certainty*.

With this View he has also attempted to expose the *empty Flourishes*, and *incoherent Rhapsodies*, by which *shallow Heads*, and *designing Hearts*, endeavour to exalt their Mistresses into *Goddesses*, in hopes of having it in their Power to sink them into the Characters of the *most Credulous* and *Foolish* of their Sex.

Orphans, and *Ladies* of *independent Fortunes*, he has particularly endeavour'd to guard against the insidious Arts of their *flattering* and *selfish* Dependents, and the *clandestine* Addresses of *Fortune-hunters*, those Beasts of Prey, as they may well be called, who spread their *Snares* for the *innocent* and *thoughtless* Heart.

These, among other no less material Objects, have been the Author's principal *Aim*: How well he has *succeeded*, must, as has been hinted, be left to the Judgment of the candid Reader.

THE

THE
CONTENTS
OF THE
LETTERS.

I. *TO a Father, against putting a Youth of but moderate Parts to a Profession that requires more extensive Abilities.* Page 1
II. *From an Uncle to a Nephew, on his keeping bad Company, bad Hours, &c. in his Apprenticeship.* 5
III. *From a Widow-Mother, in Answer to her Son's complaining of Hardships in his Apprenticeship.* 9
IV. *From an Uncle to the Youth, on the same Occasion.* 11
V. *From an Apprentice to an Uncle, about a Fraud committed by his Fellow-Apprentice.* 12
VI. *The Uncle's Answer.* ibid.
VII. *Advice from a Father to a young Beginner, what Company to chuse, and how to behave in it.* 13
VIII. *General Rules for agreeable Conversation in a young Man. From a Father to a Son.* 16
IX. *An elder to a younger Brother, who is in Love with a young Lady of great Gaiety, &c.* 18
X. *An elder to an extravagant younger Brother.* 20
XI. *To a young Man too soon keeping a Horse.* 21
XII. *Against a sudden Intimacy, or Friendship, with one of a short Acquaintance.* 25
XIII. *A young Man in Business, to a Father, desiring Leave to address his Daughter.* 26

A 4 XIV. *To*

CONTENTS.

XIV. *To the Daughter (on the Father's Allowance), apprising her of his intended Visit* Page 27

XV. *From a young Lady to her Father, acquainting him with a Proposal of Marriage made to her.* 28

XVI. *The Father's Answer, on a Supposition, that he approves not of the young Man's Addresses.* 29

XVII. *The Father's Answer, on a Supposition, that he does not disapprove of them* 30

XVIII *The young Gentleman to the Father, apprising him of his Affection for his Daughter.* 31

XIX. *From the Cousin to the Father and Mother in Commendation of the young Gentleman.* 32

XX. *From the Father, in Answer to the young Gentleman.* 33

XXI. *From the young Gentleman to his Mistress, on her Arrival at her Father's.* 35

XXII. *From a Brother to his Sister in the Country, upbraiding her for being negligent in Writing* 36

XXIII. *In Answer to the preceding.* 37

XXIV. *From the Daughter to her Mother, in Excuse for her Neglect.* 38

XXV. *From a Son-in-law to his Wife's Father, acquainting him with his Wife's Illness* ibid.

XXVI. *From a Country Chapman beginning Trade, to a City Dealer, offering his Correspondence.* 39

XXVII. *In Answer to the foregoing* 40

XXVIII. *From a Maid-servant in Town, acquainting her Father and Mother in the Country with a Proposal of Marriage, and asking their Consents.* ibid.

XXIX. *From the Parents, in Answer to the preceding.* 41

XXX. *From the same, acquainting her Parents with her Marriage.* ibid.

XXXI. *Recommending a superior Man-servant.* 42

XXXII *Recommending a Wet-nurse* 43

XXXIII. *Recommending a Cook-maid* ibid.

XXXIV. Re-

CONTENTS.

XXXIV. *Recommending a Chamber-maid.* Page 44
XXXV. *Recommending a Nursery-maid.* ibid.
XXXVI *A Father to a Son, to dissuade him from the Vice of Drinking to Excess.* 45
XXXVII. *The same Subject pursued.* 47
XXXVIII. *From an Apprentice to his Master, begging Forgiveness for a great Misdemeanour.* 49
XXXIX. *The Master's Answer* 50
XL. *From an Apprentice to his Friends, in Praise of his Master and Family.* 51
XLI. *Another from an Apprentice, where the Master is too remiss in his own Affairs.* 52
XLII *To a Country Correspondent, modestly requesting a Balance of Accounts between them.* 53
XLIII *In Answer to the preceding.* ibid.
XLIV. *A more pressing and angry Letter from a City Dealer on the same Account.* 54
XLV. *In Answer to the preceding.* 55
XLVI *To a young Trader generally in a Hurry in Business, advising* Method *as well as* Diligence. 56
XLVII. *From a Son reduced by his own Extravagance, requesting his Father's Advice, on his Intention to turn Player.* 59
XLVIII. *The Father's Answer, setting forth the Inconveniencies and Disgrace attending the Profession of a Player.* 60
XLIX. *To a Brother too captious to bear himself the Ridicule he practises upon others.* 61
L. *To a Friend, on his Recovery from a dangerous Illness* 63
LI. *On the same Occasion.* ibid.
LII. *In Answer to the preceding.* 64
LIII. *To a young Lady, advising her not to change her Guardians, nor to encourage any clandestine Address.* ibid.
LIV. *From a Mother to a Daughter, jealous of her Husband.* 67

LV. *The*

CONTENTS.

LV. *The Subject continued.* Page 68
LVI. *From a tender Father to an ungracious Son.* 71
LVII. *The Son's dutiful Answer.* 74
LVIII. *To a Friend, on Occasion of his not answering his Letters.* 76
LIX *In Answer to the preceding.* ibid.
LX. *From a Father to a Son, on his Negligence in his Affairs.* 77
LXI *The Son's grateful Answer.* 78
LXII. *A young Woman in Town to her Sister in the Country, recounting her narrow Escape from a Snare laid for her on her first Arrival, by a wicked Procuress.* 79
LXIII. *To a Daughter in a Country Town, who encourages the Address of a Subaltern [A Case too frequent in Country Towns].* 84
LXIV. *Expostulations from a grave Friend to a young Man, on his slighting and irreverent Behaviour to his Father.* 86
LXV. *Against too great a Love of Singing and Musick.* 90
LXVI. *From a Daughter to her Father, pleading for her Sister, who had married without his Consent.* 93
LXVII. *The Father's Answer.* 94
LXVIII. *To a Brother, against making his Wife and Children the constant Subject of Praise in Conversation.* 95
LXIX. *From a Father to a Daughter, in Dislike of her Intention to marry at too early an Age.* 97
LXX. *From a Father to a Daughter against a frothy French Lover.* 99
LXXI. *A modest Lover, desiring an Aunt's Favour to her Niece.* 100
LXXII. *The Aunt's Answer, supposing the Gentleman deserves Encouragement.* 101

LXXIII. *The*

CONTENTS.

LXXIII. *The Answer, supposing the Gentleman is not approved.* Page 102

LXXIV. *From a respectful Lover to his Mistress.* ibid.

LXXV. *The Answer.* 103

LXXVI. *A humorous Epistle of neighbourly Occurrences and News, to a Bottle Companion abroad.* 104

LXXVII *From a Nephew to his Aunt, on his slow Progress in a Courtship Affair.* 108

LXXVIII. *The Aunt's Answer, encouraging him to persevere.* 110

LXXIX. *A Gentleman to a Lady, professing an Aversion to the tedious Forms of Courtship.* 111

LXXX. *The Lady's Answer, encouraging a farther Declaration.* 112

LXXXI. *The Gentleman's Reply, more explicitly avowing his Passion.* 113

LXXXII *The Lady's Answer to his Reply, putting the Matter on a sudden Issue.* 114

LXXXIII. *A facetious young Lady to her Aunt, ridiculing her serious Lover.* ibid.

LXXXIV. *Her Aunt's Answer, reprehending her ludicrous Turn of Mind.* 117

LXXXV. *From a Gentleman to his Mistress, resenting her supposed Coquetry.* 119

LXXXVI. *The Lady's angry Answer.* 120

LXXXVII. *The Gentleman's submissive Reply.* 121

LXXXVIII. *The Lady's forgiving Return.* 122

LXXXIX. *Ridiculing a romantick Rhapsody in Courtship* 123

XC. *Against a young Lady's affecting manly Airs; and also censuring the modern Riding-habits.* 124

XCI. *A Father to a Daughter, relating to three Persons of different Characters proposed to him, each for her Husband; with his Recommendation of one in Years.* 126

XCII. *Her*

CONTENTS.

XCII. *Her Answer, dutifully expostulating on the Case.* Page 129

XCIII. *His Reply, urgently enforcing, but not compelling, her Compliance with his Desire* 130

XCIV. *To a rich Widow Lady with Children, dissuading her from marrying a Widower of meaner Degree, who has Children also.* 133

Instructions to young Orphan Ladies, as well as others, how to judge of Proposals of Marriage made to them without their Guardians or Friends Consent, by their Milaners, Mantua-makers, and other Go-betweens. 136

XCV. *From the young Lady, to the clandestine Proposer of the Match.* 141

XCVI. *To a young Fellow who makes Love in a romantick manner. By the Hand of a Friend* 142

XCVII. *Another less affronting on the same Occasion.* 143

XCVIII *Another still less severe, but not encouraging.* ibid.

XCIX. *To rebuke an irregular Address, when it is not thought proper wholly to discourage it.* 144

C. *Another for a Lady referring to a Guardian, or chosen Friend.* ibid.

CI. *Another to the same Purpose.* 145

CII. *From a Town-Tenant to his Landlord, excusing Delay of Payment.* ibid.

CIII. *From a Country Tenant to the same Purpose.* 146

CIV. *The Landlord's Answer.* ibid.

CV. *A threatening Letter from a Steward on Delay of Payment.* 147

CVI. *The poor Tenant's moving Answer.* ibid.

CVII. *The Steward's Reply, giving more Time.* 148

CVIII. *The poor Man's thankful Letter in Return.* 149

CIX. *An Offer of Assistance to a Friend, who has received*

CONTENTS.

received great Loſſes by a Perſon's Failure. Page 150

CX *The Friend's Anſwer, accepting the kind Offer.* ibid.

CXI *The Friend's Anſwer, ſuppoſing he has no Occaſion for the Offer.* 151

CXII. *Of Conſolation to a Friend in Priſon for Debt.* ibid.

CXIII. *In Anſwer to the preceding.* 153

CXIV. *To a Perſon of Note, in Acknowlegement of great Benefits received* 154

CXV. *Another for Favours of not ſo high, yet a generous Nature.* 155

CXVI. *An Excuſe to a Perſon who wants to borrow Money.* ibid.

CXVII. *On the ſame Subject.* 156

CXVIII. *Another on the ſame.* ibid.

CXIX. *To a Friend, in Compliance with his Requeſt to borrow a Sum of Money.* ibid.

CXX. *Another on the ſame Occaſion, limiting the Payment to a certain Time.* 157

CXXI *To a Friend, on a Breach of Promiſe in not returning Money lent in his Exigence.* ibid.

CXXII. *To a Friend, who had promiſed to lend a Sum of Money, to anſwer a critical Exigence, and drove it off to the laſt.* 158

CXXIII. *The Anſwer, excuſing the Pain he had given his Friend by his Remiſſneſs.* 159

CXXIV. *To one who, upon a very ſhort Acquaintance, and without any viſible Merit, but Aſſurance, wants to borrow a Sum of Money.* 160

CXXV. *A Gentleman to a Lady, who humourouſly reſents his Miſtreſs's Fondneſs of a Monkey, and Indifference to himſelf.* 161

CXXVI. *A Sailor to his betrothed Miſtreſs.* 162

CXXVII. *Her Anſwer.* 164

CXXVIII. *A Sea-Officer to his Wife.* 165

CXXIX. *A*

CONTENTS.

CXXIX. *A Wife to her Husband at Sea.* Page 166
CXXX. *To a Father, on his Neglect of his Childrens Education.* 168
CXXXI. *From a young Maiden, abandoned by her Lover for the sake of a greater Fortune.* 171
CXXXII. *From a Gentleman to his Mistress, who, seeing no Hopes of Success, respectfully withdraws his Suit.* 173
CXXXIII. *From a Lady to a Gentleman, who had obtained all her Friends Consent, urging him to decline his Suit to her.* 174
CXXXIV. *The Gentleman's Answer to the Lady's uncommon Request.* 176
CXXXV. *The Lady's Reply, in case of a Prepossession.* 177
CXXXVI. *The Lady's Reply, in case of no Prepossession, or that she chuses not to avow it.* 178
CXXXVII. *A Lady to a Gentleman of superior Fortune, who, after a long Address in an honourable way, proposes to live with her as a Gallant.* 179
CXXXVIII. *A Father to a Daughter in Service, on hearing of her Master's attempting her Virtue.* 181
CXXXIX. *The Daughter's Answer.* 182
CXL. *To a Gentleman of Fortune, who has Children, dissuading him from a Second Marriage with a Lady much younger than himself.* ibid.
CXLI. *The same Subject pursued.* 185
CXLII. *Against a Second Marriage, where there are Children on both Sides.* 188
CXLIII. *Against a second Marriage, where there are Children on one Side, and a Likelihood of more.* 193
CXLIV. *Advising a Friend against going to Law.* 197
CXLV. *To a young Lady, cautioning her against keeping Company with a Gentleman of bad Character.* 200

CXLVI. *From*

CONTENTS.

CXLVI. *From a Mother to her high-spirited Daughter, who lives on uneasy Terms with her Husband.* Page 201

CXLVII. *A Lady to her Friend, a young Widow Lady, who, having buried a polite and excellent Husband, inclines to marry a less deserving Gentleman, and of unequal Fortune.* 205

CXLVIII. *From a Gentleman, strenuously expostulating with an old rich Widow, about to marry a very young gay Gentleman.* 209

CXLIX. *From a young Lady in Town to her Aunt in the Country.* 1. *Describing the* Tower, Monument, St. Paul's, &c. 212

CL. 2. *Describing other remarkable Places in and about* London *and* Westminster, *which are generally shewn to Strangers.* 214

CLI. 3. *Describing* Chelsea *Hospital, and* Kensington *Palace.* 217

CLII. 4. *Describing* Greenwich *Park, and the Passage to it by Water.* 218

CLIII. 5. *Describing* Bethlehem *Hospital.* 220

CLIV. 6. *Diversions of* Vaux-hall *described.* 222

CLV. 7. *An Account of* Westminster-Abbey. 225

CLVI. 8. *Account of* Westminster-Abbey *continu'd.* 228

CLVII. 9. *On a Concert, or Musical Entertainment.* 232

CLVIII. 10. *On the Diversions of the Playhouse.* 234

CLIX. 11. *The Play, and the low Scenes of* Harlequinery *after it, described and exposed.* 236

CLX. *From a Country Gentleman in Town, to his Brother in the Country, describing a publick Execution in* London. 239

Five Letters which passed between an Aunt and her Niece, in relation to her Conduct in the Addresses made her by two Gentlemen; one a gay fluttering military

CONTENTS.

military Coxcomb, the other a Man of Senſe and Honour. Page 242

CLXI. 1 *From the Aunt to the Niece, deſiring her Niece's own Opinion of the two Lovers.* ibid.

CLXII. 2. *The Niece's Anſwer · Deſcribing the Behaviour of the ſenſible Lover.* 243

CLXIII. 3. *Continuing the Deſcription of the Behaviour of the ſame Gentleman; which occaſions a Love-quarrel.* 245

CLXIV 4. *From the ſame: Deſcribing her fluttering Pretender.* 248

CLXV. 5. *From the Aunt, containing ſolid Advice and Cautions on this Occaſion.* 250

CLXVI. *From a Lady to her falſe Lover, who, after having braved all his Friends Expoſtulations, at laſt is perſuaded to abandon her for another of larger Fortune.* 253

CLXVII. *From a Gentleman to his Lady, whoſe Over-niceneſs in her Houſe, and uneaſy Temper with her Servants, make their Lives uncomfortable.* 255

CLXVIII. *From a Gentleman who in a ſmall Fortune experiences the Slights of his Friends; but, being ſuddenly reputed to be rich, is oppreſſed with the fawning Careſſes and Adulation of thoſe who had before neglected him.* 258

CLXIX. *From one Brother to another, on the raſh Marriage of a beloved Daughter of one of them, to a profligate young Fellow.* 262

CLXX. *The afflicted Father, in Anſwer to the preceding* 264

CLXXI *To a Father, on the Loſs of his Son, who died under Age.* 265

CLXXII *To a Father, on the Loſs of a hopeful Son, who died at Man's Eſtate.* 266

CLXXIII. *To a Widow, on the Death of her Husband.* 270

Familiar

Familiar LETTERS

On the most

IMPORTANT OCCASIONS

IN

COMMON LIFE.

LETTER I.

To a Father, against putting a Youth of but moderate Parts to a Profession that requires more extensive Abilities.

Dear Sir,

OU pay me a Compliment, tho' a very obliging one, when, in the last Letter you favoured me with, you desire my Advice, with respect to the Disposition of your Son *William*; whom you are inclin'd to bring up to the Bar. If, in complying with your Request, I should say any thing you may not intirely approve, you will not have so much room to blame me, as your own wrong Choice of a Counsellor.

I need not now tell you, I have a good Opinion of *Will*; and think him a modest, grave, sober, Youth: But, for this very Reason, I hardly think him qualified for the Profession you would chuse for him; for, I doubt, he has neither Talents for the Law, nor ever will have the Presence of Mind necessary to make a Figure at the Bar. In any smooth, easy Business, he will probably succeed, and be a useful Member of the Commonwealth. And as he is not your eldest Son, I should, were it to me, put him to a Merchant, or, as we live in an Island, and Trade and Navigation are both our Riches and our Glory, I should not even scruple to put a *second* Son to a creditable wholesale Dealer, rather than fail; if he himself is not averse to such a Calling. For I know not (you'll excuse me, I'm sure) whether *Will*'s Genius is equal to that of an universal Merchant: For, the various Springs of Commerce, the Seasons for chusing proper Commodities, and numberless Incidents that make a necessary Return of Gain precarious, are full Imployment for the strongest Judgment; as a Man, by one ill-chosen Venture, often loses more than he gains by several successful ones.

But this Opinion of *Will*, should you think it just, will be no Obstacle to his succeeding in the World in some creditable easy Business. Tho' I think him unequal to the Part you seem inclinable to allot him; yet he is no Fool: And Experience teaches us, that, in some sorts of Business, ample Advantage may be made by very moderate Talents, with much Reputation. These are principally such Employments as merely consist in Buying with Prudence, and in Selling at a Market-profit: Hence we see several Wholesale Dealers gain large Fortunes with Ease and Credit, and without any other Secret than the plain Practice of

Buying

Buying at the beſt Hand, paying for their Goods punctually, and vending them always *for what they are*. In Dealings of this Kind, the Fatigues are few, and clear well-kept Books are ſufficient to ſhew, at any time, a Man's Loſs or Gain; for which, generally ſpeaking, leſs than One Forenoon in a Week is ſufficient: And yet, by a conſtant Attention, in this eaſy manner, as *good* a Character, and, very often, *more* Money is to be gained than in Profeſſions that require an extraordinary Genius, a perpetual Attention, and a cloſe and intenſe Study; which very ſeldom ſucceeds neither: For ſee you not of Hundreds of Lawyers, how very few of them make a Figure, or get genteel Bread? And how many, for want of Courage to appear at the Bar (who yet have good Parts and Knowledge in the Laws), are forced to confine themſelves to Chamber-practice, in which it is a long time before they grow noted enough to make a tolerable Livelihood?

As to what you hint, of placing him in the Phyſick Tribe; I like this no better than the other. Conſider only this one Thing, how long it is before he will be capable of entering into Buſineſs, or Reputation, as a Phyſician, if he ever does it at all For who chuſes to truſt his Health to a raw and unexperienced young Man? The Law requires a ſprightly Impudence, if I may ſo ſay, the Phyſick Line a ſolemn one, in the Perſon who would make a Figure in either. And do you think, tho' *Will* is grave enough of Conſcience, that he ever can come up to that important Deportment, that unbluſhing Parade, which is the very Eſſence of an *Engliſh* Phyſician? So he may, in either of the Profeſſions, live over all his Days, and be quite unknown; for, as *Practice* in both Faculties is the beſt Teacher, and *Theory* a moſt uncertain Guide, he may live to be Forty or Fifty Years of Age, and not come into any Bufinefs that fhall improve himfelf, or benefit his Confulters.

Whereas in the way I propofe, no fooner is he come of Age, and fit to be trufted with the Management of any Affairs at all, but his Seven Years will be expired; and if he has not been wanting to himfelf in it (and if he be, he would have been much more fo in an abftrufer Bufinefs), he will be enabled, with the Fortune you can beftow upon him, to enter upon the Stage of the World with great Advantage, and become *directly*, a neceffary and an ufeful Member of the Community. And, my good Friend, when you and I recollect, that moft of the noble Families in the Kingdom, as well as the genteel ones, had the Foundations of their Grandeur laid in Trade, I expect not, in fuch a Country as ours efpecially, that any Objection to my Advice will be form'd, either by you or your good Lady, on this Score, if you have not more fignificant Reafons proceeding from the Boy's Turn of Mind and Inclination; which, I think, fhould always be confulted on thefe Occafions. For tho' I hope it never will be fo in your Cafe, yet nothing has been more common, than that of Two Sons, the Eldeft brought up to the Eftate, the other to Trade, in the Revolution of Twenty or Thirty Years, the latter, thro' the Extravagance of the former, has made himfelf *Eldeft*, as I may fay, for, by faving while the other has been fpending, he has found Means to keep the Eftate in the Family, tho' it has been transferr'd upon the *youngeft*, and, as it has then proved, the *worthieft* Branch.

This, I think, deferves your Confideration, and by viewing *Will* in the fame Light I do, that of a well-inclined Lad, of moderate Paffions, great natural Modefty, and no foaring Genius, I believe you
will

will think it best to dispose of him in such manner as may require no greater Talents than he is possessed of, and may, in due Time, make him appear in the Face of the World fully qualified for what he undertakes. I am, Sir,

Your very humble Servant.

LETTER II.

From an UNCLE *to a* NEPHEW, *on his keeping bad Company, bad Hours,* &c. *in his Apprenticeship.*

Dear Nephew,

I AM very much concerned to hear, that you are of late fallen into bad Company; that you keep bad Hours, and give great Uneasiness to your Master, and break the Rules of his Family That when he expostulates with you on this Occasion, you return pert and bold Answers; and, instead of promising or endeavouring to amend, repeat the Offence, and have enter'd into Clubs and Societies of young Fellows, who set at nought all good Example, and make such Persons who would do their Duty, the Subject of their Ridicule, as Persons of narrow Minds, and who want the Courage to do as they do.

Let me, on this Occasion, expostulate with you, and set before you the Evil of the Way you are in.

In the first Place What can you mean by breaking the Rules of a Family you had bound yourself

self by Contract to observe? Do you think it is *honest*, to break thro' Engagements into which you have so solemnly entered; and which are no less the Rules of the Corporation you are to be one Day free of, than those of a private Family?—— Seven Years, several of which are elapsed, are not so long a Term, but that you may see it determined before you are over-fit to be trusted with your own Conduct: Twenty-one or Twenty-two Years of Age, is full early for a young Man to be his own Master, whatever you may think; and you may surely stay till *then*, at least, to chuse your own Hours, and your own Company; and, I fear, as you go on, if you do not mend your Ways, your Discretion will not *then* do Credit to your Choice. Remember, you have no Time you can call your own, during the Continuance of your Contract: And must you abuse your Master in a double Sense, rob him of his Time, especially if any of it be Hours of Business; rob him of his Rest, break the Peace of his Family, and give a bad Example to others? And all for what? Why to riot in the Company of a Set of Persons, who contemn, as they teach you to do, all Order and Discipline, who, in all Likelihood, will lead you into Gaming, Drinking, Swearing, and even more dangerous Vices, to the Unhinging of your Mind from your Business, which must be your future Support.

Consider, I exhort you, in time, to what these Courses may lead you. Consider the Affliction you will give to all your *Friends*, by your Continuance in them. Lay together the Substance of the Conversation that passes in a whole Evening, with your frothy Companions, after you are come from them; and reflect what solid Truth, what useful Lesson, worthy of being inculcated in your

future

future Life, that whole Evening has afforded you; and confider, whether it is worth breaking thro' all Rule and Order for? —— Whether your prefent Conduct is such as you would allow in a Servant of your own? Whether you are so capable to pursue your Business with that Ardor and Delight next Morning, as if you had not drank, or kept bad Hours, over Night? If not, whether your Mafter has not a double Loss and Damage from your mis-spent Evenings? Whether the taking of small Liberties, as you may think them, leads you not on to greater? for, let me tell you, you will not find it in your Power to stop when you will: And then, whether any Restraint at all will not in time be irksome to you?

I have gone thro' the like Servitude with Pleasure and Credit. I found myself my own Master full soon for my Discretion. What you think of yourself I know not; but I wish you may do as well for your own Interest, and Reputation too, as I have done for mine. And I'll assure you, I should not have thought it either creditable or *honest* to do as you do. I could have stood the Laugh of an Hundred such vain Companions as you chufe, for being too narrow-minded to break through all moral Obligations to my Master, in order to shew the Bravery of a bad Heart, and what an abandon'd Mind dared to perpetrate. A bad Beginning seldom makes a good Ending, and if you were affured that you could stop when you came for yourself, which is very improbable, how will you answer it to Equity and good Conscience, that you will not do so for your Master? There is, let me tell you, more true Bravery of Mind in forbearing to do an Injury, than in giving Offence.

You are now at an Age, when you should study to *improve*, not *divert*, your Faculties. You should now lay in a Fund of Knowlege, that in time, when ripened by Experience, may make you a worthy Member of the Commonwealth. Do you think you have nothing to learn, either as to your Business, or as to the forming of your Mind? Would it not be much better to chuse the silent, the sober Conversation of Books, than of such Companions as never read or think? An Author never commits any but his best Thoughts to Paper; but what can you expect from the laughing noisy Company you keep, but frothy Prate, indigested Notions, and Thoughts so unworthy of being remember'd, that it is the greatest Kindness to forget them?

Let me intreat you then, my dear Kinsman, for your Family's sake, for your own sake, before it be too late, to reflect as you ought upon the Course you are enter'd into. By applying yourself to Books, instead of such vain Company, you will be qualified in time for the best of Company, and to be respected by all Ranks of Men. This will keep you out of unnecessary Expences, will employ all your leisure Time, will exclude a world of Temptations, and open and inlarge your Notions of Men and Things, and, finally, set you above that wretched Company which now you seem so much delighted with. And one Thing let me recommend to you, That you keep a List of the young Men of your Standing within the Compass of your Knowlege, and for the next Seven Years observe what Fate will attend them: See, if those who follow *not* the Course you are so lately enter'd into, will not appear in a very different Light from those who *do*, and from the Industry and Prosperity of the one, and the Decay or Failure of the other (if their vain Ways do not blast them before, or as soon as they begin the World), you'll find abundant Reason every

Day

Day to justify the Truth of the Observations I have thrown together. As nothing but my Affection for you could possibly influence me to these Expostulations, I hope for a proper Effect from them, if you would be thought well of by, or expect any Favour from,

Your loving Uncle.

Your Master will, at my Request, send me word of the Success of my Remonstrance.

LETTER III.

A Widow-Mother's Letter, in Answer to her Son's complaining of Hardships in his Apprenticeship.

Dear Billy,

I AM very sorry to hear of the Difference between your Master and you. I was always afraid you would expect the same Indulgences you had met with at home; and as you know, that in many Instances, I have endeavoured to make any seeming Hardship as easy to you as I could, if this causes you to be harder to be satisfied, it would be a great Trouble to me. Your Uncle tells me, I am afraid with too much Truth, that the Indulgences you have received from me, have made your present Station more disagreeable than it would otherwise have been. What I have always done for you was intended for your Good, and nothing could so deeply afflict me as to see my Tenderness have a contrary Effect. Therefore, dear Child, to my constant Care for your Welfare, do not add the Sorrow of seeing it the Cause of your behaving worse than if it had not been bestow'd upon you, for as, before we put you to your Master, we had an extraordinary Character of him, from all his Neighbours, and those who dealt with him, and as Mr *Joseph*, who is now out of his Time, gives him the best of Characters, and declares your Mistress to be a Woman of great Prudence and good Conduct; I know not how to think they would use you ill in any respect. But consider, my Dear, you must not, in any Woman beside myself, expect to find a fond, and perhaps partial Mother; for, the little Failings which I could not see in you, will appear very plain to other Persons. My Love for you would make me wish you always with me; but as that is what your future Welfare will no way permit, and as you must certainly be a Gainer by the Situation you are now in, let a Desire to promote *my* Happiness, as well as *your own*, make every seeming Difficulty light; which, I hope, will appear much lighter for being what I intreat you to dispense with, who am

Your ever loving Mother.

I have desir'd your Uncle to interpose in this Matter, and he writes to you on this Occasion; and has promised to see Justice done you, in case your Complaints be reasonable.

LETTER

LETTER IV.

An Uncle's Letter to the Youth, on the same Occasion.

Cousin William,

I AM sorry you should have any Misunderstanding with your Master: I have a good Opinion of him, and am unwilling to entertain a bad one of you. It is so much a Master's Interest to use his Apprentices well, that I am inclinable to think that when they are badly treated, it is oftener the Effect of Provocation than Choice. Wherefore, before I give myself the Trouble of interposing in your Behalf, I desire you will strictly inquire of yourself, whether you have not, by some Misconduct or other, provoked that Alteration in your Master's Behaviour of which you so much complain. If, after having diligently complied with this Request, you assure me that you are not sensible of having given Cause of Disgust on your Side, I will readily use my best Endeavours to reconcile you to your Master, or procure you another. But if you find yourself blameable, it will be better for you to remove, by your own Amendment, the Occasion of your Master's Displeasure, than to have me, or any other Friend, offer to plead your Excuse, where you know it would be unjust to defend you. If this should be your Case, all your Friends together could promise your better Behaviour, indeed, but as the Performance must even then be your own, it will add much more to your Character to pass thro' your whole Term without any Interposition between you. Weigh well what I have here said, and remember that your future Welfare depends greatly on your present Behaviour. I am

Your loving Kinsman.

LETTER V.

An Apprentice to an Uncle, about a Fraud committed by his Fellow-Apprentice to their Master.

Dear Uncle,

I AM under greater Uneasiness than I am able to express: My Fellow-'prentice, for whom I had a great Regard, and from whom I have received many Civilities, has involved me in the deepest Affliction. I am unwilling to tell you, and yet I must not conceal it, that he has forfeited the Confidence reposed in him, by a Breach of Trust, to which he ungenerously gain'd my Consent, by a Pretence I did not in the least suspect. What must I do? My Master is defrauded: If I discover the Injury, I am sure to ruin a young Man I would fain think possessed of some Merit; if I conceal the Injustice, I must at present share the Guilt, and hereafter be Partaker in the Punishment. I am in the greatest Agony of Mind, and beg your instant Advice, as you value the Peace of

Your dutiful, tho' unfortunate Nephew.

LETTER VI.

The Uncle's Answer.

Dear Nephew,

YOUR Letter, which I just now received, gives me great Uneasiness. And as any Delay in the Discovery may be attended with Consequences which will probably be dangerous to yourself, and disagreeable to all who belong to you, I charge

charge you, if you value your own Happiness, and my Peace, to acquaint your Master instantly with the Injustice that has been done him, which is the only Means of vindicating your own Innocence, and preventing your being looked upon as an Accomplice in a Fact, to which I wish you may not be found to have been too far consenting. As to the unhappy young Man who has been guilty of so fatal an Indiscretion, I wish, if the known Clemency and Good-nature of your Master may pardon this Offence, he may let his Forgiveness teach him the Ingratitude and Inhumanity of injuring a Man, who is not only the proper Guardian of his Youth, but whose Goodness deserves the best Behaviour, tho' he be generous enough to excuse the worst. Let not a Minute pass after you receive this, before you reveal the Matter to your Master: For I am in Hopes that your Application to me, and your following my Advice, will greatly plead in your Behalf. I will very speedily call on your Master, and am, as far as an honest Regard for you can make me,

Your loving Uncle.

LETTER VII.

Advice from a Father to a young Beginner, what Company to chuse, and how to behave in it.

Dear Robin,

AS you are now entering into the World, and will probably have considerable Dealings in your Business, the frequent Occasions you will have for Advice from others, will make you desirous of
singling

singling out among your most intimate Acquaintance, one or two, whom you would view in the Light of Friends.

In the Choice of these, your utmost Care and Caution will be necessary: For, by a Mistake here, you can scarcely conceive the fatal Effects you may hereafter experience. Wherefore, it will be proper for you to make a Judgment of those who are fit to be your Advisers, by the Conduct they have observed in *their own* Affairs, and the *Reputation* they bear in the World. For he who has by his own Indiscretions undone himself, is much fitter to be set up as a Land-mark for a prudent Mariner to shun his Courses, than an Example to follow.

Old Age is generally slow and heavy, Youth headstrong and precipitate; but there are old Men who are full of Vivacity, and young Men replenished with Discretion; which makes me rather point out the *Conduct* than the *Age* of the Persons with whom you should chuse to associate; tho' after all, it is a never-failing good Sign to me of Prudence and Virtue in a young Man, when his Seniors chuse his Company, and he delights in theirs.

Let your Endeavour therefore be, at all Adventures, to consort yourself with Men of Sobriety, good Sense and Virtue; for the Proverb is an unerring one, that says, *A Man is known by the Company he keeps.* If such Men you can single out, while you improve by their Conversation, you will benefit by their Advice; and be sure remember one thing, that tho' you must be frank and unreserved in delivering your Sentiments, when Occasions offer, yet that you be much readier to *hear* than *speak*; for to this Purpose it has been significantly observed, that Nature has given a Man *two Ears,*

Ears, and but *one* Tongue. Lay in therefore by Obfervation, and a modeft Silence, fuch a Store of Ideas, that you may, at their Time of Life, make no worfe Figure than they do, and endeavour to benefit yourfelf rather by other Peoples Ills than your own. How muft thofe young Men expofe themfelves to the Contempt and Ridicule of their Seniors, who, having feen little or nothing of the World, are continually fhutting out by *open Mouths*, and *clofed Ears*, all Poffibility of Inftruction, and making vain the principal End of Converfation, which is Improvement. A filent young Man makes generally a wife old one, and never fails of being refpected by the beft and moft prudent Men. When therefore you come among Strangers, hear every one fpeak before you deliver your own Sentiments; by this means you will judge of the Merit and Capacities of your Company, and avoid expofing yourfelf, as I have known many do, by fhooting out hafty and inconfiderate Bolts, which they would have been glad to recal, when perhaps a filent Genius in Company has burft out upon them with fuch Obfervations, as have ftruck Confcioufnefs and Shame into the forward Speaker, if he has not been quite infenfible of inward Reproach.

I have thrown together, as they occurr'd, a few Thoughts, which may fuffice for the prefent to fhew my Care and Concern for your Welfare. I hope you will conftantly, from time to time, communicate to me whatever you fhall think worthy of my Notice, or in which my Advice may be of Ufe to you. For I have no Pleafure in this Life equal to that which the Happinefs of my Children gives me. And of this you may be affured, for I am, and ever muft be,

Your affectionate Father.

LETTER VIII.

General Rules for agreeable Conversation in a young Man. From a Father to a Son.

Dear William,

AS I had not an Opportunity of saying so much to you as I wished when you were last here, I send this to inform you of some Things in your general Conversation, which I think would be proper for you to observe, and amend, particularly *your excessive Itch for Talking*, which discovers itself alike on all Occasions. I have always flatter'd myself, that you do not want Sense, and am willing to hope I have not been deceived But the dangerous Self-sufficiency of most young Men, seems violently to have seized you, which, I hope, a little Reflection will remove.

The Art of rendering yourself agreeable in Conversation is worth your serious Study 'Tis an Advantage few can boast, tho' sought after by all, and nothing is so constant an Enemy to Success in those who would excel in this Art, as the harbouring an Opinion of their own Proficiency, before they have attained to any tolerable Degree of Knowlege in what they imagine themselves possessed of. Conversation, where it is rightly managed, must be so conducted, as to let each Member of the Company have a Share in the *Pleasure* and *Applause* it affords If you are Six in Number, after you have told a Story, or made any Remark which gives a general Satisfaction, you must consider it the Right of another to call *your* Attention in his Turn, and, unless particularly requested, it betrays a great Weakness to *follow yourself* No doubt but you love to be admired. And have not

others

most Important Occasions. 17

others the same Passion? You believe your Wit more brilliant than theirs Are you sure, that they are not of the same Opinion as to their own? If a Man speaks little, you must not from thence conclude him willing to give up every Claim to conversable Merit. Perhaps he cannot sing. But to be sure he is as desirous of having his *peculiar Humour*, or his *dry Joke*, applauded, as you are to be intreated another Song. If he is no Mathematician, perhaps he is versed in religious Disputation; if he despises Plays, he may admire History, tho' he understands not Geography, he may yet know how to describe the Humours of Mankind: And tho' he pretends not to Politicks, he may have a Turn for some more useful Science. When these are considered, if his Modesty is great, you cannot oblige him more than by throwing an Opportunity in his way to display his Capacity on the Subject he believes himself most able to handle with Advantage For, in order to support a thorough good Humour, a Man must be pleased with *himself* as well as with *others*. When this is properly taken care of, Conversation seldom fails to prove entertaining. And to the Neglect of this, are owing many of the *yawning* Hours spent in Companies composed of Men not incapable of behaving agreeably.

The Manner of telling a Story is also worth your Notice: You have known the Pleasure of hearing a long one well told: Mr. *Trotter* has an admirable Talent in this way. But then you must observe, that half the Pleasure he gives, arises from his happily avoiding any of the silly Digressions, which are the great Cause of a Story's seeming tedious You never hear him mingle his Relation with, *I remember very well it was the same Day that 'Squire* Trumbul's *Son came of Age,---I bought*

my

my bay Nag the very Day before, at such a Fair, being a Friday that Year;----or, I can scarce think of it without Laughing,---But, however, as I was saying.----And a hundred more such Dead-weights to Attention. Nor does he ever praise a Story before he relates it; a fatal Rock to many a good Relation: For when a Story wants a preparatory Recommendation, it ought not to be told; and even when the Relation is possible, the Generality of Auditors are apt to persuade themselves,

The Mountain labours, and a Mouse is born.

These are loose and general Hints; but by a due Improvement of them, you will find yourself very sensibly grow more and more agreeable where-ever you converse. An Ease and becoming Freedom you already have, and by the Addition of Discretion in your Use of them, and Complaisance to others, you will probably succeed in the Desire so predominant in you, of being admired by Men of Sense and Judgment. Which will be no small Pleasure to

Your affectionate Father.

LETTER IX.

An elder to a younger Brother, who is in Love with a young Lady of great Gaiety, &c.

Dear Brother,

I AM more concerned for your Welfare than you imagine. You are younger than myself: My Duty, in some Degree, requires my Care for your Good, and particularly in a Point that may
be

be so material to your whole Life, as is that of Love

Beauty has as great a Force upon my Senses, as it can have upon yours. I am near Thirty Years of Age; you are not more than Twenty Your Passions are strong, mine, Brother, are far from subsiding I admire, I love, with as much Force of Nature as you can do. My Reason ought to be stronger, and 'tis well if my Passion is not so likewise. Miss *Rooke* is amiable on many Accounts; her Features are regular, her Wit sprightly, her Deportment genteel, and Voice, — I had almost said, ravishing. Her Dress is easy and unaffected; and her Manner of Conversation has a Freedom that captivates more Hearts than yours. Yet, I greatly fear, with all these Endowments, she will not make the Wife you ought to wish for. Her airy Flights, and gay Behaviour, are pleasing, as a Partner in Conversation; but will they be equally agreeable in a Partner *for Life?* What now charms *you*, charms also *others*. You are now content with thinking yourself *one* among *many* that admire her, and are admitted to *share* the Brilliancy of her Conversation: But will a *Share* of her Wit and Humour, her Freedom and Gaiety, please hereafter as a Wife? And tho' she is delightful in Company, are you satisfied she will be as agreeable when alone with you, or when she has not an Opportunity of shewing-away in a Company that perhaps you may not approve? She now sees nobody but whom she chuses to see: If she should be a Wife, it is more than probable she may dislike Restraints. And can you approve of a diffuse Conversation in one you desire to yourself?

Think not, Brother, that I have any interested Motive for this Advice. I assure you I have not. I am not your Rival. I desire not the Lady you
seem

seem too fond of. All I mean (for I say nothing at present, with regard to your own Youth, which ought not, however, to be wholly forgotten, as very few prudent Matches are made by young Gentlemen at your Age) is, to caution you against thinking of a Gentlewoman who *may*, and I am willing to believe *will*, be a suitable Companion to a Gentleman whose Station and Choice leads him into much Company, and gay Life; but to Men whose Circumstances, if not their Inclinations, require a more retired way of Life, it is obvious, a Woman, whose Talents lie principally in Conversation, can never, for that Reason *only*, justify a young Gentleman for chusing her for a Wife.

I hope this will come time enough to put you upon guarding against the Inconveniencies that threaten the Indulgence of your present Passion. Shut not your Ears to Reason; forget not yourself; and be sure to remember, that the Pleasure of an *Hour or Two*, and of Twenty, Thirty, or Forty Years, or a *whole Life*, must arise from very different Sources. I am,

Dear Brother,

Your most affectionate, &c.

LETTER X.

An elder to an extravagant younger Brother.

Dear John,

YOU may be certain, that your Misfortunes are to me a most melancholy Subject. You are my only Brother. I own it. And your Misfortunes

most Important Occasions. 21

affect me next to my own: But there is this Difference in what I feel for you, and for myself I am sure, every Misfortune I have met with, has been occasioned by unavoidable Accidents. This Consideration has supported me under the many Afflictions I have myself endured But for those I have shared with you, I cannot boast the same Alleviation. While our Father lived, he was your constant and unwearied Support, even after your Patrimony was squander'd away While our Mother remained, she was every Week assisting your Necessities, but what might more properly be called your Levity and Extravagance. She is now, by the Divine Will, taken from us both; her Jointure, as well as the Estate my Father independently left, has devolved upon me Of this both Nature and Providence require I should make the best Use· And to serve you, I readily confess, is my greatest Care. But, my dearest Brother, how is this to be done? The generous and bountiful Assistance of our Parents, procured you no substantial Good. What then am I to do to screen you from Want and Misery?----That you are not already happy, is not owing to the Backwardness of your Friends to serve you, but, allow me to speak plainly, to your own Indiscretion. Your own Fortune maintained you not for three Years: Were I able to give you as much more, what Reason have you given me to suppose you will be a better Oeconomist than you have been? My whole Estate, let me tell you, Brother, at your Rate of Expence, would scarcely maintain you for Seven Years: And, think you as you will, I must believe it my Duty to leave enough to support my Off-spring, with prudent Conduct, to the End of Time. If I send you, as you desire, Fifty Guineas, What Good will that Sum procure you?

It

It will but serve to lengthen your Credit, and make you run deeper into Debt. I have affifted you before; and has not this always been the Cafe? And have not People given you Credit, becaufe they think I will fupport you? 'Tis Time then, my dear Brother, to hold my Hand. But yet, be affured, that when I am convinced you have thoroughly abandon'd your prefent Courfes, you fhall find in me

A truly affectionate Brother.

LETTER XI.

To a young Man too foon keeping a Horfe.

Dear Tom,

I Always take great Pleafure in hearing of your Welfare, and of every thing that makes for your Satisfaction and Comfort: But give me Leave to fay, That I am forry to hear you have fo early begun to keep a Horfe, efpecially as your Bufinefs is altogether in your Shop, and you have no End to ferve in riding out; and are, befides, young and healthy, and fo cannot require it, as Exercife. And is it worth while, think you, to keep a Horfe the whole Week, that you may have him at hand on a *Sunday* Morning, if the Day proves fair, and you have nothing to keep you in Town?

You muft confider, that tho' here, in the Country, many common Tradefmen keep Horfes, the Expence is but fmall to them; and the Diftance of one Cuftomer from another, in a manner, obliges them to it. But this can be no Plea for you; And if you do not want a Horfe for Exercife,

cife, you can only alledge the worst Reason in the World for your maintaining one, that your Neighbours all around you do the same. For, look who they are, and what their Motives, and you'll soon see the Difference, and that their Example will not justify you. Mr *Thompson*, for Instance, who lives next Door to you, is near Sixty Years of Age, of a pretty gross Constitution, and capable of no other Exercise, and moreover he had acquired, by Length of Time, and Industry, an ample Fortune, before he gave himself this Diversion. Mr. *Jenkins* has an Estate fallen to him, that sets him above the Want of Trade, and his continuing in it, is rather an Amusement than an Employment. Mr *Jackson*, Mr *West*, Mr. *Trozier*, and Mr *Kent*, are all Men of established Fortunes, and when you are as old as the youngest of them, and can as well afford it, I would be far from disuading you from keeping a Horse. But at present, you may depend upon it, you rather incur their Contempt, than gain their Esteem, by offering to appear their Equal, when they and you well know, in what relates to Expences, you ought not to be so, nor have you had a Time for it. The lower Part of the World may, perhaps, shew you more Respect for those Marks of Substance; but should a Time come (and who is exempt from Misfortunes?) when they must know they were the Effects of unthinking Levity, how despicable must you then appear in their Eyes! And let me tell you, that the Esteem of Persons of Credit and Understanding, must be gained by very different Means from Shew or Equipage, for with these, Modesty, Prudence, and good Sense only, will ever prevail.

Besides,

Besides, the Expence of the Horse is not the least thing to be considered It will in time, very probably, lead you into a more dangerous one, that of bestowing too much of your Time in the Use of it. It will unhinge your Mind, as I may say, from Business, and give your Servants Opportunity to be remiss in your Absence. And as you are a young Man, it is fit that you should lay up, by your Industry, against a more advanced Age, when the Exercise a Horse affords, will seem not only more suitable, but perhaps absolutely necessary to your Health; whereas, now, it may rather pass for Wantonness and Affectation.

You are not without a tolerable Share of Reason; let me prevail with you to use it Sell your Horse, and fear not being laugh'd at on that Account, for it will be a Credit to you more ways than one, to say, That your Business would not allow you Time to use it. And it would argue, besides, great Perverseness, to continue in an Error, for no other Reason than to support a wrong Judgment at first setting out And your reducing an unnecessary Expence in good time, will more than recover any good Opinion you may have lost by running in it

Your prudent Use of this Advice will, as it must tend to your Good, be a great Satisfaction to

Your tenderly affectionate Father.

LETTER XII.

Against a sudden Intimacy, or Friendship, with one of a short Acquaintance.

Cousin Tom,

I AM just setting out for *Windsor*, and have not time to say so much as I would on the Occasion upon which I now write to you. I hear that Mr. *Douglas* and you have lately contracted such an Intimacy, that you are hardly ever asunder, and as I know his Morals are not the best, nor his Circumstances the most happy, I fear he will, if he has not already done it, let you see, that he better knows what he does in seeking *your* Acquaintance, than you do in cultivating *his*.

I am far from desiring to abridge you in any necessary or innocent Liberty, or to prescribe too much to your Choice of a Friend. Nor am I against your being complaisant to *Strangers*, for this Gentleman's Acquaintance is not yet a Month old with you, but you must not think every Man whose Conversation is agreeable, fit to be immediately treated as a Friend. Of all Sorts, hastily-contracted Friendships promise the least Duration or Satisfaction, as they most commonly arise from Design on one Side, and Weakness on the other. True *Friendship* must be the Effect of long and mutual Esteem and Knowlege. It ought to have for its Cement, an Equality of Years, a Similitude of Manners, and, pretty much, a Parity in Circumstance and Degree. But, generally speaking, an Openness to a Stranger carries with it strong Marks of Indiscretion, and not seldom ends in Repentance.

C For

For these Reasons, I would be glad you would be upon your Guard, and proceed cautiously in this new Alliance. Mr. *Douglas* has Vivacity and Humour enough to please any Man of a light Turn, but were I to give my Judgment of him, I should pronounce him fitter for the Tea-table, than the Cabinet. He is smart, but very superficial, and treats all serious Subjects with a Contempt too natural to bad Minds, and I know more young Men than one, of whose good Opinion he has taken Advantage, and has made them wiser, though at their own Expence, than he found them.

The Caution I here give you, is the pure Effect of my Experience in Life, some Knowlege of your new Associate, and my Affection for you. The Use you make of it will determine, whether you merit this Concern from

Your affectionate Kinsman.

LETTER XIII.

A young Man in Business, to a Father, desiring Leave to address his Daughter.

SIR,

I HOPE the Justness of my Intentions will excuse the Freedom of these few Lines, whereby I am to acquaint you of the great Affection and Esteem I have for your Daughter. I would not, Sir, offer at any indirect Address, that should have the least Appearance of Inconsistency with her Duty to you, and my honourable Views to her; chusing, by your Influence, if I may approve myself to you worthy of that Honour, to commend myself to her Approbation.

Approbation. You are not insensible, Sir, by the Credit I have hitherto preserved in the World, of my Ability, by God's Blessing, to make her happy: And this the rather emboldens me to request the Favour of an Evening's Conversation with you, at your first Convenience, when I will more fully explain myself, as I earnestly hope, to your Satisfaction, and take my Encouragement or Discouragement from your own Mouth. I am, Sir, mean time, with great Respect,

Your most obedient humble Servant.

LETTER XIV.

To the Daughter (on the Father's Allowance) apprising her of his intended Visit.

MADAM,

I HAVE ventured to make known to your honoured Father, the great Desire I have to be thought worthy of a Relation to him by your Means. And, as he has not discouraged me in the Hopes I have entertained, that I may possibly be not unacceptable to him, and to all your worthy Family, I propose to do myself the Honour of a Visit to you next *Monday*. Though he has been so good as to promise to introduce me, and I make no doubt has acquainted you with it, I give you, nevertheless, the Trouble of these Lines, that I might not appear wanting in any outward Demonstration of that inviolable Respect with which I am, dear Madam,

Your most devoted humble Servant.

LETTER XV.

From a young Lady to her Father, acquainting him with a Proposal of Marriage made to her.

Honoured Sir,   *Nottingham, April* 4.

I THINK it my Duty to acquaint you, that a Gentleman of this Town, by Name *Derham*, and by Business a Linen-draper, has made some Overtures to my Cousin *Morgan*, in the way of Courtship to me. My Cousin has brought him once or twice into my Company, which he could not well decline doing, because he has Dealings with him, and has an high Opinion of him and his Circumstances. He has been set up Three Years, and has very good Business, and lives in Credit and Fashion. He is about Twenty-seven Years old, and a likely Man enough. He seems not to want Sense or Manners, and is come of a good Family He has broke his Mind to me, and boasts how well he can maintain me. But, I assure you, Sir, I have given him no Encouragement; and told him, that I had no Thoughts of changing my Condition, yet awhile; and should never think of it but in Obedience to my Parents, and I desired him to talk no more on that Subject to me. Yet he resolves to persevere, and pretends extraordinary Affection and Esteem. I would not, Sir, by any means, omit to acquaint you with the *Beginnings* of an Affair, that would be want of Duty in me to conceal from you, and shew a Guilt and Disobedience unworthy of the kind Indulgence and Affection you have always shewn to, Sir,

Your most dutiful Daughter.

My humble Duty to my honour'd Mother, Love to my Brother and Sister, and Respects to all Friends. Cousin *Morgan*, and his Wife and Sister, desire their kind Respects I cannot speak enough of their Civility to me.

LETTER XVI.

The Father's Answer, on a Supposition that he approves not of the young Man's Addresses.

Dear Polly,   *Northampton, Apr* 10.

I HAVE received your Letter dated the 4th Instant, wherein you acquaint me of the Proposals made to you, thro' your Cousin *Morgan*'s Recommendation, by one Mr. *Derham*. I hope, as you assure me, that you have given no Encouragement to him. For I by no means approve of him for your Husband. I have inquired of one of his Townsmen, who knows him and his Circumstances very well; and I am neither pleased with them, nor with his Character, and wonder my Cousin would so inconsiderately recommend him to you. Indeed, I doubt not Mr. *Morgan*'s good Intentions; but I insist upon it, that you think nothing of the Matter, if you would oblige

Your indulgent Father.

Your Mother gives her Blessing to you, and joins with me in the above Advice. Your Brother and Sister, and all Friends, send their Love and Respects to you.

LETTER XVII.

The Father's Answer, on a Supposition that he does not disapprove of the young Man's Addresses.

My dear Daughter, Northampt. *Apr.* 10.

IN Answer to yours of the 4th Instant, relating to the Addresses of Mr. *Derham,* I would have you neither wholly encourage nor discourage his Suit; for if, on Inquiry into his Character and Circumstances, I shall find, that they are answerable to your Cousin's good Opinion of them, and his own Assurances, I know not but his Suit may be worthy of Attention. But, my Dear, consider, that Men are deceitful, and always put the best Side outwards; and it may possibly, on the strict Inquiry, which the Nature and Importance of the Case demands, come out far otherwise than it at present appears. Let me advise you therefore, to act in this Matter with great Prudence, and that you make not yourself too cheap; for Men are apt to slight what is too easily obtained. Your Cousin will give him Hope enough, while you don't absolutely deny him, and in the mean time, he may be told, that you are not at your own Disposal, but intirely resolved to abide by my Determination and Direction, in an Affair of this great Importance: And this will put him upon applying to me, who, you need not doubt, will in this Case, as in all others, study your Good; as becomes

Your indulgent Father.

Your Mother gives her Blessing to you, and joins with me in the above Advice. Your Brother and Sister, and all Friends, send their Love and Respects to you.

LETTER XVIII.

The young Gentleman's Letter to the Father, apprising him of his Affection for his Daughter.

SIR,   *Notlingham, April* 12.

I TAKE the Liberty, tho' personally unknown to you, to declare the great Value and Affection I have for your worthy Daughter, whom I have had the Honour to see at my good Friend Mr. *Morgan*'s. I should think myself intirely unworthy of *her* Favour, and of *your* Approbation, if I could have a Thought of influencing her Resolution but in Obedience to your Pleasure; as I should, on such a Supposition, offer an Injury likewise to that Prudence in *herself*, which, I flatter myself, is not the least of her amiable Perfections. If I might have the Honour of your Countenance, Sir, on this Occasion, I would open myself and Circumstances to you, in that frank and honest manner which should convince you of the Sincerity of my Affection for your Daughter, and at the same time of the Honourableness of my Intentions. In the mean time, I will in general say, That I have been set up in my Business in the Linen-drapery Way, upwards of Three Years; that I have a very good Trade for the Time. That I had 1000*l.* to begin with, which I have improved to 1500*l.* as I am ready to make appear to your Satisfaction: That I am descended of a creditable Family; have done nothing to stain my Character; and that my Trade is still further improveable, as I shall, I hope, inlarge my Bottom. This, Sir, I thought but honest and fair to acquaint you with, that you might know something of a Person, who sues to you for your Countenance, and that of your good Lady, in an Affair that I hope may prove one Day the greatest Happiness of my Life, as it *must* be, if I can be blessed with that, and your dear Daughter's Approbation. In Hope of which, and the Favour of a Line, I take the Liberty to subscribe myself, good Sir,

Your most obedient humble Servant.

LETTER XIX.

From the Cousin to the Father and Mother, in Commendation of the young Gentleman.

Dear Cousins, Nottingham, *April* 12.

I GIVE you both Thanks for so long continuing with us the Pleasure of Cousin *Polly*'s Company. She has intirely captivated a worthy Friend of mine, Mr. *Derham*, a Linen-draper of this Town. And I would have acquainted you with it myself, but that I knew and advised Cousin *Polly* to write to you about it; for I would not for the World any thing of this sort should be carried on unknown to you, at my House, especially. Mr. *Derham* has shewn me his Letter to you; and I believe every Tittle of it to be true; and really, if you and my Cousin approve it, as also Cousin *Polly*, I don't know where she can do better. I am sure I should think so, if I had a Daughter he could love.

Thus much I thought myself obliged to say; and, with my kind Love to your other Self, and all my Cousins, as also my *Wife*'s, and *Sister*'s, I remain

Your affectionate Cousin.

LETTER XX.

From the Father, in Answer to the young Gentleman.

SIR,   *Northampton, April* 16.

I HAVE received yours of the 12th, and am obliged to you for the good Opinion you express of my Daughter. But I think she is yet full young to alter her Condition, and imbark in the Cares of a Family. I cannot but say, that the Account you give of yourself, and your Application to *me*, rather than first to try to engage the Affections of my Daughter, carry a very honourable Appearance, and such as must be to the Advantage of your Character. As to your Beginning, Sir, that is not to be so much looked upon, as the *Improvement*; and I doubt not, that you can make good Proof of what you assert on this Occasion. But still I must needs say, that I think, and so does her Mother, that it is too early to incumber her with the Cares of the World, and as I am sure she will do nothing in so important an Affair without our Advice, so I would not, for the World, in a Case so nearly concerning her, and her future Welfare, constrain her in the least. I intend shortly to send for her home, for she has been longer absent from us than we intended; and then I shall consult her Inclinations; and you will excuse me to say, for she is my Daughter, and a very good Child, tho' I say it, that I shall then determine myself by that, and by what shall appear to offer most for her Good. In the mean time, Sir, I thank you for the Civility and commendable Openness of Yours, and am

Your humble Servant.

The Father in this Letter referring pretty much to the Daughter's Choice, the young Gentleman cannot but construe it as an Encouragement to him, to prosecute his Addresses to *her*; in which he doubles his Diligence (on the Hint that she will soon return to *Nottingham*), in order to gain a Footing in her good Will; and she, finding her Father and Mother not averse to the Affair, ventures to give him some Room to think his Addresses not indifferent to her; but still altogether on Condition of her Parents Consent and Approbation. By the Time then that she is recall'd home (nothing disagreeable having appeared in the young Gentleman's Behaviour, and his general Character being consistent with his Pretensions), there may be supposed some Degree of Familiarity and Confidence to have pass'd between them; and she gives him Hope, that she will receive a Letter from him, tho' she will not promise an Answer; intirely referring to her Duty to her Parents, and their good Pleasure. He attends her on her Journey a good Part of the Way, as far as she will permit; and when her Cousin, his Friend, informs him of her safe Arrival at *Nottingham*, he sends the following Letter.

LETTER XXI.

From the young Gentleman to his Mistress, on her Arrival at her Father's.

Dear Madam, May 25.

I HAVE understood with great Pleasure your safe Arrival at your Father's House; of which I take the Liberty to congratulate your good Parents, as well as your dear Self. I will not, Madam, fill this Letter with the Regret I had to part with you, because I have no Reason nor Merit, at present, to expect that you should be concerned for me on this Score. Yet, Madam, I am not without Hope, from the Sincerity of my Affection for you, and the Honesty of my Intentions, to deserve, in time, those Regards which I cannot at present flatter myself with. As your good Father, in his kind Letter to me, assured me, that he should consult your Inclinations, and determine by them, and by what should offer most for your Good, how happy should I be, if I could find my humble Suit not quite indifferent to your dear Self, and not rejected by Him! If what I have already opened to him as to my Circumstances, be not unacceptable, I should humbly hope for Leave to pay you and him a Visit at *Nottingham*, or if this be too great a Favour, till he has made further Inquiry, that he would be pleased to give himself that Trouble, and put it in my Power, as soon as possible, to convince him of the Truth of my Allegations, upon which I desire to stand or fall in my Hopes of your Favour and his. For I think, far different from many in the World, that a Deception in an Affair of this weighty Nature, should be less forgiven than in any other. Since then, dearest Madam, I build my Hopes more on the Truth of Affection for you, and the Honour of my Intentions, than any other Merit, or Pretensions, I hope you will condescend, if not to become an Advocate for me, which would be too great a Presumption to expect, yet to let your good Parents know, that you have no Aversion to the Person or Address of, dearest Madam,

Your for ever obliged, and affectionate humble Servant.

My best Respects attend your good Father and Mother, and whole Family.

As this puts the Matter into such a Train, as may render more Writing unnecessary, the next Steps to be taken being the Inquiry into the Truth of the young Man's Assertions, and a Confirmation of his Character; and then the Proposals on the Father's Part of what he will give with his Daughter; all which may be done best by Word of Mouth, or Interposition of Friends; so we shall have no Occasion to pursue this Instance of Courtship further.

LETTER XXII.

From a Brother to his Sister in the Country, upbraiding her for being negligent in Writing.

My dear Sister,

I WRITE to you to acquaint you how unkindly we all take it here, that you do not write oftener to us, in relation to your Health, Diversions, and Employment in the Country.

You cannot be insensible how much you are beloved by us all; judge then if you do right to omit giving us the only Satisfaction Absence affords to true Friends, which is, often to hear from one another. My Mother is highly disobliged with you, and says you are a very idle Girl; my Aunt is of the same Opinion; and I would fain, like a loving Brother, excuse you, if I could. Pray, for the future, take care to deserve a better Character, and by writing soon, and often, put it in my Power to say what a good Sister I have. For you shall always find me

Your most affectionate Brother.

Due Respects of every one here to my Aunt, and all Friends in the Country.

LETTER XXIII.

In Answer to the preceding.

Dear Brother,

MOST kindly, and too justly, do you upbraid me. I own my Fault, and never will be guilty of the like again. I write to beg my Mother's Pardon, and that she will procure for me that of my good Aunt, on Promise of Amendment. Continue, my dear Brother, to be an Advocate for me in all my unintended Imperfections, and I will never err voluntarily for the future: That so I may be as worthy as possible of your kind Constructions, and shew myself, what I truly am, and ever will be,

Your most affectionate and obliged Sister.

LETTER XXIV.

From the Daughter to her Mother, in Excuse for her Neglect.

Honoured Madam,

I AM ashamed I staid to be reminded of my Duty by my Brother's kind Letter. I will offer no Excuse for myself, for not writing oftener, tho' I have been strangely taken up by the Kindness and Favour of your good Friends here, particularly my Aunt *Windus.* For well do I know, that my Duty to my honoured Mother ought to take place of all other Considerations. All I beg therefore is, that you will be so good to forgive me, on Promise of Amendment, and to procure Forgiveness also of my Aunt *Talbot,* and all Friends. Believe me, Madam, when I say, that no Diversions here or elsewhere shall make me forget the Duty I owe to so good a Mother, and such kind Relations, and that I shall ever be

Your gratefully dutiful Daughter.

My Aunt and Cousins desire their kind Love to you, and due Respects to all Friends. Brother *John* has great Reputation with every one for his kind Letter to me.

LETTER XXV.

From a Son-in-Law to his Wife's Father, acquainting him with his Wife's Illness.

Honoured Sir,

I AM sorry to acquaint you with the Indisposition of your dear Daughter. She was taken ill last *Monday* of a Fever, and has all the Assistance that we we can procure in thefe Parts. I hope fhe is not in Danger. However, I thought it my Duty to let you know it in time, that you may fatisfy yourfelf, that no Care is wanting; and that you may favour us with a perfonal Vifit, which will be a great Confolation to her, who craves, mean time, your Bleffing and Prayers, and alfo to, Sir,

Your dutiful Son.

This may ferve, *mutatis mutandis*, in the like Circumftance, for a Daughter to her Hufband's Father, or Mother, and in feveral other intimate Relations.

LETTER XXVI.

From a Country Chapman beginning Trade, to a City Dealer, offering his Correfpondence.

SIR, Manchefter, Oct. 20.

THE Time of my Apprenticefhip, with Mr. *Dobbins* of this Town, being expired, I am juft going to begin for myfelf in *Chefterfield*, having taken a Shop there for that Purpofe. And as I know the Satisfaction you always gave to my Mafter in your Dealings, I make an Offer to you of my Correfpondence, in Expectation that you will ufe me as well as you have done him, in whatever I may write to you for. And this I the rather expect, as you cannot difoblige Mr. *Dobbins* by it, becaufe of the Diftance I fhall be from him; and I fhall endeavour to give you equal Content with regard to my Payments, &c. Your fpeedy Anfwer, whether or no you are difpofed to accept of my Offer, will oblige

Your humble Servant.

LETTER XXVII.
In Answer to the foregoing.

SIR,

I HAVE received yours of *October* 20. and very chearfully accept the Favour you offer me I will take care to serve you in the best manner I am able, and on the same Foot with Mr. *Dobbins*, not doubting you will make as punctual Returns as he does; which intitles him to a more favourable Usage than could otherwise be afforded. I wish you Success with all my Heart, and am

Your obliged Servant.

LETTER XXVIII.
From a Maid servant in Town, acquainting her Father and Mother in the Country with a Proposal of Marriage, and asking their Consents.

Honoured Father and Mother,

I Think it my Duty to acquaint you, that I am addressed to for a Change of Condition, by one Mr. *John Tanner*, who is a Glazier, and lives in the Neighbourhood by us. He is a young Man of a sober Character, and has been set up about two Years, has good Business for his Time, and is well beloved and spoken of by every one My Friends here think well of it, particularly my Master and Mistress; and he says, he doubts not, by God's Blessing on his Industry, to maintain a Family very prettily: And I have fairly told him, how little he

has

has to expect with me. But I would not conclude on any thing, however, till I had acquainted you with his Proposals, and asked your Blessings and Consents. For I am, and ever will be,

Your dutiful Daughter.

LETTER XXIX.

From the Parents, in Answer to the preceding.

Dear Nanny,

WE have received your dutiful Letter. We can only pray to God to direct and bless you in all your Engagements. Our Distance from you must make us leave every thing to your own Discretion; and as you are so well satisfied in Mr. *Tanner*'s Character, as well as all Friends, and your Master and Mistress, we give our Blessings and Consents with all our Hearts. We are only sorry we can do no more for you. But let us know when it is done, and we will do some little Matters, as far as we are able, towards House-keeping. Our Respects to Mr *Tanner*. Every body joins with us in Wishes for your Happiness; and may God bless you, is all that can be said by

Your truly loving Father and Mother.

LETTER XXX.

From the same, acquainting her Parents with her Marriage.

Honoured Father and Mother,

I Write to acquaint you, that last *Thursday* I was married to Mr. *Tanner*, and am to go home to him in a Fortnight. My Master and Mistress have

been

been very kind, and have made me a Present towards Housekeeping of Three Guineas. I had saved Twenty Pounds in Service, and that is all. I told him the naked Truth of every thing, and indeed did not intend to marry so soon, but when I had your Letter, and shew'd it him, he would not let me rest till it was done. Pray don't streighten yourselves out of Love to me. He joins with me in saying so, and bids me present his Duty to you, and tell you, that he fears not to maintain me very well. I have no Reason to doubt of being very happy. And your Prayers for a Blessing on both our Industry, will, I hope, be a Means to make us more so. We are, and ever shall be, with Respects to all Friends,

Your most dutiful Son and Daughter.

LETTER XXXI.

Recommending a Superior Man-Servant.

SIR,

THE Bearer of this is Mr. *John Andrews,* whom I mentioned to you last time I saw you; and for whose Integrity and Ability to serve you in the way you talked of, I dare be answerable. I take the greater Pleasure in this Recommendation, as I doubt not it will be of Service to you both. And am, Sir,

Your most obedient Servant.

LETTER XXXII.

Recommen'ing a Wet-Nurse.

Madam,

THE Bearer is Mrs. *Newman*, whom I recommended to you as a Nurse for Master. You will be pleased with her neat Appearance, and wholsome Countenance. She lives just above Want, in a pleasant airy Place; and has a very honest diligent Husband, with whom she lives very happily, and the Man is exceedingly fond of Children, very sober, and good-humour'd; and they have every thing very pretty about them. You will find such Answers to the Questions that shall be put to her, as will please you in every respect that you mention'd to me, and the Woman will not tell an Untruth, or impose upon you. In a word, I know not a more proper Person, and I am glad I have this Opportunity to oblige you in so deserved a Recommendation: For I am, dear Madam,

Your most faithful Servant.

LETTER XXXIII.

Recommending a Cook-maid.

Madam,

YOU desired me to inquire for a Maid who was qualified to serve you as a Cook. The Bearer lived three Years in her last Place, and went away to her Friends in the Country, on a Fit of Illness, of which she is now perfectly recovered. As
she

she had given no Hopes of Return, they had provided themselves when she offered her Service again. They give her a very good Character, as well for Honesty and Sobriety, as for her orderly Behaviour, and obliging Temper, as also for her good Performance of what she undertakes. I therefore thought you could not wish for a properer Person; and shall be glad it proves so. For I am, Madam,

Your most obedient Servant.

LETTER XXXIV.
Recommending a Chamber-maid.

MADAM,

THE Bearer, *Jane Adams*, is well recommended to me as a diligent, faithful Body, who understands her Needle well, is very neat and housewifely, and, as you desired, no Gossip or Makebate; and has had a tolerable Education, being descended from good Friends. I make no doubt of her answering this Character. Of which I will satisfy you farther, when I have the Honour to see you. Till when I remain

Your most obedient humble Servant.

LETTER XXXV.
Recommending a Nursery-maid.

MADAM,

THE Bearer, *Sarah Williams*, is a housewifely genteel Body, who has been used to attend Children, and has a great Tenderness for them. She

She is very careful and watchful over them in all their little pretty Ways, and is a very proper Person to encourage their good Inclinations, or mildly to check their little Perversenesses, so far as you shall permit her to do the one or the other. She is come of good Friends, who have had Misfortunes; is very honest, and will, I dare say, please you much, if you are not provided; which I hope you are not, for both your sakes; for I love the Girl, and am, with great Respect, Madam,

Your obliged humble Servant.

LETTER XXXVI.

A Father to a Son, to dissuade him from the Vice of Drinking to Excess.

My dear Son,

IT is with a Grief proportioned to my Love, which is extreme, that I understand you have of late neglected your Studies, and given yourself up to the odious Vice of Drinking. What shall I say, what shall I do, to engage you to quit this pernicious Practice, before it becomes such a Habit, that it will be impossible, or at least very difficult, for you to cast it off? Let me require, let me intreat you, to give a suitable Attention to what I have to say on this Head, which I shall offer rather as a warm Friend, than an angry Father; and as I address myself to your Reason, I will leave it to yourself to judge of the Truth of the Observations I have to make to you.

In the first Place, with respect to *Health*, the greatest Jewel of this Life, it is the most destructive of all Vices. *Asthma's, Vertigoes, Palsies, Apo-*
plexies,

plexies, Gouts, Colicks, Fevers, Dropsies, Consumptions, Stone, and *Hypochondriack Diseases,* are naturally introduced by exceffive Drinking.

All the reft of the Vices, together, are not fo often punifhed with fudden Death as this one. What fatal Accidents, what Quarrels, what Breaches between Friend and Friend, are owing to it!

Then, in the fecond Place; How does it deface Reafon, deftroy all the tender Impulfes of Nature, make a wife Man a Fool, and fubject Perfons of the brighteft Parts to the Contempt of the weakeft, and even, in time, extinguifh thofe fhining Qualities, which conftitute the Difference between a Man of Senfe and a Blockhead! For, as a certain very eminent Author well obferves, Fools having generally ftronger Nerves, and lefs volatile Spirits, than Men of fine Underftandings, that which will roufe the one, will make the other either ftupid or frantick, and tho' it fometimes, while the Fit continues, ftrengthens the Imagination, yet it always depreffes the Judgment; and after the Fit is over, both thofe Faculties languifh together, till, in time, it quenches the Imagination, impairs the Memory, and drowns the Judgment.

Moft other Vices are compatible, as the fame Author obferves, with feveral Virtues; but Drunkennefs runs counter to all the Duties of Life. A great Drinker can hardly be either a good Hufband, a good Father, a good Son, a good Brother, or a good Friend: It lays him open to the worft Company, and this Company frequently fubjects him to lewd Women, Gaming, Quarrels, Riots, and often Murders. All other Vices, even the greateft of Vices, as Ambition, Unchaftity, Bigotry, Avarice, Hypocrify, deteft this unnatural and worfe than beaftly Vice; for the Beafts themfelves,

even

even the uncleanest of them, know nothing of it, much less practise it.

Other Vices indeed make Men *worse*, says this judicious Author; but this *alters* Men from *themselves*, to that degree, that they differ not more from their *present Companions*, than from their *former Selves*. A Habitude of it will make the Prudent inconsiderate, the Ambitious indolent, the Active idle, and the Industrious slothful; so that their Affairs are ruin'd for want of Application, or by being intrusted in the Hands of those who turn them wholly to their own Advantage, and, in the End, to the Ruin of those who employ them.

I have written a long Letter already. Yet have I still more to say, which, that I may not tire you, I will leave to another Letter; which the next Post shall bring you. And I am, mean time, in hopes *this* will not lose its proper Effect,

Your most indulgent Father.

LETTER XXXVII.

The same Subject pursued.

My dear Son,

BY my former you will see, that hard Drinking is a Vice, that breaks a Man's Rest, impairs the Understanding, extinguishes the Memory, inflames the Passions, debauches the Will, lays the Foundation of the worst and most dangerous Distempers, incapacitates a Person from pursuing his Studies, and from applying to the Duties of his Calling, be it what it will; begets Contempt from the World, and even if a Man's Circumstances were above feeling the Expence, which can hardly be, alters

and

and changes the Practifer of it from himself; and if he is *not* above feeling it, often reduces him to Want and Beggary: And if he has a Family, his Children, who by their Father's Industry and Sobriety might have made a creditable Figure in Life, are left to the Mercy of the World; become the Outcasts of the Earth, possibly Foot-soldiers, Livery-servants, Shoe-cleaners, Link-boys, and, perhaps, Pickpockets, Highwaymen, or Footpads; and instead of a comfortable Livelihood, and a Station above Contempt, are intitled only to Shame, Misery, and the Gallows.

And do *you* judge, my Son, how a Man can answer this Conduct to God, to his Parents and other Relations, to his Wife, to his Children, to himself, and persist in a barbarous and an unnatural Vice, which makes himself not only miserable and contemptible, but transmits the Mischief to his unhappy and innocent Children, if he has any.

Add to all this, That it is a Vice a Man cannot easily master and subdue; or which, like some others, may be cured by *Age*; but it is a Vice that feeds and nourishes itself by Practice, and grows upon a Man as he lives longer in the World, till at last, if it cuts him not off in the Flower of his Days, his Body expects and requires Liquor And so, tho' a Man, when he enters upon it, may be single, yet if he ever should marry, it may be attended with all the frightful and deplorable Consequences I have mentioned, and ruin besides an innocent and perhaps prudent Woman, rendering her, without *her own* Fault, the joint unhappy Cause of adding to the Number of the miserable and profligate Children, with which the World too much abounds, and which is owing to nothing so much as this detestable Sin in the Parents.

Con-

Consider all these things, my dear Son; and, before it be too late, get the better of a Vice that you will find difficult to subdue, when it is grown to a Head, and which will otherwise creep upon you every Day more and more, till it shuts up your Life in Misery as to yourself, and Contempt as to the World; and, instead of giving Cause even to your nearest and best Friends to remember you with Pleasure, will make it a Kindness in them to forget they ever had in the World, if a *Parent*, such a *Son*, if a *Tutor*, such a *Pupil*; if a *Brother* or *Sister*, such an unhappy *near Relation*; if a *Wife*, such an *Husband*; if a *Child*, such a *Father*; and if a *Friend*, such a *wretched one*, that cannot be thought of without Pity and Regret, for having shortened his Days, and ruined his Affairs, by so pernicious a Habit.

What a Joy, on the contrary, will that noblest of Conquests, over *yourself*, yield to all those dear Relations! And, in particular, what Pleasure will you give to the aged Heart, and declining Days, of, my dear Child,

Your indulgent and most affectionate Father!

LETTER XXXVIII.

From an Apprentice to his Master, begging Forgiveness for a great Misdemeanor.

Good Sir,

I AM so asham'd of myself for the last Occasion I have given you to be angry with me, after my repeated Promises of Amendment, that I have not the Courage to speak to you. I therefore take this Method of begging you to forgive what is past;

past; and let this Letter testify against me, if ever I wilfully or knowingly offend again for the future. You have Children of your own. They may possibly offend; tho' I hope they never will as I have done. Yet, Sir, would you not wish they might meet with Pardon, if they should, rather than Reprobation?-----My Making or my Ruin, I am sensible, lies in your Breast. If you will not forgive me, sad will be the Consequence to me, I doubt. If you do, you may save a Soul, as well as a Body, from Misery; and I hope, Sir, you will weigh this with your usual Goodness and Consideration. What is past, I cannot help; but for what is to come, I do promise, if God gives me Health and Power, that my Actions shall testify for me how much I am, good Sir,

Your repentant and obliged Servant.

LETTER XXXIX.

The Master's Answer.

JOHN,

YOUR Letter has affected me so much, that I am willing once more to pass over all you have done. Surely I may at last depend on these your solemn Assurances, and, as I hope, deep Contrition! If not, be it as you say, and let your Letter testify against you for your ingrateful Baseness; and for me, in my Readiness (which however shall be the last time) to forgive one that has been so much used to promise, and so little to perform. But I hope for better, because I yet wish you well, being, as you use me,

Yours, or otherwise.

LETTER XL.

From an Apprentice to his Friends, in Praise of his Master and Family.

Honoured Sir,

I Know it will be a great Satisfaction to you and my dear Mother, to hear that I go on very happily in my Business; and my Master, seeing my Diligence, puts me forward, and encourages me in such a manner, that I have great Delight in it, and hope I shall answer in time your good Wishes and Expectations, and the Indulgence which you have always shewn me. There is such good Order in the Family, as well on my Mistress's Part as my Master's, that every Servant, as well as I, knows his Duty, and does it with Pleasure. So much Evenness, Sedateness, and Regularity, is observed in all they injoin or expect, that it is impossible but it should be so. My Master is an honest worthy Man, every body speaks well of him. My Mistress is a chearful sweet-temper'd Woman, and rather heals Breaches than widens them. And the Children, after such Examples, behave to us all, like one's own Brothers and Sisters. Who can but love such a Family? I wish, when it shall please God to put me in such a Station, that I may carry myself just as my Master does; and if I should ever marry, have just such a Wife as my Mistress. And then, by God's Blessing, I shall be as happy as they are; and as you, Sir, and my dear Mother, have always been. If any thing can make me still happier than I am, or continue to me my present Felicity, it will be the Continuance of yours, and my good Mother's Prayers, for, honour'd Sir and Madam,

Your ever-dutiful Son.

LETTER XLI.

Another from an Apprentice, where the Master is too remiss in his own Affairs.

Honoured Sir and Madam,

YOU desire to know how I go on in my Business. I must needs say, Very well in the main; for my Master leaves every thing, in a manner, to me. I wish he did not, for his own sake. For tho' I hope he will never suffer on the Account of any wilful Remissness or Negligence, much less want of Fidelity, in me, yet his Affairs do not go on so well as if he was more in them, and less at the Tavern. But it becomes not me to reflect upon my Master, especially as what I may write or say on this Head, will rather expose his Failings, than do him Service; for as they must be his Equals that should reprove him, so all a Servant can observe to others will do more Harm than Good to him. One Thing is at *present* in my own Power; and that is, to double my Diligence, that his Family suffer as little as possible by his Remissness. And another, I hope, by God's Grace, *will* be; and that is, to avoid in myself, when my Time comes, those Failings which I see so blameable in him. And as this will be benefiting properly by the Example (for that Bee must be worse than a Drone, that cannot draw Honey from a bitter as well as a sweet Flower), so it will give you the Pleasure of knowing, that your good Instructions are not thrown away upon me, and that I am, and ever will be,

Your dutiful Son.

LETTER XLII.

To a Country Correspondent, modestly requesting a Balance of Accounts between them.

SIR,

I Find myself constrained, by a present Exigence, to beg you to balance the Account between us. Tho' Matters have run into some Length, yet would I not have apply'd to you, had I known so well how to answer my pressing Occasions any other way. If it suits you not to pay the Whole, I beg, Sir, you will remit me as much towards it as you can, without Prejudice to your own Affairs; and it will extremely oblige

Your most humble Servant.

LETTER XLIII.

In Answer to the preceding.

SIR,

I AM very glad I have it in my Power to send you now, directly, One hundred Pounds, on Account between us, which I do by our Carrier, who will pay you in Specie. I will soon remit you the Balance of your whole Demand, and am only sorry, that I gave Occasion for this Application for what is so justly your Due. When I send you the rest, which will be in a few Days, if I am not greatly disappointed, I will accompany it with an Order, which will begin a new Debt, but which I hope to be more punctual in discharging, than I have been in the last. I am, very sincerely,

Your Friend and Servant.

LETTER XLIV.

A more pressing and angry Letter from a City Dealer on the same Account.

Mr. *Barret*,

I AM sorry your ill Usage constrains me to write to you in the most pressing manner. Can you think it is possible to carry on Business after the manner you act by me? You know what Promises you have made me, and how from time to time you have broken them. And can I depend upon any new ones you make? If you use *others* as you do me, how can you think of carrying on Business? If you do *not*, what must I think of a Man who deals worse with me, than he does with any body else?----If you think you may trespass more upon *me*, than you can on *others*, this is a very bad Compliment to my *Prudence*, or your own *Gratitude*. For surely good Usage should be intitled to good Usage. I know how to allow for Disappointments as well as any Man; but can a Man be disappointed for ever? Trade is so dependent a thing, you know, that it cannot be carried on without mutual Punctuality. Does not the Merchant expect it from me, for those very Goods I send you? And can I make a Return to him, without receiving it from you? What End can it answer to give you Two Years Credit, and then be at an Uncertainty, for Goods which I sell at a small Profit, and have

not

not Six Months Credit for myself? Indeed, Sir, this will never do. I must be more punctually used by you, or else must deal as little punctually with others; and what then must be the Consequence? ------ In short, Sir, I expect a handsome Payment by the next Return, and Security for the Remainder; and shall be very loth to take any harsh Methods to procure this Justice to myself, my Family, and my own Creditors. For I am, if it be not your own Fault,

Your faithful Friend and Servant.

LETTER XLV.

In Answer to the preceding.

SIR,

I MUST acknowlege I have not used you well, and can give no better Answer to your just Expostulations, than to send you the inclosed Draught for 50 *l.* which you will be pleased to carry to my Credit; and to assure you of more punctual Treatment for the future. Your Letter is no bad Lesson to me; I have con'd it often, and hope I shall improve by it. I am ready to give you my Bond for the Remainder, which I will keep paying every Month something till 'tis all discharged; and what I write to you for, in the Interim, shall be paid for on Receipt of the Goods. This, I hope, Sir, will satisfy you for the present. If I could do better, I would; but shall be streighten'd to do this: But I think, in Return for your Patience, I cannot do less, to convince you, that I am now, at last, in Earnest. I beg you'll continue to me the same good Usage and Service I have met with from you hitherto; and that you'll believe me to be, unfeignedly,

Your obliged humble Servant.

LETTER XLVI.

To a young Trader generally in a Hurry in Business, advising Method as well as Diligence.

Dear Nephew,

THE Affection I have always borne you, as well for your own sake, as for your late Father's and Mother's, makes me give you the Trouble of these Lines, which I hope you will receive as kindly as I intend them.

I have lately call'd upon you several times, and have as often found you in an extraordinary Hurry, which I well know cannot be sometimes avoided; but, methinks, need not be always the Case, if your Time were disposed in regular and proper Proportions to your Business. I have frequently had Reason to believe, that more than half the Flutter which appears among Traders in general, is rather the Effect of their *Indolence*, than their *Industry*, however willing they are to have it thought otherwise; and I will give you one Instance in Confirmation of this Opinion, in a Neighbour of mine.

This Gentleman carried on for some Years a profitable Business; but, indulging himself every Evening in a Tavern Society or Club, which the Promotion of Business (as is usually the Case) gave the first Pretence for, he look'd upon those Engagements as the natural Consequence of the Approach of Night; and drove on his Business in the Day with Precipitation, that he might get thither with the earliest. He seldom kept very late Hours, tho' he never came home soon. The Night being gone, and his Bottle empty'd, the Morning was always wanted to dispel the Fumes of the Wine.

Whoever therefore came to him before Nine, was desired to call again; and when he rose, so many Matters waited for him, as directly threw him into a Flutter; so that from his Rising till Dinner-time, he seem'd in one continued Ferment. A long Dinner-time he always allowed himself, in order to recover the Fatigues he had undergone; and all his Table-talk was, How heavy his Business lay upon him! And what Pains he took in it! The hearty Meal, and the Time he indulged himself at Table, begot an Inappetency for any more Business for that short Afternoon; so all that *could* be defer'd, was put off to the next Morning; and long'd-for Evening approaching, he flies to his usual Solace: Empties his Bottle by Eleven Comes home: Gets to Bed; and is invisible till next Morning at Nine; and then rising, enters upon his usual Hurry and Confusion.

Thus did his Life seem, to those who saw him in his Business, one constant Scene of Fatigue, tho' he scarce ever apply'd to it Four regular Hours in any one Day. Whereas had he risen *only* at Seven in the Morning, he would have got all his Business under by Noon; and those Two Hours, from Seven to Nine, being before many People go abroad, he would have met with no Interruption in his Affairs; but might have improved his Servants by his own Example, directed them in the Business of the Day, have inspected his Books, written to his Dealers, and put every thing in so regular a Train, for the rest of the Day, that whatever had occurred afterwards, would rather have served to divert than fatigue him.

And what, to cut my Story short, was the Upshot of the Matter? Why, meeting with some Disappointments and Losses (as all Traders must expect, and ought to provide for), and his Customers not seeing him in his Shop so much as they expected, and when there, always in a disobliging petulant Hurry; and moreover, Mistakes frequently happening through the Flurry into which he put himself and every one about him; by these means his Business dwindled away insensibly; and, not being able to go out of his usual Course, which helped to impair both his Capacity and Ardor to Business, his Creditors began to look about them, and he was compelled to enter into the State of his Affairs; and then had the Mortification to find the Balance of 2000 *l*. against him.

This was a shocking Case to himself; but more to his Family; for his Wife had lived, and his Children had been educated, in such a manner, as induced them to hope their Fortunes would be sufficient to place them in a State of Independence

In short, being obliged to quit a Business he had managed with so little Prudence, his Friends got him upon a charitable Foundation, which afforded him bare Subsistence for himself, his Children were dispersed some one way, and some another, into low Scenes of Life; and his Wife went home to her Friends, to be snub'd and reflected on by her own Family, for Faults not her own.

This Example will afford several good Hints to a young Tradesman, which are too obvious to need expatiating upon. And as I dare say, your Prudence will keep you from the like Fault, you will never have Reason to reproach yourself on this score. But yet, as I always found you in a Hurry, when I called upon you, I could not but give you this Hint, for fear you should not rightly proportion your Time to your Business, and lest you should suspend to the *next* Hour, what you could and ought to do in the *present*, and so did not keep your Business properly under. Method is

every

every thing in Business, next to Diligence. And you will, by falling into a regular one, always be calm and unruffled, and have time to bestow in your Shop with your Customers; the Female ones especially; who always love to make a great many Words in their Bargainings, and expect to be humour'd and persuaded: And how can any Man find Time for this, if he prefers the Tavern to his Shop, and his Bed to his Business? I know you will take in good Part what I have written, because you are sensible how much I am

Your truly affectionate, &c.

LETTER XLVII.

From a Son reduced by his own Extravagance, requesting his Father's Advice, on his Intention to turn Player.

Honoured Sir,

AFTER the many Occasions I have given for your Displeasure, permit me to ask your Advice in an Affair which may render my whole Life comfortable or miserable. You know, Sir, to what a low Ebb my Folly and Extravagance have reduced me. Your generous Indulgence has made you stretch your Power, to my Shame I speak it, even beyond the Bounds which Wisdom, and a necessary Regard to the rest of your Family, would permit; therefore I cannot hope for further Assistance from you. Something, however, I must resolve upon to gain a Maintenance: And an Accident fell out Yesterday, which offers me, at least, present Bread.

Mr. *Rich,* Master of one of the Theatres, happened to dine at my Uncle's when I was there: After Dinner, the Subject of Discourse was, the

Art of a Comedian. On which my Uncle took Occasion to mention the little Flights in that way with which I have diverted myself in my gayer Moments; and partly compelled me to give an Inſtance of my Abilities. Mr. *Rich* was pleaſed to declare his Approbation of my Manner and Voice; and, on being told my Circumſtances, offer'd at once to take me into his Company with an Allowance ſufficient for preſent Subſiſtence, and additional Encouragement, as I ſhould be found to deſerve it. Half a Benefit he promiſed me the firſt Seaſon; which, by my (otherwiſe too) numerous Acquaintance, might, I believe, be turned to pretty good Account. I am not fond of this Life; but ſee no other Means of ſupporting myſelf like a Gentleman. Your ſpeedy Anſwer will be ever gratefully acknowleged by, honoured Sir,

Your dutiful, tho' unhappy Son.

LETTER XLVIII.

The Father's Anſwer, ſetting forth the Inconveniencies and Diſgrace attending the Profeſſion of a Player.

Dear Gilbert,

I Should be glad to have you in any Situation which would afford you a comfortable and reputable Subſiſtence: But cannot think the Life of a Stage-player proper for that End. You muſt conſider, that tho' in the gay Trappings of that Employment a Man may repreſent a Gentleman, yet none can be farther from that Character, if a perpetual Dependence be the worſt Kind of Servility. In the firſt Place, the Company you will be in a manner oblig'd to keep, will be ſuch as will tend little to the Improvement of your Mind, or

most Important Occasions. 61

Amendment of your Morals: To the Master of the Company you list in, you must be obsequious to a Degree of Slavery. Not one of an Audience that is able to *hiss*, but you must *fear*; and each single Man you come to know personally, you must oblige on every Occasion that offers, to engage their Interest at your Benefit. A Thought the most shocking to a free and generous Mind! And if to this you add the little Profit that will attend making a low Figure on the Stage, and, besides the Qualifications necessary, the incredible Fatigue attending the Support of a good Figure upon it; you will easily see, that more Credit, more Satisfaction, more Ease, and more Profit, may be got in many other Stations, without the mortifying Knowlege of being deem'd a Vagrant by the Laws of your Country. I hope this will be enough to dissuade you from farther Thoughts of the Stage. And, in any other Employment, you may yet expect some small Assistance from

Your loving Father.

LETTER XLIX.

To a Brother too captious to bear himself the Ridicule he practises upon others.

Dear Jack,

I AM glad to find you improve both in *Thought* and *Speech*. You know I am no Witch at either: But, so as we have some Wit in our Family, no matter who is at the Trouble of carrying it for what he'll get by it. I suppose you thought to give no small Pleasure to the Company last Night by your facetious Flings at all around you, not

excepting

excepting the Parson himself: But should you not have considered, that every one in the Room had a Right to return the Freedom you took, in the best manner he was able? Was it therefore well in you to resent so warmly as you did, a smart Remark made by Mr. *Crispe*, on a palpable Blunder of your own, when you had taken so much Liberty with him, as well as every body else, just before? Indeed, Brother, you must either lay aside Ridicule, or learn to bear it better; and in the present Case you should have remember'd, that, in the manner you began with that Gentleman, it was not possible for him to say any thing it would have been your Credit to resent. A Retort on these Occasions must be excused, tho' fraught with Resentment; for a Man is not always in a Humour to be jested with, and it is the Duty of him who begins, to take what follows. Your failing in this known Rule, whatever you may think, has made you appear in so mean a Light to the whole Company, that all your Acuteness will not in haste atone for it.

If I judge rightly, nothing is more delicate than Ridicule: Where it is conducted with Prudence and Humour, it is sure to please even the Man who is the Subject of it, if he is not of a morose Temper: But when, instead of that, personal Failings, or private Indiscretions, are exposed for the Entertainment of a Company, tho' you may think to raise a Laugh by it in the Unreflecting, it will bring upon you the Censure of the Considerate. It is our Duty to consult what we can *bear* ourselves, as well as what we can *inflict* on others. For my own Part, I know I cannot bear what is called a *close Rub*, as many Men can; and for that Reason I never jest with any body, unless by way of Reprisal; and that I shorten all I can, lest my Temper should not hold out.

No doubt but you have more Humour than I; but if you do not blend in it a Quantity of Temper sufficient to carry it off, you will be no Gainer by the Qualification. The Philosopher says, That to *Bear* and *Forbear*, are the highest Points of Wisdom: If so, where is his Wisdom, who will neither do the one or the other? You may not like the Freedom I have here taken; but I respect you too well to pass over your Foibles without some Observation; being

Your truly affectionate Brother.

LETTER L.

To a Friend, on his Recovery from a dangerous Illness.

Dear Sir,

GIVE me Leave to mingle my Joy with that of all your Friends and Relations, in the Recovery of your Health, and to join with them to bless God for continuing to your numerous Wellwishers the Benefit of your useful and valuable Life. May God Almighty long preserve you in Health, and prosper all your Undertakings, for the Good of your worthy Family, and the Pleasure of all your Friends and Acquaintance, is the hearty Prayer of, Sir,

Your faithful Friend, and humble Servant.

LETTER LI.

On the same Occasion.

Good Sir,

I HAVE received, with great Delight, the good News of your Recovery from the dangerous Illness with which it pleased God to afflict you. I

most

most heartily congratulate you and your good Lady and Family upon it, and make it my Prayer, That your late Indisposition may be succeeded by such a Renewal of Health and Strength both of Body and Mind, as may make your Life equally happy to yourself, as it must be to all who have the Pleasure to know you. I could not avoid giving you this Trouble, to testify the Joy that affected my Heart on the Occasion; and to assure you that I am, with the greatest Affection and Respect, Sir,

Your faithful humble Servant.

LETTER LII.

In Answer to the preceding.

Dear Sir,

I GIVE you many Thanks for your kind Congratulations. My Return of Health will be the greater Pleasure to me, if I can contribute in any measure to the Happiness of my many good Friends, and, particularly, to that of you and yours, for I assure you, Sir, that nobody can be more than I am,

Your obliged humble Servant.

LETTER LIII.

To a young Lady, advising her not to change her Guardians, nor to encourage any clandestine Address.

Dear Miss,

THE Friendship which long subsisted between your prudent Mother and me, has always made me attend to your Welfare with more than a common

mon Concern: And I could not conceal my Surprize at hearing, that you intend to remove the Guardianship of yourself and Fortune, from the Gentlemen to whom your tender Parents committed the Direction of both. I am afraid, my Dear, your Dissatisfaction arises more from sudden Distaste, than from mature Reflection. Mr. *Jones* and Mr. *Pitt* were long the intimate Friends and Companions of your Father, for more than Thirty Years he had experienc'd their Candor and Wisdom; and it was their Fitness for the Trust, that induced him to leave you to their Care; and will you reflect upon his Judgment?

They are not less wise now, than when he made his Will; and if they happen to differ from your Judgment in any thing of Moment, what Room have you to suppose yourself better able to judge of the Consequences of what you desire, than they? I do not undervalue your good Sense, and yet I must tell you, that (the Difference of Years consider'd, and their Knowlege of the World, which you can yet know little of) it would be strange if they did not understand better than you, what was proper for you, and their Honesty was never yet disputed. Upon these Considerations, who is most probably to blame, should you happen to disagree? From such Men, you will never meet more Restraints than are necessary for your Happiness and Interest, for nothing that can injure *you* in any respect, can add to *their* Advantage or Reputation. I have known several young Ladies of your Age impatient of the least Controul, and think hardly of every little Contradiction; but when, by any unadvised Step, they have released themselves, as they call it, from the Care of their try'd Friends, how often have they had Cause to repent their Rashness! How seldom do you hear
those

those Ladies, who have subjected themselves to what some reckon the greatest Restraints while young, repent the Effects of them when grown up!

To mention the single Article, about which, generally, these Differences arise, that of Marriage What good Fruits can a Lady hope, from the insidious Progress of a clandestine Address? A Man who can be worth a Lady's Acceptance, will never be ashamed or afraid to appear openly. If he deserves to succeed, or is conscious that he does, what need of concealing his Designs from her Friends? Must it not be with a View to get her in his Power, and, by securing a Place in her Affections, make her Weakness give Strength to *his* Presumption, and forward those Pretensions that he knew would otherwise be rejected with Scorn?

Let me tell you, my dear Miss, that you neither want Sense nor Beauty; and no young Gentleman can be ashamed of being *known* to love you. Consider this well, and despise the Man who seeks the Aid of back Doors, bribed Servants, and Garden-walls, to get Access to your Person. If he had not a meaner Opinion of your Understanding than he ought, he would not hope for Success from such *poor Methods*. Let him see then, how much he is mistaken, if he thinks you the giddy Girl his clandestine Conduct seems to call you. *In time,* advise with your try'd Friends. Trust no Servant with Secrets you would not have known to your Equals or Guardians; and be sure ever to shun a servile Confidant, who generally makes her Market of her Mistress, and sells her to the highest Bidder.

I hope, dear Miss, you will seriously reflect upon all I have said, and excuse the well-meant Zeal of

Your sincere Friend.

LET-

LETTER LIV.

From a Mother to her Daughter, jealous of her Husband.

Dear Bet,

I AM sorry to find you are grown jealous of your Husband. 'Tis a most uneasy Passion, and will be fatal, not only to your present Quiet, but to your future Happiness, and probably to that of your Family, if you indulge it.

You either *have*, or have *not*, Cause for it. If you have Cause, look into yourself, and your own Conduct, to see if you have not by any Change of Temper, or Disagreeableness of Behaviour, alienated your Husband's Affections; and if so, set about amending both, in order to recover them: For once he loved you, and you were satisfy'd he did, above all your Sex, or you would not have had him. If it be owing to his inconstant Temper, that is indeed unhappy; but then, so long as you are clear of Blame, you have nothing to reproach yourself with. And as the Creatures wicked Men follow; omit nothing to oblige them, you must try to avoid such uneasy and disturbing Resentments, as will make you more and more distasteful to him. Shew him, that no guilty Wretch's *pretended* Love can be equal to your *real* one: Shew him, that such Creatures shall not outdo you in *obliging Behaviour*, and *Sweetness of Temper*; and that, let him fly off from *his* Duty, if he will, you will persevere in *yours*. This Conduct will, if not immediately, in time, flash Conviction in his Face: He will see what a Goodness he injures, and will be softened by your Softness. But if you make his Home uneasy to him, he will fly both,
that

that and *you:* And to whom will he fly, but, most probably, to one who will allow his Pleas, and aggravate every thing against you, who will side with him, inflame his Passions, and thereby secure him to herself? And would *you* contribute to such a Wretch's Power over him, and furnish Opportunities for *her* to triumph over you? For while you exasperate his Passions, and harden his Mind against you, she will, by wicked Blandishments, shew him how obliging *she* can be, and so a Course of Life, that he would follow privately, and by stealth, as it were, he will more openly pursue, he will grow shameless in it; and, so common is the Vice, more's the Pity! will find those who will extenuate it for *their own* sakes, and throw the Blame on the Violence of your Temper, and say, you drive him into these Excesses. Thus much I write, supposing you have *Reason to be jealous.* I will write yet another Letter on this important Subject. I hope they will have the Weight intended them, by

Your ever indulgent Mother.

LETTER LV.

The same Subject continued.

Dear Bet,

WHAT I wrote in my former, was on a Supposition that you had too much Reason to be uneasy at your Husband's Conduct.

I will now pursue the Subject, and put the Case that you have no *Proof* that he is guilty, but your Surmizes, or, perhaps, the busy *Whisperings* of officious *Make-debates.* In this Case, take care, my *Betsey,* that you don't, by the Violence of your Passions

most Important Occasions. 69

sons, precipitate him on the Course you dread, and that you alienate not, by unjust Suspicions, his Affections from you, for then perhaps he will be ready *indeed* to place them somewhere else, whence you may not so easily draw him off; for he will, may be, think, as to *you* (if he be devoid of *superior* Considerations), that he may as well *deserve* your Suspicions, as be tiezed with them *without* deserving them.

I know it is a most shocking thing to a sober young Woman, to think herself obliged to *share* those Affections which ought to be *all her own*, with a *vile Prostitute*, besides the Danger, which is not small, of being intirely circumvented in her Husband's *Love*, and perhaps have only his *Indifference*, if not *Contempt*, instead of it. But, my Dear, at the worst, comfort yourself that *you* are not the guilty Person; for one Day he will, perhaps, fatally find his Error. And consider, besides, my *Betsey*, that your Case, from an unfaithful *Husband*, is not near so bad as his would be from an unfaithful *Wife*. For, Child, he cannot make the Progeny of a *Bastard Race* succeed to his and your Estate or Chattels, in Injury of your *lawful Children* If any such he should have, the Law of the Land *brands* them Whereas a *naughty Wife* often makes the Children of *another Man* Heirs of her Husband's Estate and Fortune, in Injury of his *own Children* or *Family*. So, tho' the Crime may be equal in *other respects*, yet this makes the Injury of the Woman to the Man, greater than *his* can be to her

These Thoughts I have thrown together, as they occurred, in two Letters, that I might not tire you with a Length, that, yet, the important Subject required. Let me briefly sum up the Contents.

If

If he be *guilty*, try by Softness and kind Expostulations to reclaim him, before the Vice be rooted in him. If it be so rooted, as that he cannot be drawn off, you know not what God may do for you, if you trust in Him, and take not upon yourself, by giving up your Mind to Violence, to be your own Avenger. A *sick Bed*, a *tender Conduct* in you, a *sore Disaster* (and who that lives is not liable to such?) may give him to see the Error of his Ways, and shew him the Foulness of his Crime, which your good Usage will aggravate, upon his sober Reflection, with the no weak Addition of *Ingratitude* to so good a Wife. The *Wretch* he has chosen for a Partner in his Guilt, may, by her sordid Ways, *awake* him, by her libidinous Deportment, *satiate* him, by her detected Commerce with *others* (for such Creatures, having once given themselves up to Vice, know no Bounds), make him abhor her. And then he will see the Difference between such a one, and a chaste Wife, whose *Interests* are bound up in *his own*, and will admire you more than ever he did; and you'll have the Pleasure, besides, in all Probability, of saving a Soul that stands in so near a Relation to your own.

But if your Uneasiness be owing to *private Talebearers*, and *busy Intermeddlers*, take care, my Dear, you are not made a Property of by such mischievous People. Take care that you make not your own *present Peace*, and your *future Good*, and that of your *Family*, and of *him* your injur'd Husband, the Sacrifices to such pernicious Busy-bodies.

Consider, my Dear, all I have said, and God bless you with a Conduct and Discretion suitable to the Occasion before you, and, at the worst, give you Comfort and Patience in *your own* Innocence. For such is this transitory Life, that all the Ill or Good we receive, will be *soon over with us*, and then

then the *Punishment* of the *former*, and the *Reward* of the *latter*, will make *all Scores even*, and what is *past* appear as *nothing*. Mean time I can but pray for you: As, my dear Child, becomes

Your ever affectionate Mother.

LETTER LVI.

From a tender Father to an ungracious Son.

Son John,

I AM under no small Concern, that your continued ill Courses give me Occasion to write this Letter to you. I was in hopes, that your solemn Promises of Amendment might have been better depended on; but I see, to my great Mortification, that all I have done for you, and all I have said to you, is thrown away. What *can* I say more than I *have said?* Yet, *once more* am I desirous to try what the Force of a *Letter* will do with one who has not suffer'd mere *Words* to have any Effect upon him. Perhaps this remaining with you, if you will now-and-then seriously peruse it, may, in some happy Moment, give you *Reflection*, and, by God's Grace, bring on your *Repentance* and *Amendment*.

Consider then, I beseech you, in time, the Evil of your Ways. Make *my* Case *your own*; and think, if *you* were to be Father of such a Son, how his Actions would grieve and afflict you. But if my Comfort has no Weight with you, consider, my Son, how your present Courses must impair, in time, a good Constitution, destroy your Health, and, most probably, shorten your Life. Consider that your *Reputation* is wounded, I hope, not mortally,

tally, as yet: That you will be ranked among the Profligates and Outcasts of the World; that no virtuous Man will keep you Company, that every one who has a Regard for his own Credit will shun you; and that you will be given up to the Society of the *worst* and *most abandon'd* of Men, when you might be improv'd by the Examples of the *best*. That no Family which values their own Honour, and the Welfare of their Child, will suffer your Addresses to a Daughter worthy of being sought after for a Wife, should you incline to marry; and that the worst of that Sex must probably, in that Case, fall to your Lot; which will make you miserable in *this World*, when you might be happy.

Then, as to *another World* beyond this transitory one, my Heart trembles for what most probably will be the Consequence to your poor Soul. For the human Mind is seldom *at a stay*. If you do not grow *better*, you will most undoubtedly grow *worse*, and you may run into those Sins and Evils, that you *now* perhaps think yourself incapable of, as *already* you are arrived at a Height of Folly and Wickedness, that once you would have thought you could not have been guilty of. Don't, my dear Son, let your poor Mother and me have the Mortification to think, that we have been the unhappy Means of giving Life to a Child of Perdition, instead of a Child of Glory; that our beloved Son with all the Pains we have taken to instil good Principles into his Mind, in hopes he would one Day prove a Credit and Comfort to his Family, should, instead of answering our longing Wishes when at Age, take such contrary Courses, as would make us join to wish he had never been born.

Consider, my dear Son, we don't want any thing of *you* but *your own Good*. We lived before you were born. You have been a great Expence to

most Important Occasions. 73

to bring you up to these Years. You cannot now live without *us*, but we can without *you*. We hope God will continue your Life to be still a *further Expence* to us. For all we live for, is our Childrens Good. Let then the *Disinterestedness* of our Plea move you. Be but good to *yourself*, that is all we require of you. Let us but have Reason to hope, that when we are *dead* and *gone*, you will support our Name with Credit, and be no Burden to your poor Sisters, nor Disgrace to our Memories. Shew us that you are of a *generous*, not of a *sordid* Nature; and will probably set yourself above future Misfortunes by reclaiming in time; and then we shall be happy. As God has done his Part by you, and given you Talents that every one cannot boast, let me beg you to consider only, how much more noble it is to be in such a Situation as shall enable you to *confer* Benefits, than such an one as shall lay you under the poor Necessity to *receive* them from others, and, perhaps, where they ought to be least expected.

I have written a long Letter. The Subject is *next my Heart*, and will excuse it. God give a Blessing to it! God give you to see the Error of your Ways before it be too late, and before you get such a Habit as you cannot alter if you would! Let your poor Mother and Sisters look upon you with *Pleasure*, rather than *Apprehension*, in case God Almighty should take me away from them: Let them think of you as a *Protector* in my stead, rather than as an ingrateful *Spoiler* among them; and you will then give Comfort to my Life, as long as God shall spare it, and alleviate, instead of aggravating, the Pangs of my dying Hour, when God shall send it.

My dear, dear Son, I conjure you, by all our past Tenderness and Affection for you, by our

E Hopes,

Hopes, and our Fears, from Infancy to Manhood, to think of all thefe Things; reflect upon the Tranfitorinefs of worldly Enjoyments, even when better chofen than yours are. Judge of the Pleafures you expect in your *prefent Courfe*, by the Vanity of the *paft*; of your *next* Affignations, by the aching Head, and undelighted Heart, which followed the *laft*, and you will find, that no Satisfaction, which is not grounded on Virtue and Sobriety, can be durable, or worthy of a rational Creature.

Your good Mother, who joins her Tears fo often with mine, to deplore the fad Profpect your ill Courfes give us, joins alfo her Prayers to mine, that this my *laft Effort* may be attended with Succefs, and that you will not let us intreat in vain. *Amen, Amen*, fays

Your indulgent and afflicted Father.

LETTER LVII.

The Son's dutiful Anfwer.

Honoured Sir,

I AM greatly affected with the tender and moving Goodnefs expreffed in your indulgent Letter. I am exceedingly forry, that all your good Advice before has been fo caft away upon me, as to render this further Inftance of your paternal Affection neceffary. I am refolved inftantly to fet about a Reformation, and to conform myfelf intirely to your good Pleafure for the future; and I beg, Sir, the Continuance of yours, and my good Mother's Prayers to God, to enable me to adhere to my prefent good Refolutions. I have fo often promifed, and fo often broken my Word

(rather

most Important Occasions.

(rather indeed thro' the *Strength* of my *Passions*, than a *Design* of Non-performance), that I think, I ought now to give you some Proof, that I am in earnest; and what better can I give, than to assure you, that I will henceforth break myself from the frothy Companions I used to take too much Delight in, and whose lewd Banters and Temptations have so frequently set aside my good Purposes? You, Sir, for the future, shall recommend the Company proper for me to keep; and I beg you will chalk out for me the Paths in which you would have me tread, and, as much as possible, I will walk in them; and when I have convinced you of the Sincerity of my Reformation, I hope, Sir, you and my honoured Mother will restore me to your good Opinions, which it shall be my constant Study to deserve. I have already broken with *George Negus,* who attempted to laugh me out of my good Resolutions. And I beg Leave to wait upon you for such a Space of Time as you shall think proper, in order to break myself from the rest of my profligate Companions, and that I may have the Benefit of your Advice and Direction for my future Conduct. God continue long (for the Benefit of us all) your Life and Health, and make me happy in contributing as much to your future Comforts, as I have, by my past Excesses, to your Trouble of Mind, is, and shall always be, the Prayer of, Honoured Sir,

Your truly penitent and dutiful Son.

LETTER LVIII.

To a Friend, on Occasion of his not answering his Letters.

Dear Sir,

IT is so long since I had the Favour of a Line from you, that I am under great Apprehensions in relation to your Health and Welfare. I beg you, Sir, to renew to me the Pleasure you used to give me in your Correspondence; for I have written three Letters to you before this, to which I have had no Answer, and am not conscious of having any way disobliged you. If I have, I will most willingly ask your Pardon, for nobody can be more than I am,

Your affectionate and faithful Friend and Servant.

LETTER LIX.

In Answer to the preceding.

Dear Sir,

YOU have not, cannot disoblige me; but I have greatly disobliged myself, in my own faulty Remissness. I cannot account for it as I ought. To say I had Business one time, Company another, was distant from home a third, will be but poor Excuses, for not answering one of your kind Letters in four long Months. I therefore ingenuously take Shame to myself, and promise future Amendment; and that nothing shall ever, while I am able to hold a Pen, make me guilty of the like Neglect to a Friend I love so well, and have

have so much Reason so to do. Forgive me then, my good, my kind, my generous Friend; and believe me ever

Your highly obliged humble Servant.

LETTER LX.

From a Father to a Son, on his Negligence in his Affairs.

Dear Jemmy,

YOU cannot imagine what a Concern your Carelessness and indifferent Management of your Affairs give me. Remissness is inexcusable in all Men, but in none so much as in a Man of Business, the Soul of which is Industry, Diligence, and Punctuality.

Let me beg of you to shake off the idle Habits you have contracted; quit unprofitable Company, and unseasonable Recreations, and apply to your Compting-house with Diligence. It may not be yet too late to retrieve your Affairs. Inspect therefore your Gains, and cast up what Proportion they bear to your Expences; and then see which of the latter you *can*, and which you *cannot* contract. Consider, that when once a Man suffers himself to go backward in the World, it must be an uncommon Spirit of Industry that retrieves him, and puts him forward again.

Reflect, I beseech you, before it be too late, upon the Inconveniencies which an impoverish'd Trader is put to, for the Remainder of his Life, which, too, may happen to be the prime Part of it; the Indignities he is likely to suffer from those whose Money he has unthinkingly squander'd, the

Contempt he will meet with from all, not excepting the idle Companions of his Folly; the Injustice he does his Family, in depriving his Children, not only of the Power of raising themselves, but of living tolerably; and how, on the contrary, from being born to a creditable Expectation, he sinks them into the lowest Class of Mankind, and exposes them to the most dangerous Temptations. What has not such a Father to answer for! and all this for the sake of indulging himself in an idle, a careless, a thoughtless Habit, that cannot afford the least Satisfaction, beyond the present Hour, if in that; and which must be attended with deep Remorse, when he comes to reflect. Think seriously of these Things, and in time resolve on such a Course as may bring Credit to yourself, Justice to all you deal with, Peace and Pleasure to your own Mind, Comfort to your Family; and which will give at the same time the highest Satisfaction to

Your careful and loving Father.

LETTER LXI.

The Son's grateful Answer.

Honoured Sir,

I Return you my sincere Thanks for your seasonable Reproof and Advice. I have indeed too much indulged myself in an idle careless Habit, and had already begun to feel the evil Consequences of it, when I received your Letter, in the Insults of a Creditor or two, from whom I expected kinder Treatment. But indeed they wanted but their own, so I could only blame myself, who had brought their rough Usage upon me. Your Letter came so seasonably upon this, that I hope it will not want the desired Effect; and as, I thank God, it is not yet too late, I am resolved to take another Course with myself and my Affairs, that I may avoid the ill Consequences you so judiciously forewarn me of, and give to my Family and Friends the Pleasure they so well deserve at my Hands; and particularly that Satisfaction to so good a Father, which is owing to him by

His most dutiful Son.

LETTER LXII.

A young Woman in Town to her Sister in the Country, recounting her narrow Escape from a Snare laid for her on her first Arrival, by a wicked Procuress.

Dear Sister,

WE have often, by our good Mother, been warned against the Dangers that would too probably attend us on coming to *London*; tho' I must own, her Admonitions had not always the Weight I am now convinced they deserved.

I have had a Deliverance from such a Snare, as I never could have believed would have been laid for a Person free from all Thought of Ill, or been so near succeeding upon one so strongly on her Guard as I imagined myself: And thus, my dear Sister, the Matter happened.

Returning, on *Tuesday*, from seeing my Cousin *Atkins*, in *Cheapside*, I was overtaken by an elderly Gentlewoman of a sober and creditable Appearance, who walked by my Side some little time before she spoke to me; and then guessing (by my asking the Name of the Street), that I was a Stranger to the Town, she very courteously began a Discourse with me, and after some other Talk, and Questions about my Country, and the like, desired to know, If I did not come to Town with a Design of going into some genteel Place? I told her, If I could meet with a Place to my Mind, to wait upon a single Lady, I should be very willing to embrace it. She said, I look'd like a creditable, sober, and modest Body; and at that very time she knew one of the best Gentlewomen that ever lived, who was in great Want of a Maid to attend upon her own Person; and that if she liked me, and I her, it would be a lucky Incident for us both.

I expressed myself thankfully, and she was so very much in my Interest, as to intreat me to go instantly to the Lady, lest she should be provided, and acquaint her I was recommended by Mrs *Jones*, not doubting, as she said, but, on Inquiry, my Character would answer my Appearance.

As that, you know, was partly my View in comeing to Town, I thought this a happy Incident, and determined not to lose the Opportunity, and so, according to the Direction she gave me, I went to inquire for Mrs. C------ in *J-----n*'s Court, *Fleet-street*. The Neighbourhood look'd genteel, and I soon found the House. I ask'd for Mrs. C----; she came to me, dress'd in a splendid manner; I told her what I came about; she immediately desir'd me to walk into the Parlour, which was elegantly furnish'd; and after asking me several Questions, with my Answers to which she seem'd very well pleas'd, a Servant soon brought in a Bowl of warm Liquor, which she call'd *Negus*, consisting of Wine, Water, Orange, &c which, she said, was for a Friend or two she expected presently; but as I was warm with walking, she would have me drink some of it, telling me it was a pleasant innocent Liquor,

and

and she always used her Waiting-maids, as she did herself. I thought this was very kind and condescending, and being warm and thirsty, and she encouraging me, I took a pretty free Draught of it, and thought it very pleasant, as it really was. She made me sit down by her, saying, Pride was not her Talent, and that she should always indulge me in like manner, if I behaved well, when she had not Company; and then slightly ask'd, What I could do, and the Wages I required? With my Answers she seemed well satisfied, and granted the Wages I asked, without any Offer of Abatement.

And then I rose up, in order to take my Leave, telling her I would, any Day she pleased, of the ensuing Week, bring my Cloaths, and wait upon her

She said, That her own Maid being gone away, she was in the utmost Want of another, and would take it kindly, if I would stay with her till next Day, because she was to have some Ladies to pass the Evening with her. I said this would be pretty inconvenient to me, but as she was so situated, I would oblige her, after I had been with my Aunt, and acquainted her with it To this she reply'd, That there was no manner of Occasion for that, because she could send the Cook for what I wanted, who could, at the same time, tell my Aunt how Matters stood.

I thought this looked a little odd, but she did it with so much Civility, and seemed so pleased with her new Maid, that I scarcely knew how to withstand her But the Apprehension I had of my Aunt's Anger for not asking her Advice, in what so nearly concern'd me, made me insist upon going, though I could perceive Displeasure in her Countenance when she saw me resolv'd.

She then ply'd me very clofe with the Liquor, which fhe again faid was innocent and weak; but I believe it was far otherwife; for my Head began to turn round, and my Stomach felt a little difordered. I intreated the Favour of her to permit me to go, on a firm Promife of returning immediately; but then my new Miftrefs began to raife her Voice a little, affuring me I fhould on no Account ftir out of her Houfe. She left the Room, in a fort of a Pet, but faid fhe would fend the Cook to take my Directions to my Aunt; and I heard her take the Key out of the outward Door.

This alarmed me very much; and, in the Inftant of my Surprize, a young Gentlewoman enter'd the Parlour, drefs'd in white Sattin, and every way genteel, fhe fat down in a Chair next me, looked earneftly at me a while, and feemed going to fpeak feveral times, but did not. At length fhe rofe from her Chair, bolted the Parlour-door, and, breaking into a Flood of Tears, exprefs'd herfelf as follows:

" Dear young Woman, I cannot tell you the
" Pain I feel on your Account, and from an In-
" clination to ferve you, I run a Hazard of in-
" volving myfelf in greater Mifery than I have yet
" experienced, if that can be. But my Heart is yet
" too honeft to draw others, as I am defir'd to do,
" into a Snare which I have fallen into myfelf You
" are now in as notorious a Brothel, as is in *Lon-*
" *don* · And if you efcape not in a few Hours, you
" are inevitably undone. I was once as innocent
" as you now feem to be. No Apprehenfion you
" can be under for your Virtue, but I felt as much
" My Reputation was as unfpotted, and my Heart
" as unvers'd in Ill, when I firft enter'd thefe guilty
" Doors, whither I was fent on an Errand, much
" like what I underftand has brought you hither. I
" was

"was by Force detained the whole Night, as you
"are designed to be, was robbed of my Virtue;
"and knowing I should hardly be forgiven by my
"Friends for staying out without their Know-
"lege, and in the Morning being at a Loss, all in
"Confusion as I was, what to do, before I could
"resolve on any thing, I was obliged to repeat my
"Guilt, and had hardly Time afforded me to re-
"flect on its fatal Consequences. My Liberty I
"intreated to no Purpose, and my Grief serv'd for
"the cruel Sport of all around me. In short, I
"have been now so long confined, that I am
"ashamed to appear among my Friends and Ac-
"quaintance. In this dreadful Situation, I have
"been perplexed with the hateful Importunities of
"different Men every Day, and tho' I long re-
"sisted to my utmost, yet downright Force never
"failed to overcome. Thus in a shameful Round
"of Guilt and Horror, have I lingered out Ten
"Months, subject to more Miseries than Tongue
"can express. The same sad Lot is intended you,
"nor will it be easy to shun it: However, as I can-
"not well be more miserable than I am, I will assist
"you what I can; and not, as the wretched Pro-
"curess hopes, contribute to make you as unhappy
"as myself."

You may guess at the Terror that seized my Heart, on this sad Story, and my own Danger; I trembled in every Joint, nor was I able to speak for some time; at last, in the best manner I could, I thanked my unhappy new Friend, and begg'd she would kindly give me the Assistance she offered: Which she did; for the first Gentleman that came to the Door, she stept up herself for the Key to let him in, which the wretched Procuress gave her; and I took that Opportunity, as she directed, to run out of the House, and that in so much Hurry and Confusion, as to leave my Hood, Fan, and Gloves behind me.

I told my Aunt every Circumstance of my Danger and Escape, and received a severe Reprimand for my following so inconsiderately, in so wicked a Town as this, the Direction of an intire Stranger.

I am sure, Sister, you rejoice with me for my Deliverance. And this Accident may serve to teach us to be upon our Guard for the future, as well against the viler Part of our own Sex, as that of the other. I am, dear Sister,

Your truly affectionate Sister.

N B This shocking Story is taken from the Mouth of the young Woman herself, who so narrowly escaped the Snare of the vile Procuress, and is Fact in every Circumstance.

LETTER LXIII.

To a Daughter in a Country Town, who encourages the Address of a Subaltern [A Case too frequent in Country Places.]

Dear Betsy,

I HAVE been under the deepest Affliction ever since I heard of your encouraging the Addresses of a Soldier, whether Serjeant or Corporal, I know not, who happens to quarter next Door to your Uncle

What, my dear Child, can you propose by such a Match? Is his Pay sufficient to maintain himself? If it be, will it be sufficient for the Support of a Family?

Consider,

most Important Occasions. 85

Confider, there will be no Opportunity for *you* to increafe his poor Income, but by fuch Means as will be very grating for you to fubmit to. Will your Hands be capable of enduring the Fatigues of a Wafh-tub, for your Maintenance? Or, will following a Camp fuit your Inclinations? Think well of the certain Mifery that muft attend your making fuch a Choice.

Look round at the Wives of all his Fellow foldiers, and mark their Appearance at their Homes, and in Publick. Is *their* abject Condition to be coveted? Do you fee any thing defirable in Poverty and Rags? And, as to the Man for whom you muft endure all this, he may poffibly indeed be poffeffed of Honefty, and a Defire to do his beft for you, at leaft you may think fo; but is it probable he will? For if he be wife and induftrious, how came he to prefer a Life fo mean and contemptible? If he was bred to any Trade, why did he defert it?

Be cautious of pufhing yourfelf into Ruin, and as I am not able to maintain you, and a young Family, do not throw yourfelf upon the uncertain Charity of *well-difpofed* People, who are already vaftly incumbered by the Miferable. I hope you will not thus rafhly increafe the unhappy Number of fuch, but will give due Attention to what I have faid; for I can have no View, but that of difcharging the Duty of

Your loving Father.

LETTER

LETTER LXIV.

Of Expostulation from a grave Friend to a young Man, on his slighting and irreverent Behaviour to his Father.

Dear Sir,

I TAKE the Freedom of a brief Expostulation with you on your Behaviour to your Father, and I hope you will receive it from me, with the same Good-will, that I mean it.

His Indulgence to you formerly, certainly claims better Returns on your Part, altho' it should be allow'd, as you fondly imagine, that his Affection to you is alienated. There may be something of Petulancy in him, which you ought to bear with; for one time or other you may be convinced by Experience, that *Age* itself has its insuperable Afflictions, that require the Allowance of every one; and more particularly of such who hope to live a long Life themselves, and still more particularly of a *Son*, whose *high Passions*, require, perhaps, at least as *much* Allowance. He may be *petulant*, but are you not *fiery* and *impetuous?* And I would fain know, whether *you* ought to bear with *him*, or *he* with *you?*

'Tis a very groundless Surmize to think his Affections are alienated from you. A Father *must* love his Son. He cannot help it. And is it credible even to yourself, on cool Reflection, that the same good Man who was wont to be delighted with your childish Vanities and Foibles (for we have all had them more or less), and even indulged and perhaps cherished those youthful Forwardnesses, that might be called the Seeds of those Passions, which
now,

now, being sprung up, give him so much Disturbance, and make you so impatient of Contradiction; Can you, I say, believe that this same good Man, without Reason, without Provocation, can change that Love into Hate?

You are grown to Man's Estate, and tho' far from the ungracious Sons, that we have seen in the World, yet ought not to be so partial to yourself, as to believe you are wholly faultless. Examine your own Conduct then, and altho' you should not be able to charge your *Intention* with any Blame, yet you must leave your *Behaviour* to be judg'd by others; and 'twill perhaps be given against you, that some Slight, some Negligence, some Inattention, if not worse, too cutting for a Father's Cares and Fondness to support, has escaped you. Then consider, Sir, what a grievous thing it must be to him to reflect, that this Behaviour of yours may be but the gradual Consequence of his former Indulgence to you; and that he is deservedly punished, for not rooting up in your childish Days those Weeds which now spread to his Uneasiness. But let me tell you, Sir, that it ought to be a more sad Reflection to a considerate young Gentleman, that *he* is to be the Instrument to punish his fond Father's faulty Indulgence to himself.

I have been a diligent Observer of the Dispensations of Providence in this respect, and have always seen the Sin of Undutifulness to Parents punished in *Kind*, more than any one Sin. I have seen the *Son* of the unc*tiful Son, revenging the Cause of his *Grandfather*, and at the same time, intail'd a Curse upon *his* Son, if he has not been taken off childless, who, in his Turn, has retorted the ungracious Behaviour; and thus a Curse has been intail'd by Descent upon the Family, from one Generation to another.

You'll say, that your Behaviour to your Father is not, you hope, of such an atrocious Nature, as to be attended with such terrible Consequences, and perhaps will add, that you do not wish for a better Behaviour from your Son, than you shew to your Father. But if this be not Partiality to your self, pray consider, that while your Father takes your present Conduct in so ill Part, and you use so little Circumspection to avoid giving him Disgust, and have so little Complaisance, as not to set him right; the thing is full as tormenting to him from the *Appearance*, as if it were *real*, nay, 'tis *real* to him, if he *believes* so

He thinks, and let me tell you, Sir, he thinks *justly*, that he ought to expect as much Deference to *his* Will and Pleasure *now*, as he has heretofore shewn you Indulgence, even in those Things that now perhaps you are so unkind to suffer to turn severest upon him. I would not recriminate But it was with very little Reverence, and indeed with an *Air* as censurable as the *Words*, that you told him, in my Hearing, that he knew not what he would have: That he expected you to be more accountable at *this* Age, than when you were a *Child*, &c. Why, dear Sir, does your being *of Age*, lessen the Duty you owe to your Father? Are not his Cares for you allowably *doubled?* And ought he not now to expect from your good Sense, and more mature Understanding (improved, as it is to be hoped, by the Education he has, at a great Expence, given you), *greater* Proofs of Duty, rather than *less?* He may forget, perhaps, what he *was at your Age*, as you irreverently told him; but how much more laudable would it be, for you, at *yours*, to enter into what you would naturally expect from *your Son*, were you in the *Place*, and at the *Age*, of *your Father!* A generous Mind will do its Duty, tho'

tho' it were not to meet with suitable Rewards or Returns; for even should your Father not do *his* by *you*, you are not absolved of *yours* to *him*; much less then ought the *natural*, the *consequential*, Infirmities of *Age*, to dissolve the Duty of a Son to an indulgent Parent.

Be convinced, my dear Sir, of your wrong Conduct, and don't think it beneath the high Spirit of a brave young Gentleman, to submit to the Will of his Father. By your Dutifulness and Circumspection you may, in all Probability, add to the Number as well as the Comfort of *his* Days to whom you owe *your* Being. But what a Woe does that young Man bring upon himself, who robs his aged Parent in *both* respects! It behoves all Children to reflect upon this timely, and with Awe.

On how many Occasions has he heretofore rejoiced to me, on, even, the smallest Openings and Dawnings of your Mind and Genius! How has he dwelt upon your Praises on even *supposed* Beauties, which have appeared such to his fond and partial Tenderness only! How has he extenuated your Failings, connived at your Faults, and extolled and brought forward into strong Light, even the remotest Appearance of Virtue in you! Such *were* always, and such, notwithstanding the Intermixtures of *Age* and *Infirmity*, and even of your continued *Slights* and *Impatience*, always *will be*, the Instances of his paternal Affection for you. And I will venture to say, that even this very Petulance, as you think it, is a Demonstration of his Regard for you, however disagreeable it may be to you, since he loves you too well to be insensible to those Parts of your Behaviour, which he thinks are owing to Slight or Negligence.

I have exceeded the Bounds I intended when I began, and would rather leave to your natural good

Sense, and cooler Reflection, what I have *already* urged, than tire you too much, with what might *still farther* be added on this Occasion. But the Affection and Friendship I have for all your Family, and the long Intimacy I have had with your good Father (who, however, knows nothing of my writeing), and the evil Consequences that may follow a wider Breach between you, will answer for my Intention, and, I hope, for my Freedom, which I will take upon me to say, *I expect* from your Candor and Education, being

Your sincere Friend to serve you.

LETTER LXV.

Against too great a Love of Singing and Musick.

Dear Cousin,

I AM sure you have the good Sense to take kindly what I am going to mention to you, in which I can have no possible View but your Benefit. When you were last with me at *Hertford*, you much obliged us all with the Instances you gave us of your Skill in Musick, and your good Voice. But as you are so young a Man, and seem to be so very much pleased *yourself* with these Acquirements, I must enter a Caution or two on this Score, because of the Consequences that may follow from too much Delight in these Amusements, which, while they are pursued as Amusements *only*, may be safe and innocent; but when they take up too much of a Man's Time, may be not a little pernicious.

In the first place, my dear Cousin, these Pleasures of *Sound* may take you off from the more desirable ones of *Sense*, and make your Delights

most Important Occasions. 91

stop at the *Ear*, which should go deeper, and be placed in the *Understanding*. For whenever a chearful Singer is in Company, adieu to all Conversation much of an improving or intellectual Nature!

In the second place, it may expose you to *Company*, and that not the *best* and *most* eligible neither; and by which your *Business*, and your other *more useful* Studies, may be greatly, if not wholly, neglected, and very possibly your *Health* itself impaired.

In the third place, it may tend (for so it naturally does) to *enervate the Mind*, and make you haunt musical Societies, Operas and Concerts; and what Glory is it to a Gentleman, if he were even a fine Performer, that he can strike a String, touch a Key, or sing a Song, with the Grace and Command of a *hired Musician*?

Fourthly, Musick, to arrive at any tolerable Proficiency in it, takes up *much Time*, and requires so much Application, as leaves but little *Room*, and, what is worse, when delighted in, little *Inclination* for other Improvements: And as Life is a *short stage*, where *longest*, surely the most precious Moments of it ought to be better employ'd, than in so light and airy an Amusement. The Time of Youth will be soon over, and that is the Time of laying the Foundation of more solid Studies. The *Mind*, as well as the *Body*, will become stiff by Years, and unsusceptible of those Improvements, that cannot be attained, but in particular Periods of it. And, when once an airy Delight engages the Faculties, a Habit is formed; and nothing but great Struggle, and absolute Necessity, if *that* will do it, can shake it off. One Part of Life is for *Improvement*, that is, *Youth*; another Part is for turning that Improvement to solid Benefits to one's self, one's Family, or Acquaintance; that is, the

middle

middle Part; another Part carries a Retrospect to a *future State*: And shall we lose the Time of *Improvement*, which can never come again; forfeit all the Benefits of it, in our *Middle life*, and imbitter our *future Prospects*, as well *mundane* as *eternal*, with Reflections on our past Neglect of Opportunities that never can be recalled? And all for what? Why, only to be deemed, for eight or ten empty Years of Life, *a good Companion*, as the Phrase is.----Tho', perhaps, a bad *Husband*, a bad *Father*, a bad *Friend*, and, of course, a bad *Man!*

Some there are, who divide Life into four Stages or Opportunities. He, they say, who is not handsome by Twenty, strong by Thirty, wise by Forty, rich by Fifty, will never be either *handsome, strong, wise,* or *rich*. And this, generally speaking, is a good and improving Observation; which should teach us, as we go along, to make a right Use of those Periods of Life, which may be proper Entrances for us into a still more important one than that behind it.

I have but lightly touched on these weighty Points, because I know you have good Sense enough to improve as much from Hints, as others can from tedious Lectures. And when I have repeated, that I am far from dissuading you from these Amusements, while they are restrained to due Bounds, and are regarded as Amusements *only*, I know you will think me, what I always desire to be thought, and what I truly am,

Your affectionate Uncle,
and sincere Friend

LET

LETTER LXVI.

From a Daughter to her Father, pleading for her Sister, who had married without his Consent.

Honoured Sir,

THE kind Indulgence you have always shewn to your Children, makes me presume to become an Advocate for my *Sister*, tho' not for her Fault. She is very sensible of *that*, and sorry she has offended you; but has great Hopes, that Mr. *Robinson* will prove such a careful and loving Husband to her, as may atone for his past Wildness, and engage your Forgiveness. For all your Children are sensible of your paternal Kindness, and that you wish their Good more for *their* sakes, than your own.

This makes it the more wicked to offend so good a Father. But, dear Sir, be pleased to consider, that it now cannot be helped, and that she may be made by your Displeasure very miserable in her own Choice, and as his Faults are owing to the inconsideration of Youth, or otherwise it would not have been a very discreditable Match, had it had your Approbation, I could humbly hope, for my poor Sister's sake, that you will be pleased rather to encourage his present good Resolutions by your kind Favour, than make him despair of a Reconciliation, and so perhaps treat her with a Negligence, which hitherto she is not apprehensive of. For he really very fond of her, and I hope will continue so. Yet is she dejected for her Fault to you, and wishes, yet dreads, to have your Leave to throw herself at your Feet, to beg your Forgiveness and

Blessing,

Blessing, which would make the poor dear Offender quite happy.

Pardon, Sir, my interposing in her Favour, in which my Husband also joins. She is *my* Sister. She is *your* Daughter; tho' she has not done so worthily as I wish, to become that Character. Be pleased, Sir, to forgive her, however; and also forgive me, pleading for her: Who am,

Your ever dutiful Daughter.

LETTER LXVII.

The Father's Answer.

My dear Nanny,

YOU must believe, that your Sister's unadvised Marriage, which she must know would be disagreeable to me, gives me no small Concern, and yet, I will assure you, that it arises more from my Affection for her, than any other Consideration. In her Education I took all the Pains and Care my Circumstances would admit, and often flattered myself with the Hope, that the happy Fruits of it would be made appear in her prudent Conduct. What she has now done is not *vicious*, but *indiscreet*; for, you must remember, that I have often declared in her Hearing, that the wild Assertion, of a Rake making a good Husband, was the most dangerous Opinion a young Woman could imbibe.

I will not, however, in Pity to her, point out the many Ills I am afraid will attend her Rashness, because *it is done*, and cannot be *helped*, but wish she may be happier than I ever saw a Woman who leap'd so fatal a Precipice.

Her Husband has this Morning been with me for her Fortune, and it was with much Temper I told

most Important Occasions. 95

told him, That as all she could hope for was wholly at my Disposal, I should disburse it in such a manner as I thought would most contribute to her Advantage; and that, as he was a Stranger to me, I should chuse to know he *deserved* it, before he had the Power over what I intended to do for her. He bit his Lip, and, with a hasty Step, was my humble Servant.

Tell the rash Girl, that I would not have her to be afflicted at this Behaviour in me; for I know it will contribute to her Advantage one way or other: If he married her for *her own sake*, she will find no Alteration of Behaviour from this Disappointment. But if he married her only for her *Money*, she will soon be glad to find it in my Possession, rather than his.

Your Interposition in her Behalf is very *sisterly*: and you see I have not the Resentment she might expect. But would to God she had acted with your Prudence! For her own sake I wish it. I am

Your loving Father.

LETTER LXVIII.

To a Brother, against making his Wife and Children the constant Subject of his Praise and Conversation.

Dear Brother,

THE Love I have always had for you, and an Unwillingness I find in myself to say any thing that may put you to Confusion, have made me take this Method of acquainting you with a small Indiscretion I have often observed in you, and which I perceive gradually to gain Ground as your Family increases.

What

What I mean, is an immoderate Inclination to make your Spouse, and your Children, the Subject of Discourse where-ever you are. Imagine not that any Pique or Dislike draws this from me. My Sister, I think, is possessed of as many valuable Qualities as most of her Sex; and all your Children are very promising. No wonder then, that this View makes a very deep Impression upon so tender a Heart as yours; and the Fondness of a Husband, and of a Father, is what must make you esteemed by all who consider the many Advantages arising from thence to Posterity. But a Mind full of Affection for what is so dear to himself, stands in need of the utmost Care, to keep what concerns *only himself*, from employing too much the Attention of *others*: What affects *you* most sensibly upon this Subject, is, even by your Friends, heard rather with an Ear of *Censure* than *Applause*. And what the tender Bias of a Father swells in your Conception to the most *witty Repartee*, to an Ear destitute of that Bias, sounds neither witty, nor uncommon, and you cannot mortify many Men more, than by dragging out an unwilling *Ay, very pretty indeed, Sir! A charming Boy!* or, *Such a Saying was far above his Years, truly*. Which kind of *yawning Applause* is sometimes, by your Attention being strongly fixed to your Story, mistaken for *Approbation*; and you thereupon launch out farther upon the same Subject, when your Hearers are scarce able to conceal their Inattention. Besides, don't you consider, that another Man may have as great Fondness for *his*, as you have for *yours*, and while your Children are the wittiest, the beautifullest, the hopefullest in *England*, do you not tacitly reflect upon every other Man's Children in the Company?

To me, I grant you full Liberty to say whatever you please; nay, several little Tricks you tell of *Patty* and *Tommy* are agreeable enough to *me*, and some I think even entertaining, but to *others*, have a close Guard upon yourself, lest when you try to get your *Children* admired, you should get *yourself* despised. Let you and me, as *Father* and *Uncle*, keep all their little Whimsies to ourselves, for as Strangers share not in the *Affection* and *Expence* attending them, why should they partake in the *Entertainment* they afford?

I hope my constant Behaviour has convinced you of my sincere Regard for your Interest and Reputation. What I have said, I mean for your Benefit. And you know me too well, to think otherwise of

Your tenderly affectionate Brother.

LETTER LXIX.

From a Father to a Daughter, in Dislike of her Intentions to marry at too early an Age.

Dear Sally,

I WAS greatly surprised at the Letter you sent me last Week. I was willing to believe I saw in you, for your Years, so much of your late dear Mother's Temper, Prudence, and virtuous Disposition, that I refused several advantageous Offers of changing my own Condition, purely for your sake. And will you now convince me so early, that I have no Return to expect from you, but that the Moment a young Fellow throws himself in your way, you have nothing else to do, but to give me Notice to provide a Fortune for you? For

that

that you intend to be of no further Use and Service to me. This, in plain *English*, is the Meaning of your Notification. For I suppose your young Man does not intend to marry you, without a Fortune. And can you then think, that a Father has nothing to do, but to confer Benefits on his Children, without being intitled to expect any Return from them?

To be sure, I had proposed, at a proper Time, to find a Husband for you; but I thought I had yet three or four Years to come. For, consider, *Sally*, you are not fully Sixteen Years of Age. And a Wife, believe me, ought to have some better Qualifications, than an agreeable Person, to *preserve a Husband's Esteem*, tho' it often is enough to *attract a Lover's Notice*.

Have you Experience enough, think you, discreetly to conduct the Affairs of a Family? I thought you as yet not quite capable to manage m, House; and I am sure, my Judgment always took a Bias in your Favour.

Besides, let me tell you, I have great Exceptions to the Person, and think him by no means the Man I would chuse for your Husband. For which, if it be not too late, I will give good Reasons.

On the Whole, you must expect, if you marry without my *Consent*, to live without my *Assistance*. Think it not hard. Your Disappointment cannot be greater than mine, if you will proceed. I have never used violent Measures to you on any Occasion, and shall not on this. But yet I earnestly hope you will not hurry yourself to Destruction, and me perhaps to the Grave, by an Action which a little Consideration may so easily prevent. I am

Your afflicted Fat!

LETTER LXX.

From a Father to a Daughter, against a frothy, French Lover.

Dear Polly,

I Cannot say I look upon Mr. *La Farriere* in the same favourable Light that you seem to do. His frothy Behaviour may divert well enough as an Acquaintance; but is very unanswerable, I think, to the Character of a Husband, especially an *English* Husband, which I take to be a graver Character than a *French* one. There is a Difference in these gay Gentlemen, while they *strive to please*, and when they *expect to be obliged*. In all Men this is too apparent; but in those of a light Turn it is more visible than in others. If after Marriage his present Temper should continue, when *you* are a careful Mother, *he* will look more like a Son than a Husband. If entering into the World should change his Disposition, expect no Medium, he will be the most insipid Mortal you can imagine. If his Spirits should be depressed by the Accidents of Life, he is such a Stranger to Reflection (the best Counsellor of the Wife), that from thence he will be unable to draw Relief. And Adversity to such Men is the more intolerable, as their Deportment is suited only to the Smiles of Success.

He *dances* well, *writes* very indifferently. Is an Artist at *Cards*; but cannot cast *Accompts*. Understands all the Laws of *Chance*; but not one of the Land. Has shewn great Skill in the Improvement of his *Person*, yet none at all, that I hear, of his *Estate*. And tho' he makes a good Figure in *Company,*

pany, has never yet studied the Art of living at *Home*. He *sings* well, but knows nothing of *Business*. He has long acted the Part of a *Lover*; but may not find the same Variety and Entertainment in acting the *Husband*. Is very *gallant*; but may not be over *affectionate*. And is so tender of *himself*, that he will have little Time to indulge *any body else* ----- These, Child, are my Sentiments of him, you are not wholly ignorant of the World. I desire to *guide*, not to *force*, your Inclinations, and hope your calm Reason will banish all farther Thoughts of this Gentleman, who, however you may like him for a Partner at a *Ball*, seems not so well qualified for a Journey through the various Trials, from which no Station can exempt the *married State*. I am

Your affectionate Father.

LETTER LXXI.

A modest Lover desiring an Aunt's Favour to her Niece.

Good Madam,

I HAVE several times, that I have been happy in the Company of your beloved Niece, thought to have spoken my Mind, and to declare to her the true Value and Affection I have for her. But just as I have been about to speak, my Fears have vanquish'd my Hopes, and I have been obliged to suspend my Purpose. I have thrown out several Hints, that I thought would have led the Way to a fuller Disclosing of the Secret that is too big for my Breast, and yet, when I am near her, is too important for Utterance. Will you be so good, Madam, to break way for me, if I am not wholly disapproved

approved of by you; and prepare her dear Mind for a Declaration that I must make, and yet know not how to begin?----My Fortune and Expectations make me hope, that I may not on those Accounts be deemed unworthy: And could I, by half a Line from your Hand, hope, that there is *no other Bar*, I should be enabled to build on so desirable a Foundation, and to let your Niece know, how much my Happiness depends upon her Favour. Excuse, dear Madam, I beseech you, this Trouble, and this presumptuous Request, from

Your most obliged and obedient Servant.

LETTER LXXII.

The Aunt's Answer, supposing the Gentleman deserves Encouragement.

SIR,

I Cannot say I have any Dislike, as to my own part, to your Proposal, or your Manner of making it, whatever my Niece may have, because Diffidence is generally the Companion of Merit, and a Token of Respect: She is a Person of Prudence, and all her Friends are so throughly convinced of it, that her Choice will have the Weight it deserves with us all. So I cannot say, what will be the Event of your Declaration to her. Yet, so far as I may take upon myself to do, I will not deny your Request, but on her Return to me Tomorrow will break the Ice, as you desire, not doubting your Honour, and the Sincerity of your Professions; and I shall tell her moreover what I think of the Advances you make. I believe she has had the Prudence to keep her Heart intirely disengaged, because she would otherwise have told me: And is not so mean-spirited, as to be able to return Tyranny and Insult for true Value, when she is properly convinced of it. Whoever has the Happiness (permit me, tho' her Relation, to call it so) to meet with her Favour, will find this her Character, and that it is not owing to the fond Partiality of,

Sir,

Your Friend and Servant.

LETTER LXXIII.

The Answer, supposing the Gentleman is not approved.

SIR,

I HAVE intimated your Request to my Niece, who thinks herself obliged to your good Opinion of her. But begs that you will give over all Thoughts of applying to her on this Subject. She says she can by no means encourage your Address. It is better therefore to know this at first, because it will save her and yourself farther Trouble. I am, Sir,

Your humble Servant.

LETTER LXXIV.

From a respectful Lover to his Mistress.

Dear Madam,

I HAVE long struggled with the most honourable and respectful Passion that ever filled the Heart of Man. I have often try'd to reveal it personally; as often in this way; but never till now could prevail upon my Fears and Doubts. But I can no longer struggle with a Secret that has given me so much Torture to keep, and yet hitherto more;

more, when I have endeavoured to reveal it. I never entertain the Hope to see you, without Rapture, but when I have that Pleasure, instead of being *animated* as I ought, I am utterly confounded. What can this be owing to, but a Diffidence in myself, and an exalted Opinion of your Worthiness? And is not this one strong Token of ardent Love? Yet if it be, how various is the tormenting Passion in its Operations! Since some it inspires with Courage, while others it deprives of all necessary Confidence. I can only assure you, Madam, that the Heart of Man never conceived a stronger or sincerer Passion than mine for you. If my Reverence for you is my Crime, I am sure it has been my sufficient Punishment. I need not say my Designs and Motives are honourable. Who dare approach so much virtuous Excellence, with a Supposition that such an Assurance is necessary? What my Fortune is, is well known, and I am ready to stand the Test of the strictest Inquiry. Condescend, Madam, to embolden my respectful Passion, by one favourable Line; that if what I here profess, and hope further to have an Opportunity to assure you of, be found to be unquestionable Truth, then my humble Address will not quite be unacceptable to you, and thus you will for ever oblige, dear Madam,

Your affectionate Admirer, and devoted Servant.

LETTER LXXV.
The Answer.

SIR,

IF Modesty be the greatest Glory of *our* Sex, surely it cannot be blameworthy in *yours*. For my own part, I must think it the most amiable Quality either Man or Woman can possess. Nor can there be, in my Opinion, a true Respect, where there is not a Diffidence of one's own Merit, and an high Opinion of the Person's we esteem.

To say more, on this Occasion, would little become me. To say less, would look as if I knew not how to pay that Regard to modest Merit, which modest Merit *only* deserves.

You, Sir, best know your own Heart; and if you are sincere and generous, will receive as you ought, this Frankness from

Your humble Servant.

LETTER LXXVI.

A humorous Epistle of neighbourly Occurrences and News, to a Bottle-Companion abroad.

Dear Bob,

I AM glad to hear you're in the Land of the Living still. You expect from me an Account of what has happen'd among your old Acquaintance since you have been abroad. I will give it you, and, 'bating that two or three Years always make vast Alterations in *mature* Life, you would be surpris'd at the Havock and Changes that small Space of Time has made in the Circle of our Acquaintance. To begin then with myself. I have had the Misfortune to lose my Son *Jo*; and my Daughter *Judy* is marry'd, and has brought me another *Jo*. *Jack Kidd* of the *Fountain*, where we kept our Club, has lost his Wife, who was a special Bar-keeper, got his Maid *Prisc.* with Child----you remember the Slut, by her mincing Airs----marry'd her, and is broke. But not till he had, with his horrid Stum, poison'd half the Society. We began to complain of his Wine, you know, before you left us, and I told him he should let *us* have Neat, who drank our

Gallons,

Gallons, if he was honeſt to *himſelf*, and, if he was to regard *Conſcience* as well as *Intereſt*, muſt do leſs Harm by diſpenſing his Rats-bane to thoſe who drank Pints, than to thoſe honeſt Fellows who ſwallow'd Gallons, and, in ſo handſome a Doſe of the one, muſt take a too large Quantity of the other: But the Dog was incorrigible, for he went on brewing and poiſoning, till he kill'd his beſt Cuſtomers, and then what could he expect?

Why, what follow'd; for, truly, *Bob*, we began to tumble like rotten Sheep. As thus The Dance was begun by that ſeaſon'd Sinner *Tim. Brackley*, the Half-pint Man, who was always ſotting by himſelf, with his *Whets* in the Morning, his *Correctives* after Dinner, and *Digeſters* at Night, and at laſt tipp'd off of one of the Kitchen-benches in an Apoplexy. 'Tis true he was not of our Club; tho' we might have taken Warning by *his Fall*, as the Saying is, but were above it. So the Rot got among us, and firſt, honeſt laughing *Jack Adams* kick'd up of a Fever. *Tom Dandy* fell into a Jaundice and Dropſy, and when his Doctors ſaid he was mending, ſlipp'd thro' their Fingers, in ſpite of their Art and Aſſurance. *Roger Harman*, the Punſter, then tipp'd off the Perch, after very little Warning And was follow'd in a Week by *Arthur Syles*. *Ralph Atkyns* bid us Good-b'ye in a few Months after him. And *Ben Tomlyns*, who, you remember, would never go home ſober, tumbled down Stairs, and broke his Collar-bone. His *Surgeon* took him firſt, a *Fever* next, then his *Doctor*, and then, as it were of courſe, *Death*. A natural Round enough, you'll ſay, *Bob*. His Widow made a handſome Burial for poor *Ben.*; took on grievouſly, and in Five Weeks married her Journeyman. *Jemmy Hawkins* was a long time ailing, yet would not leave off; ſo he dy'd, as one may ſay, of a *more natural*

natural Death. *Ralph Rawlins* fell sick, after a large Dose; and had so narrow an Escape, that he was frighten'd into a Regimen; and now drinks Asses Milk of another Complexion than that which gave him his Malady; and between *Physick* and the *Hyp,* serves for a *Memento mori* to *others,* and neither lives nor dies himself. While honest Capt. *Tinker,* who was deep gone in a Consumption, is in very little better Case And if any thing saves *him,* and *me,* and the rest of our once numerous Society, it will be the Bankruptcy of our worthy Landlord, for that has quite broke us up.

So much for the *Club,* Bob. Now to the *Neighbourhood* about us, that you and I knew next best.

Jerry Jenkyns, the prim Mercer, has had a Statute taken out against him, and 5 *s.* in the Pound is all the Result of his pragmatical Fluttering. *Dan. Pocock* the Draper has had an Estate left him, and quitted Business: While *Sam. Simpson* the Grocer has lost one in Law, and gone mad upon it. See, *Bob,* the Ups and Downs of this transitory State! *Harry Barlow* the *Turky* Merchant has left off to his Nephew, and now pines for want of Employment. *Joshua Williams* the Cheesemonger, a strange projecting Fellow, you know! is carried out of his Shop into a Sponging-House by *his own Maggots.* *John Jones* the Organist is married to *Sykes*'s Daughter *Peggy,* who proves an arrant Shrew, and has broke about his Head his best *Cremona* Fiddle, in the Sight of half a dozen Neighbours. The Wife of *Job Johnson,* our Swordcutler, has elop'd from him. You know they always liv'd like Dog and Cat. *Paul Lane*'s Daughter *Poll* has had a Bastard by 'Squire *Wilson*'s Coachman; and the 'Squire's own Daughter Miss *Nelly* has run away with her Father's Postilion. *Dick Jenkyns,* that vile Rake and Beau, is turn'd *Quaker;*

Quaker; and that still greater Libertine, *Peter Mottram, Methodist*. While old *Satan*, to make up his Loss in these two, has subdued *Will Wigley*, and *Tom Allen*, who you know used to be very hopeful young Fellows, and are now Rakes of the Town. *Tony Williams* I had like to have forgot. He has cheated all our Expectations, having escaped the Gallows, and dy'd a natural Death, after a hundred Rogueries, every one of which deserved Hanging.

Parson *Matthews* goes on preaching and living excellently, and has still as many Admirers as Hearers, but no Preferment · While old clumsy Parson *Dromedary* is made a Dean, and has Hopes, by his Sister's means, who is a Favourite of a certain great Man, to be a Bishop.

As to News of a *publick* Nature, the Papers, which no doubt you see, in the monthly Collections at least, will inform you best of that. By them however you'll find very little Judgment to be form'd of our Affairs, or our Ministers, as to the one being, or the other doing, right or wrong. For while some are made as *black* as *Devils* on one Side, they are made as *white* as *Angels* on the other. They never did *one good thing*, says the *Enemy*. They never did *one bad* one, says the Friend. For my own part, I think, considering the undoubted Truth of the Maxim *Humanum est errare*, and how much easier it is to find a Fault than to mend one, the Gentlemen in the Administration will be well off, if the Publick will *middle* the Matter between the two *Extremes* Mean time one Side goes on, *accusing* without *Mercy*; the other *acquitting* without *Shame*. 'Tis the Business of *one Set* of Papers to *bespatter* and *throw Dirt*; and of the other to follow after them, with a *Scrubbing-brush* and a *Dishclout*: And after all --- the one *bedaubs* so *plentifully*, and the other *wipes* off so *slovenly*, that, let me be hang'd, *Bob*, if I'd appear on *'Change* with the Coat on my Back that a certain great Man stalks about in, without Concern, when these *Dawbers* and *Scowerers* have done their *worst* and their *best* upon it. But 'tis a great Matter to be *used* to such a Coat. And a great Happiness, I'll warrant, your Namesake thinks it, that with all this *Rubbing* and *Scrubbing*, it does not appear *threadbare* yet, after twenty Years Wear, and a hundred People trying to pick Holes in it.

But I have done with my News, and my Politicks, in which I was ever but a Dabbler; and having written a terrible long Letter, and given you, as it were, the World in Miniature, think it time to close it; which I shall do with wishing, that now our poisoning Landlord *Kidd* is broke and gone, you were among us your old Friends now-and-then, to enliven us with your chearful Pipe, as you used to do in the Days of *yore*, when we were all alive and merry. And with this hearty Wish, I conclude myself, dear *Bob*,

Your old Bottle-Companion, and humble Servant.

LETTER LXXVII.

From a Nephew to his Aunt, on his slow Progress in a Courtship Affair.

Dear Aunt,

I HAVE made my Addresses, in the best manner I can, to Miss *Dawley*, but have not the least Room to boast of my Success. The Account you gave me of her good Sense, and many uncommon Qualifications, will not permit me to arraign her

her Conduct; and the good Opinion I have long entertained of myself, makes me very flow in blaming my own. I would have obey'd your Orders to write to you sooner, but knew not what to say; and by waiting till I began to fear you would think me negligent, I am in no better Condition. I first declared my Regard for her in a manner I thought most suitable for that Purpose. She very encouragingly made me no Answer; and when I spoke again upon the Subject, she ask'd how you did, and was glad to hear you were well. Being put out of my Play, I talk'd of indifferent Things a good while, and at last fell again upon the Reason of my attending her. She order'd the Cloth to be laid, and complaisantly hoped I would stay Supper. I had no more Opportunity for that time.

Two Days after, I repeated my Visit. She received me at first politely, but when I began to resume the Subject I came upon, she rung for the Maid, and bad her put on the Tea-kettle. About six Visits passed before I could obtain one Word to my Business: And the first Thing she answer'd upon that Head was, That Length of Time was necessary to the making of an Acquaintance that must not be either blushed at, or repented of · This she spoke with such an Air of Gravity, as put what I would have reply'd, quite out of my Head. Yet next Visit I began again. I told her how happy I should think myself, if I could be encouraged to hope for the smallest Share of her Favour. But she made me such an odd Answer, as plainly demonstrated to me, that I had more of her Contempt than Approbation. This made me as earnest as she, to wave the Subject; and so we went on upon the Weather, for a whole Week before; and when we had done that, we talk'd Politicks · So that, in short, after Two Months Study how to

accomplish

accomplish the Happiness you pointed out for me, I find myself not one single Step advanced; for when I see her now, we both talk with seeming Satisfaction, on any Subject where Love has no Part: But when that is introduced, all her easy Eloquence sinks into Reserve.

I would not determine to give up my Address, before I had your farther Advice. In Hopes of which I am, Honoured Madam,

Your dutiful Nephew.

LETTER LXXVIII.

The Aunt's Answer, encouraging him to persevere.

Nephew Robert,

I Thought you had been better acquainted with the Art of Love, than to be so easily out of Heart. That such a Lady as Miss *Dawley* has not forbid your Visits, let me tell you, is Encouragement as much as you ought to expect. She is a Lady of fine Sense, and has had the Advantage of as fine an Education; and you must not expect a Lady of her Prudence and Merit, will be won by general Compliments; or that her Affection will be mov'd by the Notion of a sudden and precipitate Passion. Her Judgment must be first touch'd, for she views Marriage as a serious Thing. By it her Mother was made happy, and her Sister undone. I in join the Continuation of your Addresses; for a more deserving Lady than Miss, does not live. And be sure, at least, to be more ambitious of appearing a *Man of Sense*, than a *Lover*. When the latter is accepted on account of the former, the Lady does Credit to her Choice. You young Fellows have such Notions of a Nine-days Courtship, that if it were indulged by all Women, none would, in a short time, be thought obliging, who did not make Modesty submit to Passion, and Discretion to Compliment. I desire to hear from you again a Month hence; and am, in the mean time,

Your affectionate Aunt.

LETTER LXXIX.

A Gentleman to a Lady, professing an Aversion to the tedious Forms of Courtship.

Dear Madam,

I Remember that one of the Antients, in describing a Youth in Love, says, he has neither Wisdom enough to speak, nor to hold his Tongue. If this be a just Description, the Sincerity of my Passion will admit of no Dispute: And whenever, in your Company, I behave like a Fool, forget not that you are answerable for my Incapacity. Having made bold to declare thus much, I must presume to say, that a favourable Reception of this will, I am certain, make me more worthy your Notice; but your Disdain would be what I believe myself incapable ever to surmount. To try by idle Fallacies, and airy Compliments, to prevail on your Judgment, is a Folly for any Man to attempt who knows you. No, Madam, your good Sense and Endowments have raised you far above the Necessity of practising the mean Artifices which prevail upon the less deserving of your Sex: You are not to be so lightly deceived, and if you were, give me leave to say, I should not think you

deserving

deserving of the Trouble that would attend such an Attempt.

This, I must own, is no fashionable Letter from one who, I am sure, loves up to the greatest Hero of Romance: But as I would hope, that the Happiness I sue for, should be lasting, it is certainly most eligible to take no Step to procure it but what will bear Reflection; for I should be happy to see you mine, when we have both out-lived the Taste for every thing that has not Virtue and Reason to support it. I am, Madam, notwithstanding this unpolish'd Address,

Your most respectful Admirer, and obedient Servant.

LETTER LXXX.

The Lady's Answer, encouraging a farther Declaration.

SIR,

I AM very little in Love with the fashionable Methods of Courtship Sincerity with me is preferable to Compliments; yet I see no Reason why common Decency should be discarded There is something so odd in your Style, that when I know whether you are in Jest or Earnest, I shall be less at a Loss to answer you. Mean time, as there is abundant Room for rising, rather than sinking, in your Complaisance, you may possibly have chosen wisely to begin first at the lowest End. If this be the Case, I know not what your succeeding Addresses may produce But I tell you fairly, that your present make no great Impression, yet perhaps as much as you intended, on

Your humble Servant.

LETTER LXXXI.

The Gentleman's Reply, more explicitly avowing his Passion.

Dearest Madam,

NOW I have the Hope of being not more despised for my acknowleged Affection, I declare to you, with all the Sincerity of a Man of Honour, that I have long had a most sincere Passion for you; but I have seen Gentlemen led such Dances, when they have given up their Affections to the lovely Tyrants of their Hearts, and could not help themselves, that I had no Courage to begin an Address in the usual Forms, even to you, of whose good Sense and Generosity I had nevertheless a great Opinion. You have favoured me with a few Lines, which I most humbly thank you for. And I do assure you, Madam, if you will be pleas'd to encourage my humble Suit, you shall have so just an Account of my Circumstances and Pretensions, as I hope will intitle me to your Favour in the honourable Light, in which I profess myself, dear Madam,

Your most obliged and faithful Admirer.

Be so good as to favour me with one Line more, to encourage my personal Attendance, if not disagreeable.

LETTER LXXXII.

The Lady's Answer to his Reply, putting the Matter on a sudden Issue.

SIR,

AS we are both so well inclined to avoid unnecessary Trouble, as well as unnecessary Compliments, I think proper to acquaint you, That Mr. *Johnson*, of *Pallmall*, has the Management of all my Affairs; and is a Man of such Probity and Honour, that I do nothing in any Matters without him. I have no Dislike to your Person, and if you approve of what Mr. *Johnson* can acquaint you with, in relation to me, and I approve of his Report in your Favour, I shall be far from shewing any Gentleman, that I have either an insolent or a sordid Spirit, especially to such as do me the Honour of their good Opinion. I am, Sir,

Your humble Servant.

LETTER LXXXIII.

A facetious young Lady to her Aunt, ridiculing her serious Lover.

Dear Aunt,

I AM much obliged to you for the Kindness you intended me, in recommending Mr *Leadbeater* to me for a Husband: But I must be so free as to tell you, he is a Man no way suited to my Inclination. I despise, 'tis true, the idle Rants of Romance; but am inclinable to think there may be an Extreme on the other Side of the Question. The

most Important Occasions. 115

The first time the *honest Man* came to see me, in the way you were pleased to put into his Head, was one *Sunday* after Sermon-time He began with telling me, what I found at *my* Fingers-ends, that it was very cold; and politely blow'd upon *his*. I immediately perceived, that his Passion for me could not keep him warm, and, in Complaisance to your Recommendation, conducted him to the Fire-side. After he had pretty well rubbed Heat into his Hands, he stood up with his Back to the Fire, and with his Hand behind him, held up his Coat, that he might be warm all over, and, looking about him, asked with the Tranquillity of a Man a Twelve-month married, and just come off a Journey, How all Friends did in the Country? I said, I hoped, very well, but would be glad to warm my Fingers. Cry Mercy, Madam!---- And then he shuffled a little further from the Fire, and after two or three Hems, and a long Pause-----

I have heard, said he, a most excellent Sermon just now: Dr. *Thomas* is a fine Man truly. Did you ever hear him, Madam? No, Sir, I generally go to my own Parish-church. That's right, Madam, to be sure. What was your Subject to-day? The *Pharisee* and the *Publican*, Sir. A very good one truly, Dr. *Thomas* would have made fine Work upon that Subject. His Text to-day was, *Evil Communications corrupt good Manners*. A good Subject, Sir, I doubt not the Doctor made a fine Discourse upon it. O, *ay*, Madam, he can't make a bad one upon any Subject. I rung for the Tea-kettle; for, thought I, we shall have all the Heads of the Sermon immediately.

At Tea he gave me an Account of all the religious Societies, unask'd; and how many Boys they had put out 'Prentices, and Girls they had taught to knit,

knit, and sing Psalms. To all which I gave a Nod of Approbation, and was just able to say (for I began to be horribly in the Vapours), It was a very excellent Charity. *O, ay,* Madam, said he again (for that's his Word, I find), a very excellent one truly, it is snatching so many Brands out of the Fire. You are a Contributor, Sir, I doubt not. *O, ay,* Madam, to be sure, every *good Man* would contribute to such a worthy Charity, to be sure. No doubt, Sir, a Blessing attends upon all who promote so worthy a Design. *O, ay,* Madam, no doubt, as you say: I am sure I have found it; blessed be God! And then he twang'd his Nose, and lifted up his Eyes, as if in an Ejaculation.

O, my good Aunt, what a Man is here for a Husband! At last came the happy Moment of his taking Leave, for I would not ask him to stay Supper: And moreover, he talk'd of going to a Lecture at *St. Helen's*. And then (tho' I had an Opportunity of saying little more than Yes, and No, all the Time; for he took the Vapours he had put me into, for Devotion, or Gravity at least, I believe) he press'd my Hand, look'd *frightfully* kind, and gave me to understand, as a Mark of his Favour, that if, upon further Conversation, and Inquiry into my Character, he should happen to like me as well as he did from my Behaviour and Person; why, truly, I need not fear, in time, being blessed with him for my Husband!

This, my good Aunt, may be a mighty safe way of travelling toward the *Land of Matrimony*, as far as I know; but I cannot help wishing for a little more *Entertainment* on our *Journey*. I am willing to believe Mr. *Leadbeater* an honest Man, but am, at the same time, afraid his religious Turn of Temper, however in itself commendable, would better suit

suit with a Woman who centres all Desert in a solemn *Appearance*, than with, dear Aunt,

Your greatly obliged Kinswoman.

LETTER LXXXIV.

Her Aunt's Answer, reprehending her ludicrous Turn of Mind.

Cousin Jenny,

I AM sorry you think Mr. *Leadbeater* so unsuitable a Lover. He is a serious, sober, good Man, and surely when Seriousness and Sobriety make a necessary Part of the Duty of a *good Husband*, a good *Father*, and good *Master* of a Family; those Characters should not be the Subjects of Ridicule, in Persons of *our Sex* especially, who would reap the greatest Advantage from them. But he talks of the *Weather* when he first sees you, it seems, and would you have him directly fall upon the Subject of *Love*, the Moment he beheld you?

He visited you just after Sermon, on a *Sunday*: And was it so unsuitable for him to let you see, that the Duty of the Day had made proper Impressions upon him?

His Turn for promoting the Religious Societies, which you speak so slightly of, deserves more Regard from every good Person; for that same Turn is a kind of *Security* to a Woman, that he who had a benevolent and religious Heart, could not make a *bad Man*, or a *bad Husband*. To put out poor Boys to 'Prentice, to teach Girls to sing *Psalms*, would be with very few a Subject for Ridicule, for he that was so willing to provide for the Children of *others*, would take ſtill greater Care of *his own*.

He gave you to underſtand, that if he liked your Character on Inquiry, as well as your Perſon and Behaviour, he ſhould think himſelf very happy in ſuch a Wife; for that, I dare ſay, was more like his Language, than that you put in his Mouth. And, let me tell you, it would have been a much ſtranger Speech, had ſo cautious and ſerious a Man ſaid, without a thorough Knowlege of your Character, that at the firſt Sight he was over Head and Ears in Love with you.

I think, allowing for the ridiculous Turn your airy Wit gives to this his firſt Viſit, that, by your own Account, he acted like a prudent, a ſerious, and a worthy Man, as he is, and as one that thought flaſhy Compliments beneath him, in ſo ſerious an Affair as this.

I think, Couſin *Jenny*, this is not only a mighty ſafe Way, as you call it, of travelling toward the *Land of Matrimony*, but to the *Land of Happineſs*, with reſpect as well to the *next World* as *this*. And it is to be hoped, that the *better Entertainment* you ſo much wiſh for, on your *Journey*, may not lead you too much out of *your Way*, and divert your Mind from the principal View which you ought to have to your *Journey's End*.

In ſhort, I could rather have wiſh'd, that you could bring your Mind nearer to *his* Standard, than that he ſhould bring down his to your *Level*. And you'd have found more Satisfaction in it than you imagine, could you have brought yourſelf to a little more of that *ſolemn Appearance*, which you treat ſo lightly, and which, I think, in *him*, is much more than *mere Appearance*.

Upon the Whole, Couſin *Jenny*, I am ſorry, that a Woman of Virtue and Morals, as you are, ſhould

should treat so ludicrously a serious and pious Frame of Mind, in an Age, wherein good Examples are so rare, and so much wanted; tho' at the same time I am far from offering to prescribe to you in so arduous an Affair as a Husband, and wish you and Mr. *Leadbeater* too, since you are so *differently* disposed, matched more suitably to each other's Mind, than you are likely to be together. For I am

Your truly affectionate Aunt.

LETTER LXXXV.

From a Gentleman to his Mistress, resenting her supposed Coquetry.

MADAM,

BEAUTY has Charms which are not easily resisted; but it is, I presume, in the Power of the finest Woman breathing, to counterbalance all her Charms by a Conduct unworthy of them. This Manner of speaking, Madam, is what I am apprehensive you have not been *enough* used to. The Advantages you possess, independently of any Act of your own, cannot be any Warrant for a Behaviour repugnant to Honour, and strict good Manners. I ventured to address myself to you, Madam, upon Motives truly honourable, and best to be defended, but suffer me to say, that I never proposed to glory in adding one to the Number of your publick Admirers, or to be so tame, as to subject myself to *any* Usage. And if this be your Intention, and this only, I shall still admire you; but must leave the Flattering of your Vanity to Gentlemen who have more Leisure, and less Sincerity, than, Madam,

Your most obedient Servant.

LETTER LXXXVI.

The Lady's angry Answer.

SIR,

BY the Letter I juſt now received from you, I fanſy you have been a little too haſty, as well as too free, in your Conjectures about my Conduct. I hope it is ſuch, and will be always ſuch, as ſhall juſtify me to Perſons of Honour of my own Sex, as well as yours. You have ſurely, Sir, a Right to act as you pleaſe; and (at preſent, however) ſo have I. How long I ſhould have this Liberty, were I at your *Mercy*, this Letter of yours gives me a moſt deſirable and ſeaſonable Intimation.

For Goodneſs ſake, Sir, let me do as *I* think proper: I ſee, *you* will. I ſent not for you, nor aſked you to be one of the Number you mention. And, if you think fit to withdraw your Name from the Liſt, can I help it, if I would ever ſo fain? But could you not do this without reſolving to affront me, and to reflect on my Conduct? I am unworthy of your Addreſs: I grant it ----- Then you can forbear it. Perhaps I like to ſee the young Fellows *dying* for me; but ſince they can do it without impairing their Health, don't be ſo very angry at me. In ſhort, Sir, you are your own Maſter; and, Heaven be thank'd, I am, at preſent, my own Miſtreſs; and your well-manner'd Letter will make me reſolve to be ſo longer than perhaps I had otherwiſe reſolved. You ſee my *Follies* in my *Conduct*. Thank you, Sir, for letting me know you do. I ſee your Sex in your *Letter*: Thank you, Sir, for that too. So being thus much obliged to you, in a double respect, can I do otherwise than subscribe myself,

Your thankful Servant?

LETTER LXXXVII.

The Gentleman's submissive Reply.

Dear Madam,

I BEG ten thousand Pardons for my rash Letter to you. I wish'd, too late, I could have recall'd it. And when I had the Favour of yours, I was under double Concern. But indeed, Madam, you treated me, I thought, too lightly; and Contempt is intolerable where a Mind is so sincerely devoted. I never saw a Lady I could love before I saw you. I never shall see another I wish to be mine; and as I must love you whether I will or no, I hope you'll forgive my foolish Petulance. I am sure it was inspired by Motives, that, however culpable in their Effects, are intitled to your Forgiveness, as to the Cause. I cannot meanly sue, tho' to you. Don't let me undergo too heavy a Penance for my Rashness. You can mould me to any Form you please. But, dear Lady, let not my honest Heart suffer the *more* Torture, because it is so devotedly at your Service. Once again, I ask a thousand Pardons.---What can I say more?---I own I am hasty, but 'tis most when I think myself slighted, or used contemptuously, by those I love. Such Tempers, Madam, are not the worst, let me tell you. And tho' I may be too ready to offend, yet am I always as ready to repent. And, dear, good Madam, let me be receiv'd to Favour this once, and I will be more cautious for the future. For

G I am,

I am, and ever muſt be, whether you'll allow it or not,

Your moſt devoted Admirer, and humble Servant.

LETTER LXXXVIII.

The Lady's forgiving Return.

SIR,

I Cannot help anſwering your Letter, becauſe you ſeem ſenſible of your Fault. If your Temper is ſo captious, your Guard againſt it ſhould be the ſtronger. It is no very comfortable View, let me tell you, that one ſees a Perſon who wants to recommend himſelf to one's Friendſhip, ſo ready to take Fire. What has a Woman to do in common Diſcretion, but to avoid, while ſhe can, a Proſpect ſo unpleaſing? For if ſhe knows ſhe cannot bear diſreputable Imputations, as indeed ſhe ought not, and that the Gentleman is not able to contain himſelf, whenever he is pleaſed to be moved, from giving them, why this, truly, affords a moſt comfortable Appearance of a happy Life! However, Sir, I cannot bear Malice for a firſt Fault, tho' yet it looks like a Temper, even in a Friend, that one would rather fear than love. But if it be never repeated, at leaſt till I give ſuch Reaſons for it, that neither Charity, nor a profeſſed Eſteem, can excuſe, I ſhall hope, that what has happen'd may rather be of good than bad Uſe to us both. But indeed I muſt ſay, that if you cannot avoid ſuch diſagreeable Inſtances of your Senſibility, it will be Juſtice to both, now we are both free, to think no more of

Your humble Servant.

LET.

LETTER LXXXIX.

Ridiculing a romantick Rhapsody in Courtship.

SIR,

MY Niece desires me to acquaint you, that she received your celestial Epistle last Night, as we were all sitting down to Supper; and she leaves it to me to answer it, according to the Effects it has produced. You must know then, that as soon as she had read it, there appear'd a more marvellous Metamorphosis in her Deportment, than any we read of in *Ovid.* She put on high Airs, and talk'd in a lofty Strain to us, as well as to the Maids; nor knew she how to behave all the rest of the Evening ---- You had so thoroughly proved her superior to all the Deities of the Antients, that she could not help fansying the homely Viands that stood before her, a Banquet of *Paradise*, and when she put to her Lips some of our common Table-drink, it became immediately, in her Fancy, *Nectar* and *Ambrosia*, and she affected to sip, rather than drink. When, by your generous Aid, she had thus raised herself far above Mortality, she began to despise our Company, and thought her Grandmother and me too highly favoured by her Preference, and spoke to us in such a Tone, as made us honest Mortals amaz'd at her sudden Elevation.

In short, Sir, as she has placed such a thorough Confidence in you, as to believe whatever you are pleased to tell her, she begs you will never so far mortify her towering Ambition, as to treat her like any thing earthly.

If then you would make yourself worthy of her Favour, you must, in order to support the Description you have given of her, at least dart thro' the Clouds, or rise with the Morning-Goddess, and attend, in her airy Chariot, at her Chamber-window, where, you say, all the Graces wait, so that you will not be displeased with your Company.

Indeed she is under a Concern, which you must supply, for what Kind of Birds you will find to draw her Chariot; for Doves and Peacocks she would scorn to borrow of *Venus* and *Juno*, whom you make so much her Inferiors.

Here she put on a Royal Air. We will conclude Our own Letter Ourself, said she; so, taking Pen in Hand, she writes as underneath.

Don't let me, when the Car is quite in Readiness, be rudely disturb'd But tell *Mercury*, I would have him tap softly at my Window. I will rise in all my Glory, whip into my starry Calash, and rush through the Regions of Light, till, despising Mortality, we shall form some new Constellation, which some happy Astrologer may, perhaps, in Honour of us both, style *The Twinklers of Moorfields* When I have chosen my new Name, I will deign to write it; till when, I can only style myself, most obliging Sir,

Your Celestial, &c.

LETTER XC.

Against a young Lady's affecting manly Airs; and also censuring the modern Riding-habits.

Dear Betsey,

THE Improvement that is visible in your Person, since your going to *Bury*, gives me much Pleasure; and the Dawning of fine Sense, and good Judgment, that difcovers itfelf in your Converfation, makes me hope to fee every Perfection of my Sifter, your late excellent Mother, revived in you.

Yet one thing the Duty of a tender Uncle obliges me to blame in you, and that is, a certain Affectation that of late obtains in your Behaviour, of imitating the Manners of the other Sex, and appearing more mafculine than either the amiable Softnefs of your Perfon or Sex can juftify.

I have been particularly offended, let me tell you, my Dear, at your *new Riding-habit*; which is made fo extravagantly in the Mode, that one cannot eafily diftinguifh your Sex by it. For you neither look like a *modeft* Girl in it, nor an *agreeable Boy*.

Some Conformity to the Fafhion is allowable. But a cock'd Hat, a lac'd Jacket, a Fop's Peruke, what ftrange Metamorphofes do they make! And then the *Air* affumed with them, fo *pert*, and fo *infipid*, at the fame time, makes, upon the Whole, fuch a *Boy-girl* Figure, that I know of nothing that would become either the *Air*, or the *Drefs*, but a young *Italian* Singer. For fuch an one, being neither *Man* nor *Woman*, would poffibly be beft diftinguifhed by this Hermaphrodite Appearance

In fhort, I would have you remember, my Dear, that as fure as any thing intrepid, free, and in a prudent Degree bold, becomes a Man, fo whatever is foft, tender, and modeft, renders your Sex amiable. In this one Inftance we do not prefer our own Likenefs; and the lefs you refemble us, the more you are fure to charm: For a *mafculine Woman* is a Character as little creditable as becoming.

I am no Enemy to a proper Prefence of Mind in Company, but would never have you appear bold, talkative, or affured. Modefty in the outward Behaviour,

Behaviour, is a strong Prepossession in a Lady's Favour, and, without it, all your Perfections will be of little Service, either as to Reputation or Preferment. You want not Sense. And, I hope, will take kindly these well-intended Hints from

Your affectionate Uncle.

LETTER XCI.

Letter of a Father to a Daughter, relating to Three Persons of different Characters proposed to him, each for her Husband: With his Recommendation of one in Years.

Dear Polly,

I HAVE three several Proposals made me on your Account, and they are so particularly circumstanced, that I cannot approve of one of them.

The first is by Mr. *Aldridge*, for his Son *John*, who, you know, is very weak in his Intellects, and so apt to be misled, that he wants a *Guardian* for him in a *Wife*, and so does you the Reputation to think you a proper Person for that Office. But I think the worst Weakness in the World in a Husband is, that of *Intellect*; and I should suffer much to have you linked to a Man who has no *Head*, and is, for that Reason, highly unworthy to be yours. A *foolish Wife* is much more tolerable, because she can be *kept up*, but a *foolish Husband* will do what he pleases, and go where he pleases, and tho' he knew nothing else, will think he knows too much to be controuled by his Wife, and will have *this* Lesson taught him by Rakes and Libertine, tines, when he is capable of *no other*. So I did not think it necessary so much as to consult you about him.

The second is from Mr. *Gough*, for his Son *Richard*, who has run thro' such a Course of Libertinism, that he has hardly his Fellow, and has neither a *sound Head*, nor a *sound Body*; and is so far from being reclaim'd, that his Father proposes a Wife, as the *last Hope*, for him, and yet knows not whether he will accept of one, if one can be found that would venture upon him. So I could not think of suffering my Daughter to stand either to the Courtesy, or lie at the Mercy, of so profligate a Rake. Tho', it seems, he *vouchsafes* to *like* you better, as his Father says, than any one he ever saw, which was the Reason of the old Man's Application to me.

The third was from Mr. *Tomkins*, whose Nephew is as bad a *Sot*, as the other is a *Rake*, but who promises to reform, if his Uncle can procure my Consent and yours. But as you had refused his Overtures when made to *yourself*, without consulting me, and for the very Reasons I should have rejected him, I would not trouble you about him, but gave a total Denial to the Request of his Uncle, who desired that the Matter might be brought on again, by my Authority and Interposition.

So, my good Girl has had hard Fortune, as one may say, in the Offers of three Persons, that it is impossible she should chuse out of One so very a *Fool*, a second so profligate a *Rake*, and the third so vile a *Sot*, that there could be no Thought of any of the three.

But I have a *fourth* Affair to mention to you, against which there can lie but one Objection; and that is, some Disparity in Years. This is my good Friend Mr. *Rowe*; as honest a Man as ever liv'd, a Man of Prudence; a Man of good Fortune, and easy Circumstance; Master of a genteel House and Business; well respected by all the World, and *most* by those who know him *best*; a good-natur'd Man, humane, compassionate, and, tho' *frugal*, not a *Niggard*.

Now, my dear Daughter, What think you of Mr. *Rowe?*---He has an high Opinion of your Prudence and Discretion; but wishes *himself*, that *you* were either Ten Years older, or *he* Ten Years younger.---Yet he thinks, if you can get over that Point, he could make you one of the fondest of Husbands, and that there is not any thing but he could and would oblige you in.

I too, my Dear, wish there was a nearer Agreement in *Years*, yet, considering the Hazards a young Woman runs, as the World goes, from *Rakes*, *Sots*, and *Fools*, of every Degree; considering that in this Matter, there is but *one* only thing to be wish'd for; and that all the *grand Desirables* of Life will be so *well* supply'd, considering too that he is a *sightly*, a *neat*, a *personable* Man, and has good *Health*, good *Spirits*, and good *Humour*, and is not yet got quite at the Top of the *Hill of Life*; considering all these Things, I say, I think that *one* Consideration might be given up for the *many* other *more* material ones, which would be so well supply'd in this Match

Say, my dear Daughter, say freely, what you think. You'll much oblige me, if you can get this Matter over. But if you cannot (and be so happy as I wish you),----why then----I don't know what to say---But I must---I think---acquiesce But yet, I could once more wish---But I will say no more till I have your Answer, but that I am

Your most indulgent Father.

LET-

LETTER XCII.

Her Answer, dutifully expostulating on the Case.

Honoured Sir,

I AM sensible of the Obligations which both Nature and Gratitude lay me under to obey your Commands, and am willing to do so at all Events, if what I have to offer be not thought sufficient to excuse my Compliance.

Mr. *Rowe* is, I believe, possessed of all the Merit you ascribe to him. But be not displeas'd, dear Sir, when I say, that he seems not so *proper* an Husband for me, as for a Woman of more Years and Experience.

His *advanced Years*, give me Leave to say, will be far from being agreeable to *me*, and will not my *Youth*, or at least the *Effects* of it, in some Particulars, be distasteful to *him*? Will not that *innocent Levity*, which is almost inseparable from my Time of Life, appear to him in a more despisable Light, than perhaps it deserves? For, Sir, is not a Likeness of Years attended with a Likeness of Humours, an Agreement in Diversions and Pleasures, and Thinking too? And can such Likenesses, such Agreements, be naturally expected, where the Years on one Side *double* the Number of the other? Besides, Sir, is not this Defect, if I may so call it, a Defect that will be far from mending by Time?

Your great Goodness, and the Tenderness I have always experienc'd from you, have embolden'd me to speak thus freely upon a Concern that is of the highest Importance to my future Welfare, which I know you have in View from more solid Motives than I am capable of entertaining. And if you still insist

insist upon my Obedience, I will only take the Liberty to observe, that if I do marry Mr. *Rowe*, it will be *intirely* the Effect of my *Duty* to the best of Fathers, and not of an *Affection* for a Gentleman that I respect in every other Light but that you propose him in. And, dear good Sir, consider then, what Misunderstandings and evil Consequences may possibly arise from hence, and render unhappy the future Life of

Your most dutiful Daughter.

I am greatly obliged to you, Sir, that you refused, without consulting me, the three strange Overtures you mention.

LETTER XCIII.

His Reply, urgently inforcing, but not compelling, her Compliance with his Desire.

Dear Polly,

I AM far from taking amiss what you have written, in Answer to my Recommendation of my worthy Friend Mr. *Rowe*, and I am sure, if I was to shew him your Letter, he would never permit you to be urged more on this Head. But, my Dear, I own my Wishes and my Heart are engag'd in *his*, shall I say, or in *your own* Favour? And I would hope, that, notwithstanding all you have written, your good Sense, and that Discretion for which you have been hitherto so deservedly noted, may, on mature Reflection, enable you to overcome the Objection that would be insuperable to lighter and airier Minds of your Sex.

Such is the Profligateness of the Generality of young Fellows of the present Age, that I own I look into the World with Affrightment, at the Risques which a virtuous young Woman has to encounter with on a Change of Condition, which makes me dwell upon the Point with the greater Earnestness. And you know, my Dear, I can have no Motive but your Good.

Then, Child, consider the Reputation this Match, to all who know Mr. *Rowe*'s Worth, will bring to your *Prudence*, and even to your *Sex*. For it is as much Credit to a *young Lady* to marry a worthy Man, *older than herself*, as it is *Discredit* for an *old Woman* to marry a young Man. Does my *Polly* take my Meaning? The Case is plain. Besides, nobody thinks Ten or Twelve Years Difference in a Man's Age any thing out of the way So, my Dear, it is not *Twenty* Years Odds; it is only *Ten* at *most*

Then, again, he is a good-natur'd Man; there's a great deal in *that*, you know.

To be sure, my Dear, it is my good Opinion of your *Prudence*, that makes me endeavour to persuade you to this. And I could be glad, methinks, to find, that I have not too high a Notion of *your* Discretion, in the Preference I am willing to give it to that of all the young Ladies I know.

But if I am mistaken, I mean, if you cannot get over this *one* Difficulty, I shall be apt to think, so surmountable does it seem to me, that you have seen somebody you like, and are prepossess'd Yet I cannot believe that neither, because you know I have so tender a Regard for your own Option, that you would have made me acquainted with it

Yet, after all, far be it from me to compel your Inclinations! But if you should be so happy as to think with me, that the many valuable Qualities

Mr. *Rowe* is possessed of, are scarcely to be hoped for in a younger Man, as the World now goes, you would make me very happy; and I am persuaded you will never repent your Choice.

One thing more let me urge, my Dear; for you see how my Heart's upon it. How many very virtuous young Maidens have married, for the sake of *Riches* only, a Man much older, much more disagreeable, waspish, humoursome, diseased, decrepit, and yet have lived Years without Reproach, and made themselves not unhappy! And will not my dear Daughter do as much to *oblige her Father* (and where Health, Good-nature, Wisdom, Discretion, and great Circumstances, meet to *inforce* the Argument), as others would do, where not one of these Advantages are in the Case, except the single Article of *Riches?* Only then, my Dear, let Mr. *Rowe* attend you, two or three times, before you absolutely set yourself against him. And, as I hope your Affections are intirely disengaged, you will soon see whether his Conversation or Proposals will not incline you in his Favour, considering all things, that is to say, considering the *one* thing AGAINST him, and the *many* FOR him. And if it cannot be, I will intirely acquiesce, being ever studious of your Happiness, as becomes

Your indulgent Father.

LETTER XCIV.

To a rich Widow Lady with Children, diffuading her from marrying a Widower of meaner Degree, who has Children alfo.

Dear Madam,

IT is with some Reluctance, and great Respect, that I prevail on myself to give you this Trouble. The frequent Visits Mr. *Clarkson* makes you, and the Airs that Gentleman gives himself, have given Birth to a Report, that a Treaty of Marriage between you is on foot; and that, in all Probability, it will be soon brought to Effect.

To be sure, Mr. *Clarkson* is not to be blam'd, to endeavour to procure for his Wife a Lady of your Prudence, good Character, and Fortune, but whether you will be able to avoid the Censure of the World, if you chuse *him* for a Husband, is another Point, which greatly concerns you to consider of, and affects me, and all who wish you well.

His Fortune, Madam, is not equal to yours, supposing it to be better than the World reports it: He has Children: So have you. What Inconveniencies may not arise from hence? Especially, as he is not thought to be one of the best and smoothest-temper'd Men in the World.----His Character is not equal, in any respect, to say the least (for I would not detract from any Man's Merit), to that of your late good Spouse, my dear Friend; who would have been much grieved, if he had had but the least Apprehension, that the Man he would not have accompany'd with, should succeed him in his Bed.

Far be it from me, dear Madam, if you are so disposed, as to wish to hinder you from a Change of Condition with a suitable Person! But as your late Spouse left *his* and *your* Children so much in your Power, methinks you should take especial Care, how and to whom you communicate any Part of that Power, and thereby give a *Right* to controul not only *them*, but yourself. Must *he* not be partial to *his own* Children? And will he not expect, that your Complaisance to him should make *you* so too; or, at least, be his Childrens Behaviour what it will, that it shall induce you to put them upon a *Par* with your own? His Daughters will be Spies upon your Conduct, and, be you ever so kind to them, will always suspect your Partiality to your own, and treat you as their *Mother-in-law*, and their Father will believe all they shall suggest, for *that* very Reason, and because he will *judge*, tho' perhaps not *allow for*, that you *ought* to prefer *your own* to *his*: And this will be the Source of perpetual Uneasinesses between you. Consider, dear Madam, whether your late affectionate Spouse deserved from you, that *his* Children and *your own* should be put upon such Difficulties, in Favour of those of *any other* Person whatever.

No doubt but you may make your own Conditions with Mr *Clarkson*. He will be glad to call you and your Fortune *his*, upon any Terms But, consider, Madam, how difficult it may be, whatever Articles you make, for a good Wife, who has been accustom'd to think her *Interest* the *same* with that of her *Husband*, to refuse to his *Importunities*, and perhaps to his *Conveniency*, if not *Necessities*, those Communications of Fortune which you may reserve in your own Power, when they will make him *easier* in Circumstance, and more complaisant in Temper And how hard it will be to deny Mr to any thing, to whom you have given your Pity, and to whom you have vowed *Duty* and *Obedie*

But if you should have the Resolution to *refuse* him, what he may not be backward to *ask*, do you think yourself so well able to bear that *Indifference*, if not *worse*, which such a Refusal may occasion? And would you chuse to have Advantage taken of your *tenderest Hours*, either to induce you to acquiesce with Importunities, which, comply'd with, may hurt your *Children*; or, to have those tender Moments dash'd with Suspicions of *Selfishness* and *Design*? For Prudence will oblige you to be on your Guard, that even the *highest Acts* of *Kindness*, and the *strongest Professions* of *Affection*, may not be preparative Arts to obtain from you Concessions you ought not to make. And how will the pure Joys which flow from an *unsuspected* Union of Minds and Interests, the Want whereof will make *any* Matrimony unhappy, be found in a State thus circumstantiated?

If, Madam, you are bent upon a Change of Condition, your Friends would wish first, that you will be pleased absolutely to ascertain the Fortunes of your Children, according to the *Design* and *Will* of their *dear Father*, as far as may *legally* be done, either by chusing Trustees for them, or by such other way as shall put it out of a *new* Husband's Power to hurt them. And when he shall know this *is done*, you will have a better Testimony of his Affection, as he will know what *is*, and what *is not* yours, and can hope for no more, because it is not in your Power to give more. But how much more is it to be wished, for your own sake, as well as your Childrens, that if you do change, it may be with a Person who has *no* Children? And then what *other* Children may be the Results of your *new Marriage*, they will be *your own* as well as *his*, and so be *more properly* intitled to your *Care* and your *Kindness*, than any Man's Children by *another Wife* can be.

By

By this means, Madam, most of the Uneasinesses we every Day see in Families, where are *two Sorts* of Children, will be prevented, or perhaps your present Children will be grown up, and out of the way, before the other can *interfere* essentially with them, or if *not*, they will be *naturalized*, as one may say, to *each other*, and, having the *same* Mother, who has an *equal* Interest in them *all*, will *expect* and *allow for* an *equal* Exertion of Tenderness and Favour to *all*.

I will trouble you with no more at present on this Head; and am confident, that when you consider maturely what I have written, and the respectful Manner in which I have ventur'd to give my Opinion, and my own Disinterestedness besides, and that I might still have urged other powerful Motives, which I forbear in *Honour* to you, you will have the Goodness to excuse the Liberty I have taken, which is so suitable to the Laws of *Friendship*, by which I am bound to be, dear Madam,

Your zealous Well-wisher, and humble Servant.

Instructions to young Orphan Ladies, as well as others, how to judge of Proposals of Marriage made to them without their Guardians or Friends Consent, by their Milaners, Mantua-makers, or other Go-betweens.

A Young Orphan Lady, of an independent Fortune, receivable at Age, or Day of Marriage, will hardly fail of several Attempts to engage her Affections. And the following general Rules and Instructions will be of Use to her on these Occasions.

In the first place, she ought to mistrust all those who shall seek to set her against her Guardian, or those Relations to whom her Fortune or Person is intrusted: And, next, to be apprehensive of all such as privately want to be introduced to her, and who avoid treating with her Guardian first for his Consent. For she may be assur'd, that if a young Man has Proposals to make, which he himself thinks would be accepted by a Person of *Years* and *Experience*, he will apply in a regular way to her Friends, but if he has not, he will hope to engage the young Lady's Affections by the means of her *Milaner*, her *Mantua-maker*, or her *Servant*; and so by Bribes and Promises endeavour to make his way to her Favour, in order to take Advantage of her Youth and Inexperience: For this is the constant Method of *Fortune-hunters*, to which many a worthy young Lady of good Sense and good Fortune has owed her utter Ruin.

The following are generally the Methods taken by this Set of Designers.

These industrious Go-betweens, who hope to make a Market of a young Lady's Affections, generally by Letter, or Word of Mouth, if they have Opportunity, set forth to the young Lady,

" That there is a certain young Gentleman of
" *great Merit*, of a *handsome Person*, and *fine Ex-*
" *pectations*, or *prosperous Business*, who is fallen
" deeply in Love with her. And very probably,
" the young Lady, having no bad Opinion of her-
" self, and loving to be admired, believes it very
" easily.

" That he has seen her at *Church*, or the *Opera*,
" the *Play*, the *Assemblée*, &c. and is impatient to
" make known his Passion to her.

" That

"That he is unwilling to apply to her *Guardian*, till he *knows* how his Addrefs will be received by *herfelf*.

"That, befides, it may very probably be the Cafe, that her Guardian may form Obftacles, which may not be reafonable on *her Part* to give into.

"That, if he has *Daughters* of his own, he would perhaps rather fee them marry'd firſt.

"That he may not care to part with her Fortune, and the *Reputation* and *Convenience* the *Management* of it may give him.

"That he may defign to marry her, when he *thinks proper*, to fome Perfon agreeable to his *own* Intereft or Inclinations, without confulting *hers* as he ought.

"That, therefore, it would be beft, that her Guardian fhould know *nothing* of the Matter, till fhe faw whether fhe could approve the Gentleman or not.

"That even *then* fhe might *encourage* his Addrefs, or *difcountenance* it as fhe *pleafed*.

"That, for her the *Propofer*'s part, fhe had no *Intereft* in the World, one way or other, and no *View*, but to ferve the young Lady, and to oblige a young Gentleman fo well qualify'd to make her happy." And fuch-like plaufible Affurances; ending, perhaps, "with defiring to bring on an *Interview*, or, if that will not be admitted, that fhe will receive a Letter from him."

This kind of Introduction ought always to be fufpected by a prudent young Lady. She ought with *Warmth* and *Refentment* to difcourage the *officious Propofer*. She ought to acquaint her,

"That fhe is refolved never to give way to a Propofal of this Importance, without the *Confent* and *Approbation* of her *Guardian* or *Friends*.

"That her good Father or Mother, who had
" *seen the World*, and had *many Years* Experience
" of her Guardian's *Honour* and *Qualifications* for
" such a Trust, knew what they did, when they
" put her under his Care

" That he had always shewn an *honest* and *gene-*
" *rous* Regard for her Welfare

" That she took it very unkindly of the Pro-
" poser, to offer to inspire her with *Doubts* of his
" *Conduct*, when she had *none* herself, nor *Reason*
" for any.

" That it was Time enough when he gave her
" *Reason*, to be apprehensive of his sinister Designs,
" or of his preferring his *own* Interest to *hers*.

" That it was a very strange Attempt to make
" her mistrust a *Friend*, a *Relation*, a *Gentleman*,
" who was chosen for this Trust by her *dear Pa-*
" *rents*, on *many Years Experience* of his Honour
" and Probity, and of whose Goodness to her, *for*
" *so long time past*, she herself had many Proofs:
" And this in Favour of a Person who had a *visible*
" *Interest* to induce him to this Application;
" whose *Person* she hardly *knew*, if *at all*, whose
" *Professions* she could not *judge* of, who began by
" such mean, such groundless, such unworthy Insi-
" nuations Who *might*, or *might not*, be the Per-
" son he pretended, and who wanted to induce
" her to prefer *himself*, on *no* Acquaintance at all,
" to a *Gentleman* she had so many Years *known*,
" and whose *Honour*, good *Character*, *Reputation*,
" and *Conscience*, were all engaged to her as so
" many Pledges for his honourable Behaviour to
" her

" That she the *Proposer*, and the young Gentle-
" man *too*, must have a very indifferent Opinion
" of her *Gratitude*, her *Prudence*, her *Discretion*,
" to make such an Attempt upon her.

" That

"That if he could approve himself to a Man of *Years* and *Experience*, who was not to be imposed upon by *blind Passion*, in the Light he wanted to appear in to *her*, why should he not apply to *him first?*

"That surely it was a very *ungenerous* as well as *suspicious* Method of Proceeding, that he could find no *other way* to give her an Opinion of *himself*, but by endeavouring to depreciate the Character of a *Gentleman*, who, by this Method, plainly appeared to his *own Apprehension* to stand in the way of his Proceedings, and *that t s before* he had *try'd him*, and which shewed, that he himself had not hope of succeeding, but by *Arts of Delusion*, *Flattery*, and a *clandestine Address*, and had nothing but her *own Inadvertence* and *Inexperience* to build upon.

"That, therefore, it behoved her, had she no other Reason, to reject with *Resentment* and *Disdain* a Conduct so affrontive to her *Understanding*, as well as *selfish* and *ungenerous* in the Proposer.

"That, therefore, she would not countenance any *Interview* with a Person *capable* of acting in such a manner, nor receive any *Letter* from him

"And lastly, that she desires never to hear of this Matter again, from her the *Proposer*, if she would have her retain for her that good Opinion which she had hitherto had."

This prudent Reasoning and Conduct will make the Intervener quit her Design upon the young Lady, if she is not wholly abandoned of all Sense of Shame, and corrupted by high Bribes and Promises; and in this Case, the young Lady will judge how unfit such a Person is either for her *Confident* or *Acquaintance*. Nor will the Lady lose an humble Servant *worthy* of being *retain'd* or *encourag'd:* For if he be the Person he *pretends*, he will directly apply to her *Guardian*, and have a high Opinion of her Prudence and Discretion; and if she hears no more of him, she may conclude, he could not make good his Pretensions to a Person of *Discernment*, and will have Occasion to rejoice in escaping his designing Arts with so little Trouble to herself.

If a Lady has had actually a Letter delivered her from such a Pretender, and that by means of a Person who has any Share in her Confidence, and wants a Form of a Letter to send to the Recommender to discourage the Proceeding; the following, which has been sent with good Effect, on a like Occasion, may be proper.

LETTER XCV.

Mrs. Pratt,

I Inclose the Letter you put into my Hands, and hope it will be the last I shall ever receive from you or any body else on the like Occasion. I am intirely satisfied in the Care and Kindness of my Guardian, and shall encourage no Proposal of this sort, but what comes recommended to me by *his* Approbation. He knows the World. I do not, and that which is not fit for *him* to *know*, is not fit for *me* to *receive*; and I am sorry either you or the Writer looks upon me in so weak a Light, as to imagine I would wish to take myself out of the Hands of so *experienced* a *Friend*, to throw myself into those of a *Stranger*. Yet I would not, as this is the first Attempt of the kind from you, and that it may rather be the Effect of Inconsideration, than Design, shew it my Guardian, because he would not perhaps impute it to so favourable a Motive in you, as I am willing to do, being

Your Friend and Servant.

If there be no Go-between, but that a young Fellow takes upon himself to send Letters to tease a young Lady to encourage his Address, by his romantick Professions of his Affection and Regard for her, and attributing such Perfections to her, as no one Woman ever had; and if she is desirous, but knows not how, to get rid of his troublesome Importunity, and that even a contemptuous Silence, which it is prudent for a young Lady to shew on such an Occasion, has no Effect upon him; nor yet that he will desist, tho' she returns his Letters *un open'd*, or in a *blank Cover*, after she happens to have read them; then let the Lady get some Friend to write to him, looking upon him as beneath her own Notice. For even a *Denial*, if given in *Writing* under *her own Hand*, will encourage some presumptuous Men, or at least they may make some Use of it to the Lady's Disadvantage; and ought not to have it to boast, that they have received a Letter from her, tho' ever so much to their own Discredit, if it were shewn. And the following may be the Form:

LETTER XCVI.

SIR,

YOU have thought fit to write to Miss K——, twice or thrice in a very troublesome manner. She cannot possibly so far forget what belongs to Herself and Character, as to answer you any other way than by the Contempt of Silence. Yet since she cannot, it seems, be free from your Impertinence, she wishes you may be told, That you must have as mean an Opinion of *her* Judgment, as all who read your Epistles, must have of *yours*, if you can expect Success from such inconsistent Rhapsodies.

I will from myself venture to give you one Piece of Advice; That the next Person you pretend to address with your bright Compositions, you don't in them forget one Ingredient, which is *Common Sense*, tho' you should be forced to borrow it. I am

Yours, unknown.

Or, if this be thought too affronting, the following

LETTER XCVII.

S I R,

YOU are desired to send no more of your elaborate Epistles to Miss *Knollys*. You are quite mistaken in the Lady. She knows *herself*, and by your Letter she knows *you*, so well, that she sends it back, that you may find some other Person to send it to, whose Sentiments and Understanding are better proportion'd to your own. I am, Sir, &c.

If the Letters of the young Fellow deserve less Severity, and are such as have not their Foundation in Romance and Bombast, but yet the Lady thinks not proper to encourage his Address, this Form may serve.

LETTER XCVIII.

S I R,

I AM desir'd to acquaint you, that Miss *Knollys* thinks herself obliged to every one who has a good Opinion of her, but begs, that you will not give yourself, or her, the Trouble of any more Letters. For Things are so circumstanced, that

she

she has neither Inclination nor Power to encourage your Addreſs. I am, Sir,

Your humble Servant, *unknown*.

If the Lady has a mind to rebuke the Attempt of a clandeſtine Addreſs to her, and yet thinks the Propoſal not abſolutely unworthy of Attention, did it come *regularly* to her, by means of her *Father*, *Mother*, *Guardian*, &c. this Form may be obſerved.

LETTER XCIX.

S I R,

MISS *Knollys* deſires you ſhould be informed, which ſhe preſumes you did not know, That ſhe can never think herſelf at her own Diſpoſal, while ſhe has ſo near and ſo good a Friend to adviſe with as Mr. *Archer*, whoſe Wiſdom ſhe much prefers to her own, as his Experience in the World, and Kindneſs to her, make him deſerve to be conſulted, in all her Affairs of Moment. Whatever ſhall appear fit to him, will have great Weight with her, and there is but that one poſſible way to engage her Attention. I am, Sir,

Yours, &c.

Or, if the Lady has not a Guardian, or Father, or Mother, but ſome Friend in whom ſhe can confide, the following may be a proper Form

LETTER C.

S I R,

IT may not be amiſs to acquaint you, that Miſs *Knollys* is ſo happy as to have a Friend of Experience and Probity, without whoſe Advice ſhe undertakes nothing of Consequence. It is Mr. *Salter*, of *Grace-church-street*. And she will not care to admit of any Proposal of Moment to her that has not passed his Approbation. This, she hopes, will save her and yourself the Trouble of any further Application. I am

Your humble Servant.

Or this:

LETTER CI.

SIR,

MR. *Salter*, of *Grace-church-street*, being a Gentleman that Miss *Knollys* consults in all her Affairs, she refers to him all Proposals that are or may be of Importance to her, and desires to receive no more Letters or Messages from you, by any other Hand. I am

Your humble Servant, unknown.

LETTER CII.

From a Town-Tenant to his Landlord, excusing Delay of Payment.

Honoured Sir,

I AM under a great Concern, that I cannot at present answer your just Expectations. I have sustained such heavy Losses, and met with such great Disappointments of late, that I must intrude another Quarter on your Goodness. Then, whatever Shifts I am put to, you shall hear to more Satisfaction than at present, from, Sir,

Your most humble Servant.

H LET-

LETTER CIII.

From a Country Tenant to the same Purpose.

Honoured Sir,

THE Season has been so bad, and I have had such unhappy Accidents to encounter with in a sick Family, Loss of Cattle, &c. that I am obliged to trespass upon your Patience a Month or two longer. The Wheat-harvest, I hope, will furnish me the Means to answer your just Expectations, which will be a great Contentment to

Your honest Tenant, and humble Servant.

LETTER CIV.

The Landlord's Answer.

Mr. Jacobs,

I HAVE yours I hope you'll be as good as your Word at the Expiration of the Time you have mentioned. I am unwilling to distress any *honest* Man; and I hope, that I shall not meet with the *worse* Usage for my Forbearance. For *Lenity* abused, even in generous Tempers, provokes Returns, that some People would call *severe*, but should not be deemed such, if *just*. I am

Yours, &c.

LETTER CV.
A threatening Letter from a Steward on Delay of Payment.

Mr. Atkins,

I HAVE mentioned your Case to Sir *John*, as you requested. He is exceedingly provoked at your Usage, and swears bloodily he'll seize, and throw you into Gaol, if he has not 20 *l.* at least paid him by Quarter-day, which is now at hand. So you know what you have to trust to; and I would have you avoid the Consequences at any rate; for he is resolved otherwise to do as he says. Of this I assure you, who am

Yours, &c.

LETTER CVI.
The poor Tenant's moving Answer.

Good Mr. Taverner,

I AM at my Wits-end almost on what you write. But if I *am* to be ruined, with my numerous Family, and a poor, industrious, but *ailing* Wife, how can I help it? For I cannot possibly raise 20 *l.* any manner of way by the Time you mention. I hope Sir *John* won't be hard-hearted. For if God Almighty, our *common* Landlord, should be *equally* hard upon us, what would become of us *all*? Forgive my Boldness to talk of God Almighty to his *Honour*, in this free manner.

I would do it, if it was to be done; but you know, Sir, what a *Season* we have had. And an honester Tenant his Honour will never have, that I am sure of. But if Money wis'n't rise, what can I do?

I do? Should I sell my Team, and my Utensils for Labour, there is an End of *all*. I shall have no Means left me then wherewith to pay his *Honour*, or *any body* else. If his Honour will not be moved, but *will* seize, pray, good Mr. *Taverner*, prevail on him not to throw me into Gaol, for a Prison pays no Debts; but let my poor Wife and Six small Children lie in the Barn, till I can get a little Day-labour; for that must be all I can have to trust to, if his Honour seizes. I hear my Man *William* that was, has just taken a Farm; may be, he will employ his poor ruin'd Master, if I am not 'prison'd. But if I be, why then the Parish must do something for my poor Children, tho' I hoped they would never trouble it. Lay these things before his Honour, good Sir, and forgive this Trouble from

His Honour's honest, tho' unfortunate Tenant.

LETTER CVII.

The Steward's Reply, giving more Time.

Mr. Atkins,

I HAVE laid your Letter and your Case before Sir *John*. He is moved with it, and says he will have Patience another Quarter, to see what you'll do. Consider, Man, however, that Gentlemen live at a great Expence, are obliged to keep up their Port, and if their Tenants fail *them*, who then they must fail their *Tradesmen*, and suffer in their *Credit*. You have good Crops of all Kinds on the Ground, and surely may, by next Quarter, raise 40 or 50 *l.* tho' you could not make 20 *l.* in a Fortnight. This Sir *John* will expect at least, I can tell you. And you may comply with it from the Produce of so good a Farm, surely. I am

Yours, &c.

LETTER CVIII.

The poor Man's thankful Letter in Return.

GOD bless his Honour, and God bless you, Mr. *Taverner*, that's all I can say. We will now set our Hands to the Plough, as the Saying is, with chearful Hearts, and try what can be done. I am sure, I, and my Wife and Children too, tho' three of them can but lisp their Prayers, shall, Morning, Noon and Night, pray to God for his Honour's Health and Prosperity, as well as for you and yours, and to enable me to be just to his Expectations. I'm sure it would be the Pride of my Heart to pay every body, his Honour especially. I have not run behind-hand for want of Industry, that all my Neighbours know, but Losses and Sickness I could not help, and nobody could live more frugal and sparing than both my Wife and I. Indeed we have hardly allowed ourselves Cloaths to our Backs, nor for our Children neither, tight, and clean, and wholsome as they may appear to those who see them. And we will continue to live so low as may only keep us in Heart to do our Labour, until we are got before-hand; which God grant. But all this I told you before, Mr. *Taverner*; and so will say no more, but I will do all I can, and God give a Blessing to my Labours, as I mean honestly. So no more, but that I am, Sir,

Your ever-obliged Servant.

LETTER CIX.

An Offer of Assistance to a Friend who has received great Losses by a Person's Failure.

Dear Sir,

I AM exceedingly concerned at the great Loss which you have lately sustained, by the Failure of Mr. *Tranter.* I hope you behave under it like the Man of Prudence you have always shewn yourself, and as one who knows how liable all Men are to Misfortunes. I think it incumbent, on this Occasion, not to console you by Words *only*; but in the Spirit, and with the Chearfulness, of a most sincere Friend, to offer my Service to answer any *present* Demand, so far as 200 *l.* goes, which you shall have the Use of freely for a Twelve-month, or more, if your Affairs require it; and will even strain a Point rather than not oblige you, if *more* be necessary to your present Situation. You'll do me great Pleasure in accepting this Offer as *freely*, as it is *kindly* meant by, dear Sir,

Yours most faithfully.

LETTER CX.

The Friend's Answer, accepting the kind Offer.

My dear Friend,

HOW shall I find Words to express the grateful Sense I have of your Goodness? This is an Instance of true Friendship indeed! I accept most thankfully of some Part of your generous Offer, and will give you my Bond, payable in a Year, for 100 *l.* which is, at present, all I have Occasion for,

for, and if I did not know I could then, if not before, answer your Goodness as it deserves, I would not accept of the Favour. This Loss is very heavy and affecting to me, as you may suppose; yet your generous Friendship is no small Comfort to me in it. For so good a Friend is capable of making any Calamity light. I am, dear Sir,

Your most faithful and obliged humble Servant.

LETTER CXI.

The Friend's Answer, supposing he has no Occasion.

Dear Sir,

A Thousand Thanks to you for your generous Offer, and kind Advice. I have been not a little affected at the unexpected Failure of a Man all the World thought as good as the Bank. But, at present, I have no Occasion for your friendly Assistance. If I should, I know no one in the World I would sooner chuse to be obliged to; for I am, dear, kind Sir,

Your most obliged humble Servant.

LETTER CXII.

Of Consolation to a Friend in Prison for Debt.

Dear Sir,

I AM exceedingly concerned to hear, that the Severity of your Creditors has laid you under Confinement. But there is one Comfort results from it, that the utmost Stretch of their Revenge cannot carry them farther; and that when a Man is got to the undermost Part of Fortune's Wheel, he *may rise,*

rise, but *cannot* sink lower. You now know the worst, and have nothing to do, but to support your Misfortune with that true Magnanimity which becomes a noble Mind. Long, very long, have you been labouring under great Difficulties, and so have been inured to Misfortunes; and you have *looked forward* with such Anxiety and Pain to the hard Lot that has now befallen you, that 'tis impossible the *bearing* of it can be equal to the *Apprehensions* you had of it. You see all around you too many unhappy Objects reduced to the same Distress; and you see them either extricating themselves from those Difficulties (as I hope you soon will), or learning to bear them with a true Christian Resignation For well does the wise Man observe, that *the Race is not to the Swift, nor the Battle to the Strong, nor Riches to a Man of Understanding*. And it will yield you some Consolation, when you reflect, that *this* Life is but a State of *Probation*, and he that meets with Misfortunes *here*, may, by a *proper Use* of them, and by *God's Grace*, be intitled to a blessed Hope; when a *prosperous State* may make a Man forgetful of his Duty, and so reap no other Good but what he finds in this *transitory* Life. Remember, my Friend, that the *School of Affliction* is the *School of Wisdom*; and so behave under this *trying* Calamity, as to say, with the Royal Prophet, *It is good for me, that I was afflicted.*

I think myself, however, not a little unhappy, that my Circumstances will not permit me to assist you on this grievous Occasion, in the way a Friend would chuse to do, if he was able; but if, by my personal Attendance on any of your Creditors or Friends, I can do you Pleasure or Service, I beg you to command me. For, in whatever is in my poor Power, I am, and shall ever be,

Your faithful Friend and Servant

LETTER CXIII.

In Answer to the preceding.

Dear Sir,

I Now experience fully the Truth of the honest *English* Phrase, That *a Friend in Need is a Friend in Deed*. You have filled me with such unspeakable Comfort, to find that I am not abandon'd by *all* my old Acquaintance, that, in a great measure, your seasonable Kindness will enable me to pursue the Advice you give me.

It is too late to look back now on the Steps that have brought me to this abject Condition. No doubt, were I to live my Life over again, I could do much better for myself than I have done, and should hardly run into some of the Failings that have help'd to bring such heavy Misfortunes upon me. But my Comfort is, I ever had an *honest Intention*, and never was a *Sot* or a *Spendthrift*. But yet, who knows, if I had avoided *some* Mistakes, that I might not have fallen into *as bad* another way? So I must acquiesce in the Dispensation, and pray to God, in his own good Time, to deliver me from it.

What is most grievous to me in this Matter is, my *poor Wife* and *Children*, who have deserved a happier Fate, had it been in my Power to have done better for them, than now I am ever likely to do.

As to your kind Offer, my dear Friend, I will beg to see you as often as may not be detrimental to *your own* Affairs. I care not how seldom I see my dear Wife. Neither *her* Heart nor *mine* can bear the Grief that oppresses us when we think of our *happier* Days and Prospects, and see them all

concluded

concluded within these *Bars*, and *Bolts*, and *Lattices*; so that we sink one another still lower every doleful Visit the dear good Woman makes me. But *your* Visits, my Friend, will be of singular Use and Comfort to *me* (as your Presence and kind Advice will be to *her*, as often as you can), to save us both the Mortification of seeing one another so often as my Affairs will otherwise require her to come to this dismal Place; for I cannot open my Mind to any body but you and her. I will also get you to go to Mr. *Maddox*, my principal Creditor, and one or two more; I will tell you about what; and only fear I shall be too troublesome to you. But you are so kind as to offer your Service in this way, and I am reduced to the sad Necessity of pushing myself upon you, without the least Hope of ever having it in my Power to shew you, as I wish to do, how much I am

Your ungrateful, tho' unhappy Servant.

LETTER CXIV.

To a Person of Note, in Acknowlegement of great Benefits received.

Honoured Sir,

PERMIT me to approach you with the thankful Acknowlegements of a grateful Heart, on the Favour and Benefit your Goodness has conferred upon me. It shall be the Business of my whole Life, to the utmost of my Power, to deserve it; and my whole Family, which you have made happy by your Bounty, will every Day join with me in Prayers to God, to bless you with the Continuance of your valuable Health, a long Life,

most Important Occasions.

Life, and all worldly Honour; for so it will become us to do, for the unmerited Favours confer'd upon, honoured Sir,

Your most dutiful Servant.

LETTER CXV.

Another for Favours of not so high, yet of a generous Nature.

Worthy Sir,

I Should appear ungrateful, if I did not add this further Trouble to those I have already given you, of acknowleging your Goodness to me, in this last Instance of it. May God Almighty return to you, Sir, one hundredfold, the Benefit you have conferr'd upon me, and give me Opportunity, by my future Services, to shew my grateful Heart, and how much I am, worthy Sir,

Your for-ever obliged and dutiful Servant.

LETTER CXVI.

An Excuse to a Person who wants to borrow Money.

SIR,

I AM very sorry, that your Request comes to me at a time when I am so press'd by my own Affairs, that I cannot with any Conveniency comply with it. I hope, Sir, you will therefore excuse

Your most humble Servant.

LETTER CXVII.

On the same Subject.

SIR,

I HAVE, on an urgent Occasion, been obliged to borrow a Sum of Money myself within ten Days past. Hence you'll judge of my Want of *Capacity*, rather than *Inclination*, to comply with your Request. For I am

Your sincere Friend.

LETTER CXVIII.

On the same Subject.

SIR,

IT is with no little Pain, that I am obliged to lay open to you, on occasion of the Loan you request of me, my own Inability. I shall make very hard Shift to answer some necessary Demands, which must be comply'd with by a certain Time, and so can only say, I am sorry I have it not in my Power to shew how sincerely I am

Your most humble Servant.

LETTER CXIX.

To a Friend, in Compliance with his Request to borrow a Sum of Money.

SIR,

YOU have highly obliged me in the Request you make me. I most chearfully comply with it, and inclose a Note for the requested Sum, payable on Sight; and am not a little glad it is in my Power to shew you how much I am

Your faithful Friend and Servant.

LETTER CXX.

Another on the same Occasion, limiting the Repayment to a certain Time.

SIR,

THE Intimation you give me, that the Sum of 50 Pounds will be of great Use to you, and that you shall be able to repay it in Four Months, makes me resolve to put myself to some Difficulty to oblige you. Accordingly, I inclose a Bank Note to that Amount. But I must, in the *Name of Friendship*, beg of you to return it to me *unused*, if you cannot keep your Word in the Repayment; for my accommodating you with this Sum is rather, at present, a greater Testimony of my *Inclination* than *Ability* to serve you: For I am

Your affectionate Friend and Servant.

LETTER CXXI.

To a Friend, on a Breach of Promise in not returning Money lent in his Exigence.

SIR,

WHEN you apply'd to me, in your Streights, for Assistance, and made such strong Promises of returning in Four Months what I advanced; little did I think, you would give me the irksome Occasion, either of reminding you of your Promise, or of acquainting you with the Streights in which my Friendship for you has involv'd myself. I have always endeavour'd to manage my Affairs with so much Prudence, as to keep *within myself* the Power of answering Demands upon me, without troubling my *Friends*; and I told you, I must expect you would keep your Word exactly to the Four Months, or else I should be distress'd, as bad as you were when you apply'd to me. *Six* Months passed, and you took no manner of Notice of the Matter, when I was forced to remind you of it, having been put to it, as I told you I should. You took a Fortnight longer, under still stronger Promises of Performance. And *Three Weeks* are now expir'd, and your *second* Promises are still as much to be performed as your *first*. Is this kind, is this friendly, is it *grateful*, Sir, let me ask you? And ought I to be made to suffer in *my* Credit, who was so ready to save *yours?*---When, too, mine had been in no Danger, had I not put out of my own Power what actually was then in it? I will only say, That if any Consideration remains with you for one so truly your Friend, let me immediately be paid, and take from me the cruel Necessity of reproaching *you* for Ingratitude, and *myself* for Folly. Who am, Sir,

Your unkindly used, &c.

LETTER CXXII.

To a Friend, who had promised to lend a Sum of Money, to answer a critical Exigence, and drove it off to the last.

Dear Sir,

YOU were so kind as to tell me, a Fortnight ago, that you would lend me One hundred Pounds on my Bond, to answer a Demand that my Credit would be otherwise a Sufferer by. And you were pleased to say, you would have me look no further,

further, and that I should certainly have it in time. I have looked no further, Sir; and the Day of Payment approaching, you cannot imagine how my Mind has suffered by being not *absolutely sure* of having the Money to answer the Demand. I hope, Sir, nothing has happen'd to make you alter your Mind, for, at this short Notice, I shall not know to whom to apply to raise it. In the utmost Perturbation of Mind, for fear of the worst, my Credit being wholly at Stake, I beg your Answer, which I hope will be to the Satisfaction of, Sir,

Your obliged humble Servant.

LETTER CXXIII.

The Answer, excusing the Pain he had given his Friend by his Remissness.

Dear Sir,

I WILL attend you this Afternoon with the Money, which I had always great Pleasure in the Thought of supplying you with; and I am most heartily vexed with myself, for giving you the Pain and Uneasiness that must have attended a Mind so punctual as yours, and in a Case so critically circumstanced. But I hope you'll forgive me, tho' I can hardly forgive myself. I am, Sir, as well on this, as on any other Occasion in my Power,

Your sincere Friend and Servant.

LETTER CXXIV.

To one who, upon a very short Acquaintance, and without any visible Merit but Assurance, wants to borrow a Sum of Money.

SIR,

YOU did me the Favour of inquiring for me two or three times while I was out of Town. And among my Letters I find one from you, desiring the Loan of 50 Guineas. You must certainly have mistaken *yourself* or *me* very much, to think we were enough known to each other for such a Transaction. I was twice in your Company; I was delighted with your Conversation: You seemed as much pleased with mine: And if we both acted with Honour, the Obligation is mutual, and there can be no room to suppose me your Debtor. I have no churlish nor avaritious Heart, I will venture to say; but there must be Bounds to every thing; and Discretion is as necessary in conferring as in receiving a Kindness. To a Friend, my helping Hand ought to be lent, when his Necessities require it: You cannot think our Intimacy enough to commence that Relation; and should I answer the Demands of every *new Acquaintance*, I should soon want Power to oblige my *old Friends*, and even to serve *myself*. Surely, Sir, a Gentleman of your Merit cannot be so little beloved, as to be forced to seek to a new Acquaintance, and to have no better Friend than one of *Yesterday*. I will not do you the Injury to suppose, that you have not *many*, who have the *best* Reasons from long Knowlege, to oblige you: And, by your Application to *me*, I cannot think *Bashfulness* should stand in your way to *them*. Be this as it may, it does not at all suit my Conveniency to comply with your Request; and so I must beg you to excuse

Yours, &c.

LETTER CXXV.

A Gentleman to a Lady who humourously resents his Mistress's Fondness of a Monkey, and Indifference to himself.

Madam,

I MUST be under the less Regret, for the Contempt with which you receive my Addresses, when your Favour is wholly engrossed by so wretched a Rival. For ought a *rational Man* to wonder he is received with Neglect and Slight by a Lady who can be taken up with the Admiration of a *chattering* Monkey? But pray be so good as to permit me to reason the Matter a little with you. I would ask you then, By what extraordinary Endowment this happy Creature has found Means to engross your Favour? Extravagance is never commendable: But while I am dying beneath your Frowns, how can you be profuse in your Caresses to so mean a Competitor? Condescend to view us in the same Light. What valuable Qualification is Mr. *Pug* endowed with, which I am destitute of? What can he do, which I cannot perform, tho' with less Agility, to full as good Purpose? Is it a Recommendation in him, that he wears no Breeches? For my part, I will most willingly surrender mine at your Feet. Be impartial for once: Place us together before you: View our Faces, our Airs, our Shapes, and our Language. If he be handsomer than I, which,

which, on a strict Scrutiny, I hope will not be allowed him neither, pray try our Wits: However acute he may be, I can assure you I reckon myself no Fool, if I was, I should less resent the Preference you give against me I will sing or dance with him for his Ears Turn him loose to me, I will fight him, if that be necessary to obtain your Favour; or do any thing in the World to shew you how much I am, and shall ever be, if you'll permit it,

Your very humble Admirer.

LETTER CXXVI.

A Sailor to his betrothed Mistress.

My dear Peggy,   Barbados, Oct 9.

IF you think of me half so often as I do of you, it will be every Hour; for you are never out of my Thoughts, and, when I am asleep, I constantly dream of my dear *Peggy*. I wear *my* Half bit of Gold always at my Heart, ty'd to a blue Ribband round my Neck; for *True Blue*, my dearest Love, is the Colour of Colours to me. Where, my Dearest, do *you* put *yours?* I hope you are careful of it, for it would be a bad Omen to lose it.

I hope you hold in the same Mind still, my dearest Dear; for God will never bless you, if you break the Vows you have made to me. As to your ever faithful *William*, I would sooner have my Heart torn from my Breast, than it should harbour a Wish for any other Woman besides my *Peggy*. O my dearest Love! you are the Joy of my Life! My *Thoughts* are all of *you*; you are *with me* in all I *do*; and my *Hope* and my *Wish* are only to be *yours*. God send it may be so!

Our

most Important Occasions. 163

Our Captain talks of failing foon for *England*; and then, and then----my deareſt *Peggy!*---O how I rejoice, how my Heart beats with Delight, that makes me I cannot *tell how,* when I think of arriving in *England,* and joining *Hands* with my *Peggy,* as we have *Hearts* before, I hope! I am ſure I ſpeak *for one.*

John Arthur, in the good Ship *Elizabeth,* Capt. *Winterton,* which is returning to *England* (as I hope *we* ſhall ſoon), promiſes to deliver this into your own dear Hand; and he will bring you too, Six Bottles of Citron-water, as a Token of my Love. It is fit for the fineſt Ladies Taſte, it is ſo good; and it is what, they ſay, Ladies drink, when they can get it.

John ſays, he will have one ſweet Kiſs of my deareſt *Peggy,* for his Care and Pains. So let him, my beſt Love; for I am not of a jealous Temper. I have a better Opinion of my *Deareſt,* than ſo.---- But, Oh! that I was in *his* Place!----*One* Kiſs ſhould not ſerve *my Turn,* tho' I hope it *may his!*--- Yet, if he takes *two,* I'll forgive him; one for *me,* and one for *himſelf.* For I love *John* dearly, and ſo you may *well* think. Well, what ſhall I ſay *more?* ----Or, rather, what ſhall I ſay *next?* For I have an hundred things crouding in upon me, when I write to my Deareſt, and, alas! one has ſo few Opportunities! But yet I muſt leave off, for I have written to the Bottom of my Paper. Love then to all Friends, and Duty to both our Mothers, concludes me

Your faithful Lover till Death.

LET-

LETTER CXXVII.

Her Answer.

Dear William,

FOR so I may call you now we are *sure*; and so my Mother says. This is to let you know, that nothing shall prevail upon me to alter my Promise made to you, when we parted. With heavy Hearts enough, that's true. And yet I had a little Inkling given me, that Mr. *Alford*'s Son the Carpenter would be glad to make Love to me. But, do you think I would suffer it? No, indeed! For I doubt not your *Loyalty* to me, and do you think I will not be as *loyal* to you!----To be sure I will. *These Sailors run such sad Chances,* said one that you and I both know. *They may return, and they may not.* Well, I will trust in God for that, who has return'd safe to his Friends, their dear *Billy,* so many a time, and often. *They will have a Mistress in every Land they come to,* said they. All are not such naughty Men, said I; and I'll trust *Billy Oliver* all the World over. For why cannot *Men* be as faithful as *Women*, tro'? And for *me*, I am sure no Love shall ever touch my Heart but *yours*.

God send us a happy Meeting! Let who will speak against *Sailors*; they are the Glory and the Safeguard of the Land. And what would have become of *Old England* long ago but for *them?* I am sure the lazy good-for-nothing *Land-lubbers* would never have protected us from our cruel Foes. So Sailors are, and ever shall be, esteemed by me, and, of *all* Sailors, my dear *Billy Oliver.* Believe this Truth from

Your faithful, &c.

P S.

P.S. I had this Letter writ in Readiness to send you, as I had Opportunity. And the Captain's Lady undertakes to send it with her's. That is very kind and condescending. Is it not?

LETTER CXXVIII.
A Sea-Officer to his Wife.

Port-Mahon, October 31.

My dear Life,

I TAKE the Opportunity afforded me by Captain *Copythorne*, who is returning to *England*, to let you know that I am in perfect Health at present, God be praised; tho' I have, with many of the Crew, been down of the *Bloody-Flux*, occasioned by being a little too free with the new Wines and Fruit of these Countries; and yet I thought I was very moderate in both. Our Captain continues very civil and kind, and places his principal Confidence in me, and I endeavour so to behave on the Occasion, as to avoid incurring the Envy of every one, and, indeed, have the good Fortune to be generally respected.

Captain *Copythorne* is so kind as to carry to you a Token of my Affection; which is a small Parcel of *Cyprus* Wine, that I believe will be agreeable to your best Friend Mrs. *Simpson*, to whom therefore you may present half, and keep the other for your own Use. The Captain has also Fifty Dollars to present you with, from me, only paying out of them the *Duty for the Wine*; for it is but *just*, that it should be so, if he cannot meet with Favour in so small a Parcel, for what the Law of the Land, which protects us all, gives to the King, is as much its Due (however other People act), as any Part of my private Property, which is secured to me by the same Law, is mine: And I am convinc'd, that if every one acted up to this just Principle, there need not be so many Taxes as there are; and the fair Trader, and all honest Men, would be the better for it.

I hope, my dear *Jackey* and *Nancy* continue in good Health, and dutiful, and come on in their *Schooling*; for that will stand them in stead, perhaps, when the poor Matters we are enabled to do for them, may not be worth trusting to.

I long to see my dear *Betty*. God give us a happy Meeting, if it be his blessed Will. But, I believe, it will hardly be till we have humbled the proud *Jack Spaniard*: Which God also grant. For that Nation has been very vile and base to us honest *Englishmen*. This concludes me at present

Your ever-loving Husband.

Love and Service to all Friends.

LETTER CXXIX.

A Wife to her Husband at Sea.

My Dear,

I Think it a long Time since I have had the Comfort and Satisfaction of hearing of your Welfare. Often and often do I reflect on the Unhappiness of us poor Women, who are marry'd to Seafaring Men. Every *Wind* that blows, every *Pirate* we hear of, and now, in *Time of War*, every Hour of our Lives, the Dread of *Enemies* alarms us. God Providence is our Reliance, and so it ought, for nothing else can sustain us thro' our different Apprehensions every Day we live. But to be sure the Unhappiness is still greater to such as love one another

other, as we always did. I hope, when it shall please God to return you safe to my Wishes, that you will take no more of these very long Voyages, if you can help it. The Trips to *Holland* or *France* are so pretty, that they rather add to, than diminish one's Comforts: But, Oh, these long, long Voyages! Yet, in Time of War, People cannot do as they will. And I must be contented; and the more, when I see, that the fine Ladies of Captains, Commodores, and Admirals, are no better off than your poor *Jenny*.

We have had the Misfortune to lose Uncle *James* since you went: He was a *Landman*, out of the Dangers *you* run; yet, as I hope, God has preserved *you*, while *he* is dead and *gone*. So we see there is nothing to be said for it, when our Time is come. They talk of my Aunt's marrying again, and she has a Courtier comes to her, because she is aforehand in the World, and yet Uncle *James* has not yet been dead three Months. Fie upon her, I say, tho' she is my Aunt! for she had a good Husband of him. As to you and me, my Dear, I hope God will spare us to one another; for you are my *First* Love, and shall be my *Last*. Cousin *Barns* had the Misfortune to break his Leg, but is in a good way. *Jenny Adams* is to be marry'd next Week to *John Lascells*. This is all the News among our Acquaintance, for I am sure it is none, to tell you, that I am

Your faithful and loving Wife.

LETTER CXXX.

To a Father, on his Neglect of his Childrens Education.

Dear Sir,

I AM under a Concern to see such a Remissness, as every body takes notice of, in the Education of your Children. They are brought up, 'tis true, to little Offices in your Business, which keep them active, and may make them in some degree of *present*, tho' *poor* Use to *you*; but, I am sorry to say, of *none* to *themselves*, with regard to their *future Prospects*, which is what a worthy Parent always has in View.

There is a proper Time for every thing; and if Children are not early initiated into their Duty, and those Parts of Learning which are proper to their particular Years, they must necessarily be discouraged, and set behind every one of their School-fellows, tho' much younger than themselves, and you know not, Sir, what a laudable Emulation you by this means destroy, than which nothing is of greater Force to Children, to induce them to attend to their Book; nor what a Disgrace you involve them in with respect to Children among Children, for the Biggest and Eldest to be so much outdone by the Least and Youngest.

Nor is the Consequence of this Defect confin'd to the School-age, as I may call it, for as they grow up, they will be look'd upon in an equally discouraging and disadvantageous Light, by all who converse with them. Which must of course throw them into the Company of the Dregs of Mankind; for how will they be able to converse or correspond with those whose Acquaintance is most worth their while to cultivate? And indeed they will probably be so conscious of their Unfitness to bear a Part in worthy Conversation, that, to keep themselves in Countenance, they will, of their own Accord, shun the *better* Company, and associate with the *worst*. And what *may* be the Consequence of this, a wise Man, and a good Father, would tremble to think of, especially when he has to reflect upon himself as the *Cause* of it, let it be what it will.

Then, Sir, it is to be consider'd, that without a tolerable Education they can be only fit for mean and sordid Employments. Hear what the Wise Man says to this very Purpose. "How can he get "Wisdom, that holdeth the *Plough*, and that glo-"rieth in the *Goad*, that driveth *Oxen*, and is oc-"cupied in their Labours, and whose Talk is of "*Bullocks?* He giveth his Mind to make *Fur-*"*rows*, and is diligent to give the *Kine Fodder*. So "every *Carpenter* and *Workmaster*, that laboureth "Night and Day----The *Smith* also sitting by the "Anvil, and considering the Iron-work, the Va-"pour of the Fire wasteth his Flesh----The *Noise* "of the *Hammer* and the *Anvil* is ever in his Ears "----So doth the *Potter* sitting at his Work, and "turning the Wheel about with his Feet----He "fashioneth the Clay with his Arm, and boweth "down his Strength before his Feet." These, as he observes, are useful in their way; but their Minds being *wholly* engross'd by their Labours, "they shall not be sought for in *publick Council*, "nor sit *high* in the *Congregation*----they can-"not declare *Justice* and *Judgment*, and they "shall not be found where *Parables* are spoken." That is, they shall be confin'd to the Drudgery of their own *servile Station*, and will be intitled neither to *Honour* nor *Respect*, as they might

have

have been, had they had an Education to qualify them for more respectable Businesses. And you will consider, Sir, in a closer Light, as to us who live in the *present Age*, and in this *great City*, that there is hardly a *creditable* or *profitable* Employment in *London*, where a tolerable Knowlege of *Accompts*, and *Penmanship*, in particular, is not required. Consider also, what Opportunities they may lose by this Neglect of their Education, in case they should fail in the Business they are put to, of getting comfortable and genteel Bread in some Merchant's Compting-house, or in some one of the several Offices about this great Metropolis; as *Book-keepers*, *Clerks*, *Accomptants*, &c.

And with regard more immediately to *yourself*, how can you expect, when they know you could do better for them, but that their Behaviour to *you* will be of a Piece with the rest? For if they are not polish'd by Learning, but are left to a kind of *Instinct* rather, is it to be expected, that they should behave to *you*, and their *Mother*, with that Sense of their Obligations which Learning inculcates? Nor, indeed, will they *have* those Obligations to you, which other Children have to *their* Parents, who take care to give them Opportunities of Improvement, which are deny'd to yours. Consider, dear Sir, what a contemptible Character, even among the sordid Vulgar, that of an *illiterate Fellow* is, and what Respect, on the contrary, a *Man of Letters* is treated with, by his *Equals*, as well as *Inferiors*· And when you lay all these plain Reasons and Observations together, I make no doubt but you will endeavour to retrieve lost Time, and be advised in this material Point (which I can have no Interest in) by

Your sincere Friend and Servant.

LET-

LETTER CXXXI.

From a young Maiden, abandon'd by her Lover for the sake of a greater Fortune.

Mr. John,

I MUST take up my Pen and write, tho' perhaps you will only scoff at me for so doing, but when I have said what I have to say, then I shall have eased my Mind, and will endeavour to forget you for ever. I have had so many Cautions given me against the false Hearts of Men, and was so often told how they will vow and forswear themselves, that I ought to have been on my Guard, that's true. And indeed, so *I was* a great while: You know it well. But you courted me so long, vowed so earnestly, and seem'd so much in Love with me, that it was first *Pity* in me, that made me listen to you, and, Oh! this *nasty Pity*, how soon did it bring-----But I won't say *Love* neither. I thought, if all the young Men in the World besides proved false, yet it was impossible *you* should. Ah! poor silly Creature that I was, to think, tho' every body flatter'd me with being sightly enough, I could hold a Heart so sordidly bent on *Interest*, as I always saw *yours* to be! But that, thought I, tho' 'tis a Meanness *I don't like*, yet will it be a Security of his making a frugal Husband in an Age so fruitful of *Spendthrifts*.

But at length it has proved, that you can prefer *Polly Bambridge*, and leave *poor me*, only because she has a greater Portion than I have.

I say nothing against *Polly*. I wish *her* well. Indeed I do. And I wish *you* no Harm neither. But as you knew *Polly before*, why could you not have made to yourself a Merit with *her*, without

going

going so far with *me?* What need you have so often begg'd and pray'd, sigh'd and vow'd (never leaving me, Day nor Night), till you had got me foolishly to *believe* and *pity* you? And so, after your Courtship to me was made a *Town-talk*, then you could leave me to be laugh'd at by *every one I slighted for you!* Was this just, was this well done, think you?

Here I cannot go out of Doors but I have some one or other *simpering* and *sneering* at me, and I have had two *Willow-garlands* sent me, so I have---But what poor Stuff, in some of my *own Sex* too, is this, to laugh at and deride *me* for *your* Baseness? I can call my Heart to witness to my Virtue in Thought, in Word, and in Deed; and must I be ridiculed for a *False-one*, who gives himself Airs at *my* Expence, and at the Expence of his own Truth and Honour? Indeed you cannot say the least Ill of me, that's my Comfort. I defy the World to say any thing to blast my Character. Why then should I suffer in the *World's Eye*, for *your* Baseness?

I seek not to move you to return to the Fidelity you have vow'd; for by this Time, mayhap, you'd be as base to *Polly* as you have been to *me*, if you did; and I wish *her* no *Willow garlands*, I'll assure you. But yet, let me desire you to speak of me with Decency. That is no more than I deserve, well you know. Don't (to brave thro' the Perfidy you have been guilty of) mention me with such Fleers, as, I hear, you have done to several; and pray call me none of *your poor dear Girls!* And, *I hope she won't take it to Heart, poor Thing!* --- with that Insolence that so little becomes you, and I have so little deserved. I thought to have appeal'd to your *Conscience*, on what has passed between us, when I began. I thought to have

put

put the Matter *home* to you! But I have run out into this Length, and now don't think it *worth while* to write much more: For what is *Conscience* to a Man who could *vow* as you have done, and *act* as you have done?

Go then, Mr. *John*, naughty Man as you are! I will try to forget you for ever. Rejoice in the Smiles of your *Polly Bambridge*, and glad your Heart with the Possession of an Hundred or Two of Pounds more than I have, and see what you'll be the *richer* or *happier* a *few Years* hence. I wish no Harm to you. Your *Conscience* will be a greater Trouble to you than I wish it to be, if you are capable of *reflecting*. And for *your sake*, I will henceforth set myself up to be an Adviser to all my Sex, never to give Ear to a *Man*, unless they can be sure that his *Interest* will be a *Security* for his *pretended Affection* to them. I am, tho' greatly *injured* and *deceived*, naughty Mr *John*,

Your Well-wisher.

LETTER CXXXII.

From a Gentleman to his Mistress, who seeing no Hopes of Success, respectfully withdraws his Suit.

MADAM,

I Make no doubt but this will be the welcomest Letter that you ever receiv'd from me, for it comes to assure you, that it is the last Trouble you will ever have from me. Nor should I have so long with-held from you this Satisfaction, had not the Hope your Brother gave me, that in time I might meet with a happier Fate, made me willing to try every way to obtain your Favour. But I see, all the Hopes given me by his kind Consideration for me, and those that my own Presumption had made me entertain, are all in vain. And I will therefore rid you of so troublesome an Importuner, having nothing to offer now but my ardent Wishes for your Happiness; and these, Madam, I will pursue you with to my Life's latest Date.

May you, whenever you shall change your Condition, meet with a Heart as passionately, and as sincerely, devoted to you as mine! And may you be happy for many, very many Years, in the Man you can honour with your Love! For, give me leave to say, Madam, that in *this*, my End will be in part answer'd, because it was most sincerely *your* Happiness I had in View, as well as *my own*, when I presumptuously hoped, by *contributing* to the *one*, to *secure* the *other*. I am, Madam, with the highest Veneration,

Your most obedient humb'e Servant.

LETTER CXXXIII.

From a Lady to a Gentleman, who had obtained all her Friends Consent, urging him to decline his Suit to her.

SIR,

YOU have often importun'd me to return Marks of that Consideration for *you*, which you profess for *me*. As my Parents, to whom I owe all Duty, encourage your Address, I wish I could. I am hardly treated by them, because I cannot. What shall I do? Let me apply to you, Sir, for my Relief,

Relief, who have much good Sense, and, I hope, Generosity. Yes, Sir, let me bespeak your *Humanity* to *me*, and *Justice* to *yourself*, in this Point; and that shall be all I will ask in my Favour. I own you deserve a much better Wife than I shall ever make; but yet, as Love is not in one's own Power, if I have the Misfortune to know I cannot love you, will not *Justice* to yourself, if not *Pity* to me, oblige you to abandon your present Purpose?

But as to myself, Sir, Why should you make a poor Creature unhappy in the Displeasure of all her Friends at present, and still more unhappy, if, to avoid that, she gives up her *Person*, where she cannot bestow her *Heart*? If you love me, as you profess, let me ask you, Sir, Is it for *my sake*, or is it for *your own*?----If for *mine*, how can it be, when I must be miserable, if I am forced to marry where I cannot love?--- If for *your own*, reflect, Sir, on the Selfishness of your Love, and judge if it deserves from me the Return you wish.

How sadly does this Love already operate! You love me so *well*, that you make me miserable in the Anger of my dearest Friends!----Your Love has already made them think me undutiful, and instead of the Fondness and Endearment I used to be treated with by them, I meet with nothing but Chidings, Frowns, Slights, and Displeasure.

And what is this Love of yours to do for me hereafter?----Why hereafter, Sir, it will be turned to *Hatred*, or *Indifference* at least. For then, tho' I cannot give you my *Heart*, I shall have given you a *Title* to it, and you will have a lawful Claim to its Allegiance. May it not then, nay, *ought* it not to be treated on the Foot of a Rebel, and expect Punishment as such, instead of Tenderness? Even were I to be treated with *Mercy*, with *Goodness*, with *Kindress* by you, and could not *deserve* or *return* it, what a Wretch would your *Love* make me! How would it involve me in the crying Sin of *Ingratitude!* How would it destroy my *Reputation* in the *World's Eye*, that the *best* of Husbands had the *worst* of Wives!----The *kindest* of Men, the *unkindest* of Women!

Cease then, I beseech you, this hopeless, this cruel Pursuit!----Make some *worthier* Person happy with your Addresses, that can be happy in them!----By this means, you will restore me (if you decline as of your *own* Motion) to the Condition you found me in, the Love of my Parents, and the Esteem of my Friends. If you *really* love me, this may be a hard Task; but it will be a most generous one----And there is some Reason to expect it; for who, that *truly* loves, wishes to make the Object of his Love miserable? This must I be, if you persist in your Address, and I shall know by your Conduct on Occasion of this *uncommon* Request, how to consider it, and in what Light to place you, either as the most *generous*, or the most *ungenerous* of Men. Mean time I am, Sir, most heartily, tho' I cannot be what you would have me,

Your Well-wisher, and humble Servant.

LETTER CXXXIV.

The Gentleman's Answer to the Lady's uncommon Request.

Dear Madam,

I AM exceedingly concern'd, that I cannot be as acceptable to you, as I have the good Fortune to find myself to your honour'd Parents It,

Madam,

Madam, I had Reason to think it was owing to your Prepossession in some happier Man's Favour, I should utterly despair of it, and should really think it would be unjust to *myself*, and ungenerous to *you*, to continue my Address. As therefore you have, by your *Appeal* to me, in so *uncommon* a way, endeavour'd to make me a *Party* against *myself*, and I have shewn so much Regard to you, as to be willing to oblige you, as far as I *can*, may I not hope the Favour of you to declare generously, whether I owe my Unhappiness to such a *Prepossession*, and whether your Heart is given to some *other* ?----If this be the Case, you shall find all you wish on my Part; and I shall take a Pride to plead against myself, let me suffer ever so much by it, to your Father and Mother. But if not, and you have taken any other Disgusts to my Person or Behaviour, that there may be Hope my utmost Affection and Assiduity, or a contrary Conduct, may, in time, get the better of, let me implore you to permit me still to continue my zealous Respects to you; for this I will say, that there is not a Man in the World who can address you with a sincerer and more ardent Flame, than, dear Madam,

Your affectionate Admirer, and humble Servant.

LETTER CXXXV.

The Lady's Reply, in case of a Prepossession.

SIR,

I Thank you for your kind Assurance, that you will befriend me in the manner I wish; and I think I owe it to your Generosity to declare, that there is a Person in the World, that, might I be left to my *own* Choice, I should prefer to all other Men.

Men. To this, Sir, it is owing, that your Address cannot meet with the Return it might otherwise deserve from me. Yet are Things so circumstanc'd, that while my Friends prefer *you*, and know nothing of the *other*, I should find it very difficult to obtain their Consents. But your generous Discontinuance, without giving them the *true* Reason for it, will lay an Obligation greater than I can express, on

Your most humble Servant.

LETTER CXXXVI.

The Lady's Reply in case of no Prepossession, or that she chuses not to avow it.

SIR,

I AM sorry to say, that my Disapprobation of your Address is insuperable----Yet I cannot but think myself beholden to you for the Generosity of your Answer to my earnest Request. I must beg you, Sir, to give over your Application: But how can I say, while I cannot help being of *this* Mind, that it *is* or is *not* owing to *Prepossession*; when you declare, that in the one Instance (and that is very generous too) you *will* oblige me, but in the other you *will not?* If I cannot return *Love* for *Love*, be the Motive what it *will*, pray, Sir, for your own *sake*, as well as *mine*, discontinue your Address - In case of *Prepossession*, you say you *can*, and you *will* oblige me. Let my *Unworthiness*, Sir, have the same Effect upon you, as if that *Prepossession* were to be avow'd. This will inspire me with a Gratitude that will always make me

Your most obliged Servant.

LETTER CXXXVII.

A Lady to a Gentleman of superior Fortune, who, after a long Address in an honourable way, proposes to live with her as a Gallant.

SIR,

AFTER many unaccountable Hesitations, and concealed Meanings, that your Mind seem'd of late big with, but hardly knew how to express, you have, at last, spoken out all your Mind; and I know what I am to trust to! I have that Disdain of your Proposal that an honest Mind ought to have. But I wish, for my own sake (and I will say, for *yours* too, because your Honour is concern'd in it so deeply), that I had had, at my first Acquaintance with you, such an Instance of your *Plain-dealing*, or, rather, *Baseness* Then I should have had no Regret in letting you know how much I scorn'd the *Proposer*, and the *Proposal* Tho' I hope, as it is, a little Time and Reflection will make me, for the sake of the *latter*, abhor the *former*.

However, Sir, I must say, you are very cruel to use me thus, after you had, by all the alluring Professions of an honourable Love, inspired me with a grateful Return, and brought me to the Freedom of owning it-----Nor yet will I be an Hypocrite, or deny my honest Passion, for that would be to lessen your Guilt. God is my Witness, I lov'd you beyond all your Sex, yet I lov'd you *virtuously*; I lov'd you because I thought you *virtuous*. And now, tho' it may take some Time, and too much Regret, to get over, yet do I hope, your Behaviour will enable me to conquer my fond Folly

Ungenerous Man! to take Advantage of your superior Fortune to insult me thus, when you had gained my Affections! What, tho' I am not bless'd with a worldly Circumstance equal to what you might expect in a *Wife*, can you think my Mind so base as to submit to be yours on unworthy Terms? Go, unworthy Man, and make your Court to Miss *Reynolds*, as you seem to threaten. She has a Fortune equal to your own, and may you be happy together! I should have been so, had I never known you. I never deceived you. You knew my scanty Fortune, and yet pretended to prefer me to all my Sex.

On me you might have laid the highest Obligation, by raising me to a Condition I was humble enough to think above me, and I should have been, on that Account, all Gratitude, all Duty, all Acknowlegement. On Miss *Reynolds* you will confer none, her Fortune will quit Scores with yours, and you must both, in your Union, be Strangers to the inexpressible Pleasure of *receiving* or *conferring* of Benefits: But this is a Pleasure which none but generous Minds can taste. That yours is not so, witness your detested Proposal, after such solemn Professions of faithful and honourable Love. And I have one Consolation, tho' a Consolation I did not wish for, that I am under no Obligation, but the contrary, to such a Man. And am as much your Superior, as the Person who would do no Wrong, is to one that will do nothing else. Send me, however, my Letters, that I may be assured my fond Credulity will not be the Subject of fresh Insult, and that perhaps to the *Person* that shall be what you made *me* expect *I* should be. I will send you all yours, the last only excepted. Which, as it may assist me to conquer my fond Folly for you, I hope you'll allow

allow me to keep, tho' it is the Abhorr'd of my Soul----May *you* be happier than you have made *me!*----is the laſt Prayer you will have from
> *Your too credulous Well-wiſher.*

LETTER CXXXVIII.

A Father to a Daughter in Service, on hearing of her Maſter's attempting her Virtue.

My dear Daughter,

I Underſtand, with great Grief of Heart, that your Maſter has made ſome Attempts on your Virtue, and yet that you ſtay with him. God grant that you have not already yielded to his baſe Deſires! For when once a Perſon has ſo far forgotten what belongs to himſelf, or his Character, as to make ſuch an Attempt, the very Continuance with him, and in his Power, and under the ſame Roof, is an Encouragement to him to proſecute his Deſigns. And if he carries it better, and more civil, at preſent, it is only the more certainly to undo you when he attacks you next. Conſider, my dear Child, your Reputation is all you have to truſt to. And if you have not already, which God forbid! yielded to him, leave it not to the Hazard of another Temptation; but come away directly (as you ought to have done on your own Motion) at the Command of

> *Your grieved and indulgent Father.*

LETTER CXXXIX.

The Daughter's Answer.

Honoured Father,

I Received your Letter Yesterday, and am sorry I stay'd a Moment in my Master's House after his vile Attempt. But he was so full of his Promises of never offering the like again, that I hop'd I might believe him; nor have I yet seen any thing to the contrary. But am so much convinced, that I ought to have done as you say, that I have this Day left the House; and hope to be with you soon after you will have receiv'd this Letter. I am

Your dutiful Daughter.

LETTER CXL.

To a Gentleman of Fortune, who has Children, dissuading him from a Second Marriage with a Lady much younger than himself.

Worthy Sir,

YOU are pleased to inform me of your Thoughts in relation to a Change of your Condition, and to command me to give you freely my Opinion of the Conveniencies and Inconveniencies, that may follow from the Inequality of Years between you, and the young Lady you think of making your second Wife. Indeed I am so much concerned for your Happiness, that had I heard of such your Intention, and had not your Commands to be free on this Head, I think I should have run the

Risque

Risque of being thought impertinent and officious, rather than not have expostulated with you on this Occasion. My Objections, Sir, are not so much to the Gaiety of the Lady, as to her Youth, and the Children you have already by your late excellent Lady: And when you remember, that Miss *Fanny*, your eldest Daughter, is near as old as the Lady you think to make her Mother; I beg, Sir, you will consider, how your Reputation, as to Prudence, will suffer in the Eye of the World *without you*, as well as the Look it will have to your *Children* and *Domesticks*.

Nature, Justice, Decency, and every Branch of human Prudence, plead strongly against the Union of lively Youth with maturer Years. *Her* Temper may be very agreeable: So, indeed, is *yours*-----But may they be so to *each other*, when they meet together in so close an Union? You are *yet* blest with a good State of *Health*; but can you expect, that it will be *always* so?---Or rather, will not *every Year* take from *your* Constitution, what it will add to *hers*, for several Years to come? Your Years make *you* serious and solemn, and you are past a *Relish* for those Pleasures and Amusements, which are but suitable to *hers*, and which at the *same Age* you yourself delighted in. Can you recal *Time past*? Will it become you to *resume* the Part which *Judgment* has made you quit? How aukwardly, if you attempt it, will you do this! What Censure will *this* subject you to! How will it embolden the gay young Fellows to make Attempts, that may, notwithstanding the most unexceptionable Conduct in the *Lady*, give *you* great Uneasiness!

If you cannot join in the *innocent Gaieties* which you have long *disused*, it would be, in some measure, cruel, to *deprive* a young Lady of her Share of them,

at

at an Age that will naturally make her *expect* and *require* them: And yet will not even *innocent* Liberties be Matter of Reproach to *her*, and Uneasiness to *you*, if she takes them without you? And would you chuse to bear her Company, and indulge a *young-old* Taste for gay Scenes long contemn'd, and so appear in a Light, to all that beheld you together, either as her *Father*, or her *jealous Keeper*, and make it look to the World as if you *yourself* doubted her Virtue out of your own *Presence?* Suppose the Scene at a gallant Comedy, that sprightly free Joke which will make *her* smile, will make *you* frown; and so on in every other Scene of Life and Amusement between you. For a *Defect* or *Inequality*, of whatever kind, whenever a Man is *conscious* of it, let him *carry it off as he may*, will always be *present* with him, and, like another Conscience, stare him in the Face.

Your Fortune, 'tis true, is so considerable, that you may amply provide for *all* your Children, and yet make it worth a young Lady's while, who would study her *Interest*, preferably to any *other* Consideration, to oblige you: But, Sir, let me ask you, Can you, who lived so happily with your *late dear Lady*, and had such constant Proofs of her *inviolable* Affection to your Person, content yourself with a *counterfeit* Passion, a mere *selfish* Affection, in a *Wife?* And can you think, that so *young* a Lady can love you, like *her* who grew on in Life, in Hope, in Desires, *with you*, and who, from a reciprocal Youth passed agreeably together, grew *equally* mature, and had *both* but *one* View between you; to wit, a young Family growing up, the *common* Offspring of your *mutual* Affections; and who were the *binding*, and, so long as her Life lasted, the *indissoluble* Cement of your *Loves* and your *Interests?*----If she *can*, she will be

a Con-a Contradiction to all *Experience*, and you will be happy against all reasonable *Expectation*----If she *cannot*, will you be content with a *selfish*, an interested *Civility*, instead of *true Love*; and which cannot possibly so much as look *like* Love, but by the Dissimulation and Hypocrisy of your *Bosom Companion*?

When I look back on what I have written, I begin to be afraid of your Displeasure on a double Account, for the *Nature*, and for the *Length* of this Epistle, tho' you have commanded me to speak my Mind. Yet having several other material Points to touch upon, and relying upon your Excuse for my good Intentions (for what View can I have in the Liberty I take, but your Happiness?), I will beg Leave to pursue the Subject in another Letter, and to conclude this, tho' a little abruptly, with the Assurance, that (as you request) nobody shall see what I write but yourself, and that I am, Sir,

Your affectionate humble Servant.

LETTER CXLI.

The same Subject pursued.

SIR,

I WILL now take the Liberty to continue my Subject, and my humble Expostulations upon it. And I will suppose two Cases very, if not equally, probable; to wit, that you *may*, or may *not*, have Children by your new Lady; and to judge in both Cases, how the Happiness of your remaining Life may be affected by either. In the first place, if you should have Children by her (to say nothing of the Misunderstandings and Jealousies loufies this may create between your Lady, and your prefent Children, which may greatly affect your own Happiness), are you fo well able to fupport, at *thefe* Years, with Credit and Satisfaction, that Character which fo peculiarly befits a *young* Hufband to a *young* Wife? And will it not naturally ftrike you, that your own Children by *that* time will make a *better* Figure in fuch a Circumftance than yourfelf? Will you be fo well able to go thro' the *fame* Troubles, the *fame* Anxieties, the *fame* Hopes, Fears and Affections, both to the pregnant Mother, and afterwards to the Infant Progeny, that you have fo *happily* got over? And will not what was then called *laudable Love*, be now deem'd *Dotage* and *Uxoriousness*?

Providence feems to have defign'd the *youthful* Portion of a Man's Life, for mutual Endearments, and Propagation of his Family; the *maturer* Part, for Education, Counfel or Advice. And will you, Sir, *invert* the Defign of it? Will you *call back* the Days of *Senfe*, into the Years of *Intellect*, watch over the Baby in the *Cradle*, when you fhould form the Mind of the *grown Perfon*?----How unequal will you be to this Part, to what you *once* were!----As you will not have the *fame* Difpofitions about you, you cannot have the *fame* Joy at a pleafing Incident, but will have poffibly a *fuperadded* Weight of Sorrow on any fad Event, as *Years* will have *added* to your *Reflection*, as *Experience* will have *contracted* your *Hope*, and as you will have *feen* the Vanity of all worldly Expectations.

Then, my dear Sir, confider, if you fhould even get over this *refumed* Province happily, and have no material Uneafinefs from the Lady, on the Account I have intimated to you; is it not too probable, that you may not live to fee this young Race brought up? And if you fhould, what Animofities, mosities, what Uneasinesses may not ensue, from the different Interests into which your Family will be divided ! And it may, moreover, be possible for you to have Grandchildren older than some of your own by your new Lady.

But if we suppose, that the *Occasion* for this may happen, will the Matter be mended by it?----All young Ladies expect and wish for Children, when they marry. If she should not have any, she will hardly be induced to think it *her* Fault, but the *Difference* of Years will *tell* her, and all the World will *join* in it, where to lay the Blame, *deserved* or *not*. She will, for want of so *necessary* an Employment, look *abroad* for Amusements and Diversions, which, however innocent in her first Intentions, may not *always* end so, and if they *do*, will be very unsuitable to your Disposition and Liking. Childbed *matronizes* the giddiest Spirits, and brings them to Reflection sooner than any other Event. Its Consequences fill up the Time, and introduce different Scenes of Pleasure and Amusement in the Mind of a Lady. It draws her Attention to more *serious* Affairs, it *domesticates* her, as I may say, and makes her associate with graver Persons, and such as are in the same Scenes of Life. But where this is *not*, she *continues* her youthful and giddy Acquaintance, *classes* herself, as to her *Company* and *Diversions*, as if in the *single* State still, and looks for Amusements *out of herself*, and *out of her House*. And you will be obliged to connive at a good deal more than you otherwise would, because the Difference of Years will give as much *Consciousness* to *you*, as it will *Presumption* to *her*; and if there be any Grievance between you, she'll think, after all you can do, it is of *her* Side. Nor will *Time* and *Years* mend the Matter, but, contrarily, make it *worse* and *worse*.

Then

Then another Inconvenience may arise: The Lady, if she has no Children by you, to prevent lying at the *Mercy of yours*, as she will call it, will be making a *separate* Interest to herself: She will grow upon your Indulgence and Fondness; she will *cajole*, she will *reproach*, she will *teize* you into Acts of Bounty and Profusion to her. She will endeavour to build up a Fortune out of yours, to the Prejudice of *your Family*. And all this for what End?----Only to make her a *rich Widow*, and to give her Opportunity to triumph, in Conjunction, perhaps, with some *young Rake* or *Profligate*, over *your Ashes*, and to make Comparisons *grievous to Reflection*, at the Expence of your Fortune and Memory, in the *new* Man's Favour.

Forgive me, dear Sir, these free Hints. My full Mind, which is thus ready to overflow thro' the Zeal I have for your *Honour* and *Welfare* suggests many *more* to me, which your cool Reflection will not want. And I have been already so prolix, that I will only farther say, that I am, and shall ever be,

Your faithful and most affectionate
Friend and Servant.

LETTER CXLII.

Against a Second Marriage, where there are Children on both *Sides.*

Dear Sir,

YOU ask my Opinion as to the Thoughts you have entertained of making your Addresses to the *Widow Lockyer*. Do you really ask it with an Intent to take it? Or, like the Generality of the World, only in hopes, that my Judgment, falling in with

with your own, may be a kind of Justification or Excuse for what you intend to do, and are, perhaps, already resolved upon? If so, what do you do, but lay a Snare for me, which may put an End to our Friendship? For Men least of all bear Controul or Contradiction in Points of this Nature, when their Hearts are actually determined; and then Indifference begins, and Disgust ends the best-cemented Friendships.

To say the Truth, I never was a Friend to Second Marriages, where there are Children on one Side, and a Likelihood of more; but, especially, where there are Children on *both*. I have nothing to say, as to the Person or Character of the Lady. You, whom it most concerns, are well satisfy'd of both, or you would not have gone so far, as to ask a Friend's Advice on this Occasion. But since you do put it to me, I will throw a few Reasons together, which have always had Weight with me on these Occasions, and I hope, you'll not think the worse of your Friend, if he happen to differ a little from your own Judgment.

It must be confess'd, in the Case you put, That the Circumstances, on both Sides, are pretty equal: That there is no great Disparity in Years. That she has Three Children, and you have Four; a round Family, however, when they come together! That she is very fond of her Children, and you, at *present*, of yours: That you are not an ill-temper'd Man, and she is a good-temper'd Woman, and was a loving Wife to her late Spouse, as you were an affectionate Husband to yours. Well, so far is very well, and, you'll think perhaps, very promising of a happy Union; and possibly you may think right, at least you have much better Grounds for it than many that do marry upon much worse, and more unequal Prospects.

But

But consider, Sir, what Security have you, that Persons who have been always good-temper'd, when they have nothing to thwart or try their Temper, will be still so, when they have something that will?---Here, at the very Threshold of this Adventure, is a Cause of great Trial; a Trial which neither of you had before, and consequently, which neither of you knew how you shall behave in: She loves *her* Children. So she ought. You love *yours*. It is right so to do. But see you not, before I speak, that this laudable *separate* Love of *either*, may become matter of great Uneasiness to *both?* You cannot, either of you, possibly expect more than common Civility, and outside Kindness, from the other, *she* to *yours*, *you* to *hers*. And it will be happy enough, if this Task do but sufficiently try the Discretion of *both*.

It is impossible, my Friend, but you must have very different Views on each other.---A pretty Prospect to set out with in a matrimonial Adventure! Her Praises of her own Children will be very sincere and lavish. Her Praises of yours, if she *ever* praises, will be very suspicious and sparing. And perhaps you must be as discreet as possible, in the Praises of your own. The very Cloaths each wear, the Victuals they eat, nay, the very Looks of either Parent, as they shall appear kind to their own, or reserved to the other's, will afford room for inward Heart-burnings, if not outward Janglings. I have seen many Instances of these Kinds.

Their different Capacities; one shall take their Learning, another not---Their different Tempers, one shall be mild, another insulting; one smooth, another rough-----Their different Ages, which will make one dictate, while the other will not be prescribed to----will all afford Cause of Difference And when they come to an Age fit for
setting

setting them out in the World; if Boys, to Apprentice; you put *Jackey* to a better Trade than *Tommy*, and give more Money with him! And yet one Trade or Master may apparently deserve or require it, the other, not. If Girls, in Matrimony; Why should *Betsey* be married before *Thomasine?* --Let the Eldest go first! Tho' perhaps the one has an humble Servant, the other none----Ay, I see poor *Thomasine* must be contented with any body, or any thing, while *Betsey* must be a Lady! ---These are all still fresh Causes of Difference and Uneasiness to you both.

Then will she actually, or you will suspect it (and that is as bad to your Peace), be constantly *progging*, as the Women call it, for her Children, in order to make a private Purse for them, on any Occasion that may happen, or in case he shall outlive you.

And if there be a *third* Race of Children from this Marriage, worse and worse still. Then the two former Sets, if they never join'd together before, now will make a common Cause, in this single Point, against the new Race; and must not this double your own and your Wife's Comforts, think you?-----Then must you be glad to lessen your Family at home, that you may lessen the Number of so many Spies and Enemies to your Repose. The Boys must be hurry'd out to the first Thing that offers for them, whether suitable or unsuitable to their Genius or Capacity, and they generally thrive accordingly. The Girls to the first Men that will take them, whether he can provide for them or not, as he ought, and after a while they may come back to you, tho' fitted out with a great Expence, quite destitute and undone, with a further Increase to your Family, the too frequent Consequences of precipitate Marriages. And then

will

will a new Scene commence; for all the unprovided-for will join against the poor unhappy one.

This, you'll say, is looking a great way forward. It is so. And what may never happen. Possibly, it never may, as to the last Case, but as it too often has happen'd, and daily does happen, a wise Man will think a little about it, while it is in his Power to prevent it all.

I have touch'd but upon a few of the Consequences that may too probably follow from a new Engagement. Yet, I believe, these, if you are *not* absolutely determined, will make you think a little, if you *are*, why then, all the Reasons that can be urged will signify nothing. And in this Case, you should not have laid a Snare for me to disoblige a Person who is to step in between your Friendship and mine, and who will look upon me (if she knows my Mind, as very probably she will, for I hardly ever knew a Secret of this kind kept) as her Enemy; and so create a Coolness and Indifference between us, which you cannot help, if you would. For if ever it be so, and your *Lady* receives me, in a way that I have not been used to in your *House*, I shall be very shy of visiting either you or her.

If you require it, and it will have any Effect upon you, I can enter still farther into this Subject, but I fansy I have said enough, and perhaps more than you'll thank me for. But be that as it will, I have answer'd your Request; and shewn you (peradventure, at the Expence of my Discretion), that I am, in all Things,

Your sincere Friend, and Well-wisher

LETTER CXLIII.

Against a second Marriage, where there are Children on one Side, and a Likelihood of more.

Dear Sir,

YOU are inclined, you tell me, to give your *Children* a *Mother*, instead of the good one they have lost; or rather, in plain *English*, you should have said, *yourself* a *Wife*, to supply your *own Loss*: And you ask my Opinion on the Subject, without naming the Person, only intimating, that she is a maiden Lady, no more than Seven Years younger than yourself, and has a pretty middling Fortune.

I am glad you have not named the Lady; for now I shall stand clear of any Imputation of personal Prejudice, let me say what I will. I will therefore freely tell you my Mind, that I am always against second Marriages, where there are Children on one or both Sides, and likely to be more. Unless there are such worldly Reasons as make it absolutely prudent for a Person to marry to establish his Circumstances. This is not your Case. For you are very easy in the World, and besides, the Ladies of this Age are so brought up, that a Man must not look for very extraordinary Assistances in a Wife, with relation to her *own* Children, much less the Children of *another* Woman. Well, but *this* Lady is highly prudent, good-humour'd, an excellent Oeconomist, and what not? And so they are *all*, my Friend, or, at least, we are apt to persuade ourselves so, before they are marry'd.

But we'll suppose her all you say, and all you think; yet she will hardly, I presume, be divested of the Passions common to human Nature. Can you expect, that tho' you give your Children a Mother, you give them an *own* Mother? She may have Prudence enough to do what *she* will think her Duty by them; but must she not be her own Judge, of what that is?----And are you sure, that what she calls so, nay, and, for Peace-sake, what you will be willing to call so too, will be called so by your Children, as they grow up, and even by the rest of the World? But Children, you'll say, may be unreasonable, and undutiful----Very well, Sir----we'll suppose it so; but will this make you happy, let them have Reason, or not, for their Surmises? And as she cannot plead *Nature* for the Regulator of her Conduct towards them, but common Civility, and Prudence only, at the very best; will there not be two to one on the Childrens Side, that they may be right? But whoever may be right or wrong, if you are made unhappy by it, that's the essential Point to you, who by this second Marriage have been the Cause of it all.

This is most certain, *her* Views must be quite contrary to those of your *Children* 'Tis true, theirs will of Consequence be likewise contrary to hers; and yet both may be very reasonable too, according to the Character of each. And is not this a pretty Situation for you, do you think? For which Side *can* you, *must* you take? The Children, as they grow up, will be jealous of ill Offices from her with you. She will interpret those Things which a natural Mother would think nothing of, as studied Slights. And will not their constant Bickerings make you uneasy in your own Family, where Uneasiness is the least tolerable, as it is the Place to which a Man should retire for Comfort, when the World gives him Cause of Displeasure?

most Important Occasions.

And what, pray, may this probably end in? Why, for Quietness-sake, you will possibly be obliged to separate them. The Mother-in-law, should *she* be in *Fault*, you *cannot* part with. The Children then must turn out, of course. You must study, after reconciling and patching up a hundred Breaches, to make some other Provision for *them*. And thus, perhaps, they are precipitated into a wide World, and exposed to a thousand dangerous Temptations: And how can you forgive yourself, if they should by the means become a Prey to the designing Attempts, the *Boys*, of *vicious Women*; the *Girls*, of *profligate Men*? And how would it have grieved the Heart of their indulgent Mother, could she have foreseen, that her beloved Spouse, instead of supplying the Loss of a *Mother* to them, should take from them his own *immediate* Protection, and that, perhaps, at a Time of Life when it was most necessary for their future Good?

This may, very probably, be more or less the Case, if there be no other Difficulties than what may arise between your Children and their Mother-in-law. But if, as is most likely, you should have Children by this your second Wife, the Case may be still worse. She will then look upon yours by your first, not only with a *more indifferent*, but probably with a *jealous* Eye. She will be continually carking and laying up for her *own*, and grudge every thing you lay out upon the *others* And when they are both grown up to any Bigness, what Clashings and Jarrings may not ensue between the Offspring of the *same* Father, and two *different* Mothers? How will you be obliged to give a Preference to the Children of the *latter* Wife, against those of the *former*; because the Mother of the one is *present* and *partial*, and perhaps *clamorous*,

K 2

in *their* Favour----that of the other, *absent, silent, dead, forgotten!*

If Love hides a Multitude of Faults, as no doubt it does, and *Indifference*, or, perhaps, as it may be, *Hatred*, is quick-sighted to every little Slip, how will *hers* be all Angels! *Yours*----the worst she can call them!----Yet how can you *help* this? You are married to the *Temper*, as well as to the *Woman*, and Opposition, 'tis likely, will but make matters worse, for what the Sex cannot carry by Reason or Argument, they will by Obstinacy and Teizing.

Then in the Matter of making Provision respectively for their future Good, how will your Solicitudes for the *one* be constantly lessened, for the *other* perpetually importun'd! Nor must your own Judgment, in *either* Case, be so much the Rule of your Conduct, as the fond Partiality of your second Wife for hers. And it is far from being impossible, that she may use your first Children *worse* than she would do *mere Strangers*, for no other Reason, but because they have a better Title to your *Regard*, and stand *more* in the way of her Interest and Views.

These, my good Friend, are some of the Reasons I have to allege against second Marriages, where there are Children on one Side, and a Probability of having a second Race. As I hinted, there may be Reasons, where a Person's Circumstances stand in need of the Assistance that may be procur'd by this means, to overbalance many of the Inconveniencies I have hinted at. The lesser Evil, in this Case, is to be chosen, and the Party must make the best of the rest. But this is not your Case. And so I refer the Whole to your mature Consideration, and am, Sir,

LETTER CXLIV.
Advising a Friend against going to Law.

Dear Sir,

I AM sorry to hear, that the Difference between you and Mr. *Archer* is at last likely to be brought to a Law-suit. I wish you'd take it into your serious Consideration before you *begin*, because it will hardly be in your Power to *end* it, when you please. For you immediately put the Matter out of your own Hands, into the Hands of those whose *Interest* it is to protract the Suit from Term to Term, and who will as absolutely prescribe to you in it, as your Physician in a dangerous Illness.

The Law, my good Friend, I look upon, more than any one thing, as the *proper* Punishment of an over hasty and perverse Spirit, as it is a Punishment that follows an Act of a Man's own seeking and chusing. You will not consent, perhaps, *now* to submit the Matter in Dispute to Reference, but let me tell you, that, after you have expended large Sums of Money, and squandered away a deal of Time in Attendance on your Lawyers, and Preparations for Hearings, one Term after another, you will probably be of another Mind, and be glad *Seven Years* hence to leave it to that Arbitration which now you refuse. He is happy who is wise by other Mens Misfortunes, says the common Adage. And why, when you have heard from all your Acquaintance, who have try'd the Experiment, what a grievous Thing the Law is, will you, notwithstanding, pay for that Wisdom, which you may have at the Cost of others?

The Representation that was once hung up as a Sign in the *Rolls* Liberty, on one Side, of a Man all in Rags wringing his Hands, with a Label, importing, *That he had lost his Suit*, and on the other, a Man that had not a Rag left, but stark naked, capering and triumphing, *That he had carry'd his Cause**, was a fine Emblem of going to Law, and the infatuating Madness of a litigious Spirit.

How excellent to this Purpose is the Advice of our Blessed SAVIOUR, rather than seek *this Redress* against any who would even *take one's Coat, to give him his Cloak also!* For, besides the Christian Doctrine inculcated by this Precept, it will be found, as the Law is managed, and the Uncertainty that attends, even in the *best-grounded* Litigations, that such a pacifick Spirit may be deemed the *only* way to preserve the rest of one's Garments, and to prevent being stript to the Skin.

Moreover, what wise Man would rush upon a Proceeding, where the principal Men of the Profession (tho' the Oath they take, if Serj---nts, obliges them not to sign a sham Plea, nor plead in a Cause against their own Opinion) are not ashamed, under the specious, but scandalous Notion, of doing the *best they can for their Client*, to undertake, for the sake of a paltry Fee, to *whiten* over the *blackest* Cause, and to defeat the *justest*? Where your Property may depend altogether upon the Impudence of an eloquent Pleader asserting *any thing*, a perjured Evidence swearing whatever will do for his Suborner's Purpose? Where the Tricks and Mistakes of Practisers, and want of trifling Forms, may Nonsuit you? Where Deaths of Persons made Parties to the Suit may cause all to begin again? What wise Man, I say, would sub-

---

* 'Tis said, That Sir *John Tr------*, Master of the Rolls, caused this Sign to be taken down, on the Clamour it occasion'd among the Lawyers.

ject

most Important Occasions. 199

ject himself to these Vexations and common Incidents in the Law, if he could any way avoid it; together with the intolerable Expences and Attendances consequent on a Law-suit? Besides, the Fears, the Cares, the Anxieties, that revolve with every Term, and engross all a Man's Thoughts? Where *legal* Proofs must be given to the *plainest* Facts, that a living Man is living, and identically himself, and that a dead Man is dead, and buried by Certificate, where Evidence must be brought at a great Expence to Hands and Seals affixed to Deeds and Receipts, that never were before question'd; till a Cause shall be split into several Under-ones, these try'd Term by Term, and Years elapse before the main Point comes to be argued, tho' originally there was but one single Point, as you apprehended, in the Question. As to the Law-part only, observe the Process. First, comes the Declaration; 2dly, a Plea, 3dly, Demurrer to the Plea, 4th'y, a Joinder in Demurrer. 5thly, a Rejoinder, 6thly, a Sur-rejoinder, which sometimes is conclusive, sometimes to begin all over again. Then may succeed Tryals upon the *Law* Part, and Tryals upon the *Equity* Part, oftentimes new Tryals, or Rehearings, and these followed by Writs of Error.

Then you may be plung'd into the bottomless Gulf of Chancery, where you begin with Bills and Answers, containing Hundreds of Sheets at exorbitant Prices, 15 Lines in a Sheet, and 6 Words in a Line (and a Stamp to every Sheet), barefacedly so contriv'd to pick your Pocket. Then follow all the Train of Examinations, Interrogatories, Exceptions, Bills amended, References for Scandal and Impertinence, new Allegations, new Interrogatories, new Exceptions, on Pretence of insufficient Answers, Replies, Rejoinders, and Sur-rejoinders, till, at last,

K 4 when

when you have danced thro' this blessed Round of *Preparation*, the *Hearing* before the Master of the Rolls comes next, Appeals follow from his Honour to the Chancellor, then from the Chancellor to the House of Lords, and sometimes the Parties are sent down from thence for a new Tryal in the Courts below----Good Heavens! What wise Man, permit me to repeat, would enter himself into this confounding *Circle of the Law?*----

I hope, dear Sir, you will think of this Matter most deliberately, before you proceed in your present angry Purpose; and if you shall judge it proper to take my Advice, and avoid a Law-suit, I am sure you will have Reason to thank me for it, and for the Zeal wherewith I am

Your sincere Friend and Servant.

LETTER CXLV.

To a young Lady, cautioning her against keeping Company with a Gentleman of a bad Character.

Dear Cousin,

THE great Respect I have, and always had for you, obliges me to take this Freedom, to let you know, that the Neighbourhood begins to talk pretty freely of you and Mr. *Lory*. You have been seen with him at the Play, and, after that, at the R---- Tavern, a House of no good Repute, I assure you; where you have staid with him till near Twelve o'Clock at Night. You have likewise been with him at *Vipont's* in *Hampstead*, at *Vaux-hall*, *Cuper's-gardens*, *Mary-le-bon*, &c.

I am sorry for these Things, because he has none of the best of Characters; having, as I am well inform'd, already ruin'd Two, if not Three, worthy Tradesmens Daughters: And it is but too probable, that he has no honourable Design upon you For, whatever he may promise you, I am credibly assur'd, that he is actually engaged with Miss *Knapper*, whom you know very well Indeed, it is said, he has 200 *l. per Ann.* but if it be so, he is very much involved in the World; and, at the Rate he lives, had he three times that Estate, would never be out of Debt, for he is downright extravagant, a Man of no Conduct, a perfect Rattle, whose Words are not to be rely'd on in any respect, and makes a common Boast of the Favours he has receiv'd from our Sex, whose faulty Fondness is the constant Subject of his Ridicule.

For all these Reasons, I beg of you, dear Cousin, to avoid his Company; for tho' I am confident you will preserve your *Virtue*, yet, my Dear, think what you will, you may receive an incurable Wound in your *Reputation*. I hope you'll excuse this Liberty, which no other Motive but Zeal for your Credit and Welfare has occasioned. And believe me to be *Your faithful Friend,*
as well as affectionate Kinswoman.

LETTER CXLVI.

From a Mother to her high-spirited Daughter, who lives on uneasy Terms with her Husband.

Dear Nanny,

I AM sorry, with all my Heart, to hear of the frequent Misunderstandings between your Husband and you. I hoped much better things from your

your Prudence. From *my* Prudence, you'll say perhaps! as if I thought all the Fault was yours. But, my Dear, I don't think so, I can't think so, and yet I may find Fault with your want of Prudence too. For Prudence will oblige a good Wife to bear a little Contradiction from her Husband, tho' not always just, perhaps, as well as to avoid giving Offence. Suppose he is peevish, petulant, uneasy in his Temper, and on slight or no Occasions, as you may think, must *you* be peevish and petulant, because *he* is so? How do you know what Things may have happened to him abroad, in the way of his Business, to make him so?----Or, if it be *only* Humour, why must you be as bad as he that you find Fault with? Is an ill Temper in a Husband, so taking a thing, that the Wife, who finds it intolerable to her, must nevertheless imitate or assume it?

The Reason why you will not allow him to be oftener in the Right, and why you condemn as causeless his Petulance and Waspishness, must proceed, in a great measure, from a slender Opinion, if not Contempt, of his Judgment. If you think him a Man of Sense, 'tis impossible but you should allow, that there may be some Cause, tho' you don't immediately penetrate it, why he should be disturbed, and it would be kind in you to suppose the best, as, that his Tenderness for you will not let him communicate it to you, rather than to imagine he is always in the wrong, and always angry without Reason. But were it actually to be so, are you commissioned to punish him with Provocations and Resentments *as* wrong, and even *more* unbecoming in a Wife? If you love him as you ought, you will extenuate his Failings, and draw into an advantageous Light those Actions which may be interpreted in his Favour.

But

But if, as I heard you once say, *you will give him as good as he brings*, that *you will not bear his unaccountable Humours*, and such-like vulgar and provoking Expressions, it must come to this Point: Either *you* or *he* must give way, one of your Tempers must be subdued, and over-aw'd by the other. If it be *his* Case, tir'd out by your resolute and sturdy Behaviour, to succumb, do you think this will either be a Credit to *him* or to *you*? What an abject (*henpeck'd*, the Vulgar call it) Wretch will he be deem'd! What a *Termagant* you! He'll be the Jest of his Companions, and you be thought to excel----in what? In a Quality the most infamous to a Woman, next to that of an Adultress.

But this I aver, that Meekness, Condescension, Forbearance, are so far from being despisable Qualities in our Sex, that they are the *Glory* of it. And what is *Meekness*, my Dear, if you are not to be try'd by Provocations? What is *Condescension*, if you must always have your own way? What is *Forbearance*, if you are to return Injury for Injury, with the hostile Spirit of a fierce Enemy, rather than to act with the sweet Complacency of a tender Wife, who has vow'd Obedience and Duty?

But, Obedience and Duty, you'll say, in Return for *ill Nature* and *ill Usage*! Yes, my Dear, even were it to be so, you *ought*. For, do you think you are never to condescend, or give up your own Humour to your Husband? A pretty Sort of *Obedience* that, which shall be only shewn where you are *not* thwarted, but never where you *are*! Would not this be Obedience to your own headstrong Passions, and not to him?----So long as you can have your way in every thing, you will be a Mirror of Condescension, but when once you come to be contradicted, why then you are at Liberty to contradict again. If he is out of the way in his Hu-

mour,

mour, you will never be in the way in yours. If he gives you *one* unkind Word, he shall have *two* in Return; for *you will give him as good as he brings*. If he is passionate, you will be so too. You will return provoking Answers for reflecting Words, and so make your House a constant Scene of Confusion, and your Life uncomfortable. And for what? Why to shew how *bravely* you can return Injury for Injury; how *nobly* you can contend for Victory over your Husband; and how you can make him despised in his Family, as well by Children as Servants, and yourself discredited by the poor Victory, suppose you were to win it by breaking his Spirit.

Is this, my Dear, the Part of a tender *Wife* to a *Husband?* Nay, is it the Part of a *Christian* to a *Christian*, where there is *not* the matrimonial Obligation? For are we not commanded to return *Good for Evil*, and to *pray for them that despightfully use us?*----And is not the Wife's *Conversation to be coupled with Fear?* And do we not vow *Reverence* to a Husband as our *Head?*----How can all this be, if you are to return Evil for Evil, to make yourself your own Judge, and Jury, and Executioner too, by acquitting yourself, condemning him, sentencing him, and punishing him with all the Severity of licentious Speech, provoking Snappishness, or the still more affecting Deportment of sullen contemptuous Silence? Let me, on the Whole, beseech you, for *my* sake, who would be loth to be thought to have set you any bad Example, for your *Family's* sake, for your *Reputation's* sake, as well as *his*, to resolve on a different Conduct. Make the good Rule yours, of never being out of Humour when he is so. First soften him by good Temper; then, when soften'd, expostulate mildly on the Unreasonableness of his Anger. If you convince him

thus,

thus, he will take care of the like Error; or his *present* Confeſſion will ſtrengthen your mild Arguments againſt him in any thing elſe for the *future*. He will ſee you adviſe him for his Good. He will have a greater Opinion of *your* Prudence, and be more doubtful of *his own*. He will ſee you contend not for Victory, or Contradiction-ſake; but for his own ſake. And depend upon it, you will both reap the happy Fruits of it in the Comfort of your Lives; in the Love of your own Children; in the Reverence of your Servants (who will otherwiſe be liſted in each Contender's Quarrel, and be inſolent Judges of the Conduct of both); in the Reſpect of your Neighbours and Friends; and in the Pleaſure you will give to your Relations, who will viſit and be viſited by you both, with that Delight which nobody knows how to eſtimate ſo much, as, my dear *Nanny*,

Your ever-affectionate Mother.

LETTER CXLVII.

A Lady to her Friend, a young Widow Lady, who, having bury'd a polite and excellent Husband, inclines to marry a leſs deſerving Gentleman, and of unequal Fortune.

Dear Madam,

WERE I to lay it down for a Maxim, that *Maids* often mend their Circumſtances by Marriage, *Widows* very rarely, I believe I might be juſtify'd by every one's Experience. To what can the Truth of this Obſervation be owing? Is it to be ſuppoſed, that Widows have ſtronger Paſſions than Maids? Shall the proud lordly Sex have it to boaſt, that they are ſuch eſtimable Creatures, that when once one of them has had the Fortune to be chosen by a Lady, and has been taken from her by Death, she cannot live without taking another, and finds herself obliged to accept of the next that offers, thro' all Disadvantages, and every Degree of Inequality? Surely this cannot be the Case! Surely a prudent, a modest Lady, will not say this, *in so many Words!*----Much less, then, ought she to confess it by her *Actions*, which are much stronger than *Words*. For I believe no Woman who ever enter'd the Pale of Matrimony with sprightly Hopes about her, found the Possession (*Sex only* consider'd) equal to her Expectations. The Maid may hope, may fansy much, in the Commerce between the Sexes, from her meditating on the heighten'd Scenes which pernicious Novels, and idle Romances, the Poison of Female Minds, abound with. But the Widow *knows* 'tis all *Free-masonry*, all empty Hope, flashy, foolish, unworthy, unpermanent, and, but for the Law of Nature, despicable.----Whence is it then, that the *wishing*, expecting Maid, should be more prudent than the *knowing*, experienced Widow? Should be better Proof, with raised Imaginations, against Courtship or Persuasion, than one who well knows the transitory Vanity and Unsatisfactoriness of the End to which that Courtship or Persuasion tends?

If it be said, That *this* Point is not so much the Case, as the *settled* Life of Matrimony, which has been once so satisfactorily experienced, let the Circumstances of a Lady who abounds in every thing, answer this poor, but common Excuse, and let the Choice she makes of the Person and Fortune of her second Husband (which is generally, as I have observed above, in both Cases, far short of her former Choice) acquit or convict her, as her Conduct shall deserve.

If a young Widow, indeed, advantages *herself*, and worsts not her *Children* (if she has any), in her second Adventure, let her proceed: She is justified to worldly Prudence. But this, as I have said, is so seldom the Case, even with Widow Ladies of Modesty, and *Discretion* in other respects, that I must own I have been often puzzled and confounded how to account for the Motives of such an one, reputably, especially when she appears to me and all the World, neither to have done Honour to the Memory of her late Spouse, to her Family, to herself, nor, as sometimes has been the Case, paid any regard to common Decency. How, I say, shall this be accounted for, in a Lady of Prudence and Virtue? Is it, that, as one Extreme is said to border on another, *extreme Joy* treads on the Heels of *extreme Sorrow?* It cannot be; for as, on one hand, I am sure there can be no *extreme Joy* in the matrimonial Commerce; so, I fear, where a Woman can soon forget her departed Spouse, she cannot be sensible of *extreme Grief* for his Loss. And if she will take upon her this latter Part of the Character, and own the first was thus indifferent to her, she shall have my Consent to do any thing she has a mind to do, and I will exempt her willingly from the Observation of every other Rule of Prudence and Decency.

But in a Case the direct Reverse of this, how shall we account for such a Behaviour? How, in particular, if the charming, the blooming Miss *Birdish*, who was so coy a Maiden, and with so much Difficulty won by the late amiable and considerable Mr *Brookes*, with a Fortune superior to her own, should, within a few Months after his Decease, when blest with an Affluence left her by his Generosity and Affection for her, be won by Mr. *Townes,*

Fownes, a Man less accomplish'd as to Knowlege, less amiable in his Person, less polite in his Conversation, and of a Fortune so much beneath what was even her maiden one, that her Friends then would never have thought him worthy of her?----How, I say, shall we account for this, if it should be so? Is there a secret Sympathy in Tempers and Dispositions, that attracts each its Like by Motives imperceptible, and unaccountable? It cannot be in *this* Case, surely. For can the polite Mrs. *Brookes* be **less** polite for having been marry'd to one of the best-bred and best-behav'd Gentlemen in *England?* And can she so soon get over Forms as a *Widow*, for *such* a Suitor as Mr. *Fownes*, which as a *Maid* were so long before they could be dispensed with in Favour of *such* a Lover as Mr. *Brookes?*----Is her soft and delicate Mind, as we all think it, after *all*, more on a Level with that of the one Gentleman, than that of the other *far more* excellent one? Has she, will the Licentious ask, stronger Incentives to a married State as a Widow, than she had as a Maid?----It cannot be!----What then shall we say to all this?----For after all, two Years won not Miss *Bendish*, to a Gentleman of exalted Worth; and two Months seem to have made a great Progress with Mrs. *Brookes!*----And that in Favour of a Gentleman, whom we all think unworthy of her at all.

My dear Bosom-friend, my School-fellow, my Companion, as well in the *maiden* as in the *matrimonial*, tho', I bless God, not in the *vidual* State, resolve me these Questions; answer to me for this Conduct; account to me for these seeming unaccountable Motives; and thereby justify yourself to your *Reputation*, to the *Memory* of the *dear Departed*, to your *own Sex*, to the *other Sex* (so attentive as they *both* are to your Conduct in this

Par-

Particular), and, lastly, which will for ever oblige me, to

   Your affectionate and
     Faithful Friend and Servant.

LETTER CXLVIII.

From a Gentleman, strenuously expostulating with an old rich Widow, about to marry a very young gay Gentleman.

Madam,

I AM very sorry to hear of the Encouragement you give to the Visits of young Mr. *Barnes*, because of the great Difference in Years between you. I cannot help giving you the Trouble of this Expostulation, tho' I am told (and much affected I am with the News, if it be true), that the Matter between you is so far gone, that all I can say may too probably prove ineffectual.

Our Sex, Madam, in all your late Husband's Time, has received an Advantage and a Credit from your Conduct in the marry'd State; and now, I wish it may not receive as great a Disparagement, since the prudent Mrs. *Bates* thinks fit to countenance the Addresses of one who was born after she was marry'd, and a Mother, and who can possibly have no other Inducement than your Fortune. I believe, Madam, you never knew one happy Marriage of this sort in all your Life: And you will reflect, that you will not be intitled to Pity, nor the young Man to Censure, if he should prove the worst and most profligate of Husbands to you. For every one will censure *you*, and acquit *him*, should he even treat you with personal Abuse and Barbarity.

Besides, it is well known, that Mr. *Barnes* is a young Man of no very promising Inclinations. Some young Gentlemen are as grave and discreet at Twenty-five, as others at Thirty five. But he has all the Vanity, the Gaiety, the Affectation, of any one at his Time of Life. And can you expect, that he will treat *you* well, that was never noted for treating his *own Mother* very dutifully, who, by the way, is *younger* than yourself? Advanced Years are the constant Subject of Ridicule with such wild young Fellows, to their Shame be it spoken! And what can you expect, when the very Motives by which you shall be supposed to be acted in such a Match, will involve you in the deepest Censure, will make you the Contempt of Persons of all Ages, and both Sexes, and expose you to the low Buffoonry even of the Man you have chosen, who, instead of being your Protector, as a Husband ought to be, will probably be the Person who will *lead the Jest* that all will join in upon you, in order to excuse his own sordid Choice?

You owe it, Madam, give me Leave to say, to the *Memory* of your late worthy *Husband*, you owe it to your *Sex*, you owe it to *yourself*, and your own *Interest*, and *future Good*; nay, to *Decency*, I will venture to add, to proceed no further in this Affair. It seems to me, to be next to a Degree of Incest for a Woman all hoary and grey-goosed over by Time, or who will be soon so, to expose herself to the Embraces of a young Fellow, who is not so old as her first Son would have been, had he lived. Forgive me, Madam, but I cannot help this Plain-dealing on the Occasion. If you proceed in giving Encouragement to the Boy's Address, I expect not, nor can I desire, to be forgiven, or

to

to stand upon common Terms with you. If otherwise, I am ready to ask your Pardon, but I cannot with Patience think, that Mrs. *Bates*, who has passed thro' every Station *hitherto* with so much Applause, as well that of the prudent *Widow*, and exemplary *Matron*, as the affectionate *Wife*, should give so great a Wound to our Sex as she will do, if she makes such a Boy as Mr. *Barnes* the Successor to her late worthy Husband, and the Master of her Person and Fortune. By which Act she will vow Obedience to one who was in a Cradle, when she had Children of her own who were rising from it; and who would undoubtedly despise her in this Light, were it not for her Wealth, all of which, that he can get at, by Force, or fair Means (if he acts by you as others generally have done in the same Circumstances), will be squander'd away upon rival Objects more suitable to his Youth, while you will be the *Laughing-stock* and Scorn of such as will revel in *your* Spoils, and triumph over you by the Help of your own *Fortune* Mean time you will be so far from engaging the Pity of your Sex, that the more considerate of them will shun and contemn you, as one who has brought a Disgrace upon it. The Men will despise and flout you, and you will have nothing to do but to hide in a contemn'd Obscurity that grey-green Head, which has so inconsiderately involved you in so much Distress, and to turn Penitent for it, and pray for an End to a miserable Life, which, come when it will, will give Cause of Joy and Triumph to your young Husband, and very little Sorrow to any other Person.

But I hope still for better things; and I hope for Pardon for this Freedom, for fain would I be thought by Mrs. *Bates*,

Her affectionate and faithful Friend,
and humble Servant.

The

The following Eleven Epistles may serve as Models for Letters to write by, on the like Occasion; likewise to give a brief Description of London *and* Westminster, *to such as have not seen those Cities; and to point out to those who never were in Town before, what is most-worthy of Notice in it.*

LETTER CXLIX.

From a young Lady in Town to her Aunt in the Country.

I. *Describing the* Tower, Monument, St. Paul's, *&c.*

Honoured Madam,

YOU will have me write you down Accounts of what I see remarkable in and about *London*, to keep me, as you say, out of Idleness, and to entertain my good Friends in my Absence. I will obey, tho' your good Opinion of me, I am sensible, will be no small Disadvantage to me, for I shall convince you more effectually than ever of my Defects, and Want of that Ability to entertain my absent Friends, which their Partiality had made them expect from me.

To begin then, my Aunt and Cousins carried me, in the first Place, to see the Tower of *London*, which we have heard so much Talk of in the Country; and which no one that visits this great Town, omits seeing. 'Tis situated by the *Thames* Side, surrounded with an old Wall, about a Mile in Compass, with a broad deep Ditch, which has generally more Mud in it than Water. All round the

the outward Wall are Guns planted, which on extraordinary Occasions are fired; as, on more common ones, they fire only Rows of others, which are fixed in the Ground, on the Wharf by the *Thames*. At the Entrance on the Right-hand, we saw the Collection of wild Beasts kept there; as Lions, Panthers, Tygers, &c. also Eagles, Vulturs, &c.

We were then carried to the Mint, where we saw the manner of coining Money, and striking Medals, &c. From thence we went to the Jewel-house, and were shewn the Crown, and the other Regalia; which gave me no small Pleasure, as I had never seen these Things before, and heard so much Talk of them.

The Horse-Armory is a fine Sight; for here they shew Fifteen of our *English* Monarchs on Horseback, all in rich Armour, attended with Guards: But I think this Sight not comparable to the small Armory; for here Pikes, Musquets, Swords, Halberds, and Pistols (enow, as they told us, for threescore thousand Men), are all placed in such beautiful Order, and such various Figures, representing the Sun, Star and Garter, Half-moons, and such-like, that I was greatly delighted with the Sight, all the Arms being bright, and shining.

We saw the Train of Artillery, in what they call the Grand Storehouse; filled with Cannon and Mortars, all very fine, a Diving-bell, and other Curiosities, and I thought, upon the Whole, that this great Magazine of Curiosities and Stores was the most worthy of the Notice of a Stranger to *London*, of any thing I had been shewn.

From hence they carried me to the *Monument*, built in Remembrance of the Fire of *London*, a very curious Pillar, from the Gallery of which we had a Survey of the whole City. But as it stands low,

low, I cannot say, but I liked the Prospect from *St. Paul's* Cupola much better, when I was carried up thither, which was Yesterday; for that being the highest Situation in the City, and more in the Centre of *London* and *Westminster*, commands a finer View over both Cities, *Hampstead* and *Highgate* Hills, *Surrey*, the River, &c. The Cathedral is a most noble Building, and I admired it not a little, for its Choir, Chapels, Dome, Whispering-place, Vaults below, and other Curiosities too tedious to mention.

This, Madam, may serve for one Letter, and to shew you how much I am desirous, by my Obedience to your Commands, to approve myself

Your dutiful Niece.

LETTER CL.

From the same.

II. *Describing other remarkable Places in and about* London *and* Westminster, *which are generally shewn to Strangers.*

Honoured Madam,

I HAVE seen the Custom-house, a Place of Hurry and Business, with a crouded and inconvenient Key, compared to that of *Bristol*, *St. Thomas's* and *Guy's* Hospitals, *Southwark*, all most noble Charities; *St. Bartholomew's*, a still nobler, but which, by its additional Buildings, seems to be in a way to swallow up its own Revenues, by pulling down their Tenants Houses, which contributed Means to support the Charity; *Smithfield* also, a spacious Market for live Cattle, &c. as, I should have said, I had *Leaden-hall* Market, a Prodigy of its Kind, and the Admiration of Foreigners. *Sadler's-wells*, at *Islington*, I have been at, and seen there the Diversions of Rope-dancing, Volting, Singing, Musick, &c. which I thought well enough for once. *Islington-wells*, or the *New Tunbridge*, I have been at; the Walks and Rooms neat enough, and good Decorum observ'd in both.

The Blue-coat Hospital I have also seen, another noble Charity; and the pretty Sight of the Children at Church, and at Supper on *Sunday* Night, which much pleased me. The Charter-house too, another noble Charity.

Also the *Guildhall* of *London*, a handsome Building, adorn'd with Pictures, and with the Trophies of the Duke of *Marlborough*'s Victory over the *French*; and the preposterous wooden Figures of the two famous Giants. The Royal Exchange likewise, a very fine Edifice; but they say the Statues of the Kings and Queens there, are ill done, except that of *Charles* II. in the Middle of the Area, and one or two more.

I have also been carried to *Westminster-hall*, and the two Houses where the Lords and Commons meet. They are by no means answerable to what I expected, tho' the House of Commons is the neatest, and very convenient for hearing and seeing too. *Westminster-hall*, like *Guildhall*, is adorned with the Duke of *Marlborough*'s Trophies, and it has Shops on each Side for Milaners, Booksellers, and such-like Trades. Here the Coronation-Feast is kept, and here are held, as you know, the Courts of Chancery, King's-Bench, Common-Pleas, and up Stairs the Court and Offices of the Exchequer.

The Abbey we are to see another time, being obliged to dine at *Westminster* with a Friend of my Cousin's.

Somerset-house, in the *Strand*, I have seen, noted for its pleasant Garden fronting the River; and it is, indeed, a fine Palace itself, designed for the Residence of the Queens Dowager of *England*, when we have such a Personage. *Marlborough* House in the Park, is finely furnished and adorned with Pictures of the Duke's Battles. *St. James's* House is a poor Palace for a King of *England*; but it seems convenient on the Inside. *Buckingham-house* stands better than that, for commanding the beautiful Park and Canal. The Treasury, a fine new Building. *White-hall*, whose Glory is the Banquetting-house, justly admir'd for its Architecture by *Inigo Jones*, and Inside Painting by *Rubens*. It is a noble Situation for a Palace, which, were it to be built like this, would be the most magnificent in the World.

We took Coach another time, and were carried thro' the principal Squares and new Buildings about *London* and *Westminster*, which are highly worth seeing; such as *Lincoln's-Inn* Square, *Lincoln's-Inn* Fields, *St. James's* Square, *Soho* Square, *Hanover* Square, *Cavendish* Square, and *Grosvenor* Square, with the Multitude of stately Buildings, and noble Streets contiguous to the latter; a Sight worthy of Admiration.

This, Madam, may serve for a second Letter, and another Instance, tho' a poor one, of that Obedience which will always bind me to be

Your dutiful Niece.

LETTER CLI.
From the same.
III. *Describing* Chelsea *Hospital, and* Kensington *Palace.*

Honoured Madam,

I HAVE been carried, by my obliging Cousins, to *Chelsea* College, about a Mile from *St. James's* Park, and to *Kensington* Palace, about two Miles West from *London*.

The College, you know, was founded by King *Charles* II. and finished by the late King *William*, for the Reception of superannuated Officers and Soldiers. It is situated on the Banks of the *Thames*, its Gardens extending quite down to the River. It is a neat and stately Building; the Front, looking to the *Thames*, has a fine Hall on one Side, and a neat Chapel on the other, with a noble Pavilion, as they call it, between them. The two Sides are four Stories high, and have two Wards in each Story, containing thirty-six neat Bed-rooms each, for so many Soldiers. Each Corner of this main Building is adorned with a fine Pavilion, being the Governor's Lodging and Council-chamber; Lodgings for Officers, &c. In the Middle of the Square is a Brass Statue of King *Charles* II. on a Marble Pedestal.

There are, besides, four other large and uniform Wings, one is the Infirmary for the Sick, a second for maimed Officers, a third for Officers of the College, the fourth for Servants. The Whole is a neat, convenient, and airy Building, well worth a Stranger's View.

Kensington Palace is a very pretty Summer Retirement for the Court: It is adorn'd with fine Pictures,

L rich

rich Hangings, and other Ornaments. But the Gardens, which have been much augmented of late Years, are delightful, and we diverted ourselves in walking round them, which gave me great Pleasure; and I could not but wish, that you, Madam, were with me, because you love walking, and would have been much pleased with these charming Gardens, which abound with fine Walks, &c. A noble Piece of Water, called the *Serpentine* River, but for what Reason I know not (it being a strait, and not winding Piece), presents itself to View; and there is lately a new Road made thro' *Hyde-park* to *Kensington*, by the late Q. *Caroline*, to keep the Gardens clear from Dust in the Summer, and make them more private from Horses, Passengers, Coaches, &c.; for the old Road, in one Part, ran almost close to the Wall. A Row of Lamps from one End to the other of this Road, is placed on each Side of it, when the Court is there, which is a Beauty, as well as Convenience.

Will this, Madam, serve for a third Letter on the Subject you have prescribed to

Your ever-dutiful Niece?

LETTER CLII.

From the same.

IV. *Describing* Greenwich *Park, and the Passage to it by Water.*

Honoured Madam,

LAST *Tuesday*, being *Easter Tuesday*, I went with my Uncle, Aunt, and Cousins, down the River, on what they call a *Party of Pleasure*, but with Design principally to see *Greenwich* Park and Hospital. We

We took Water at the Tower, which I describ'd in my first Letter. I was pretty much afraid of Danger from Anchors, Cables, and such-like, as we passed by the great Numbers of Ships, that lay in our Way at first setting out. But afterwards the River looked very pleasant, and the Number of Boats all rowing with the Tide, made the River look very agreeably.

After sailing not many Miles, we come within Sight of the Dock-yard at *Deptford*, where several large Ships upon the Stocks afforded a fine Prospect; as the naval Strength of *England* is both its Glory, and its Defence.

Next to *Deptford*, I was greatly pleased with the Prospect of the Royal Hospital at *Greenwich*, for Seamen grown old in the Service of their Country. When we landed, we went into this fine Building; and in the *Inside*, every thing, in my Judgment, was perfectly agreeable to the Magnificence of the *Outside*; allowing the one to be designed to do Honour to the Nation, the other to support a Number of necessitous People, who ought to be the publick Care. The great Hall, and the Paintings in it, are admirable; but I know not whether they would not better suit a *Palace*, than an *Hospital* And, indeed, this may be said of the whole Building.

From thence we went into the Park; where I beheld divers odd Scenes of Holiday-folks. Here appeared a rakish young Fellow, with two or three Women who look'd like Servant-maids; the Hero delighted, the Nymphs smiling round him----There a careful-looking Father with his Children on each Side; Trains of admiring Lovers, ready-pair'd, followed one another in thronging Crouds at the Gate; a Sea-Officer, with a Lady not over-burdened with Modesty in her Behaviour: A Croud of City Apprentices, some with, some without their Lasses: Half a dozen Beaux ogling all they met: And several seemingly disconsolate Virgins walking alone. The Concourse of middling Objects pressed chiefly toward a high Hill in the Middle of the Park; where, as they arriv'd, their Business was to take hold of Hands, and run down as fast as possible, amidst the Huzza's of a Multitude of People, who earnestly expected to see the Women fall, in hopes that their Cloaths would not lie so conveniently, when they were down, as might be wished.

This, Madam, is a Diversion you would not expect so near the polite City of *London*; but I assure you, such a Levity possessed almost every body assembled on this Occasion, as made the Park, tho' most beautiful in itself, no way entertaining to

Your most dutiful Niece,

LETTER CLIII.

From the same.

V. *Describing* Bethlehem *Hospital.*

Honoured Madam,

YOU tell me, in your last, that my Descriptions and Observations are very superficial, and that both my Uncle and yourself expect from me much better Accounts than I have yet given you. For I must deliver my *Opinion*, it seems, on what I see, as well as tell you what I have been shewn. 'Tis well I left my bettermost Subjects to the last; such, I mean, as will best bear Reflection, and I must try what I can do, to regain that Reputation which your Indulgence, rather than my Merit, had formed for me in your kind Thoughts

Thoughts----Yet, I doubt, I shan't please you, after all. But 'tis my Duty to try for it, and it will be yours, I had almost said, to forgive Imperfections which I should have conceal'd, but for your undeserv'd good Opinions of me, which draw them into Light.

I have this Afternoon been with my Cousins, to gratify the odd Curiosity most People have to see *Bethlehem*, or *Bedlam* Hospital.

A more affecting Scene my Eyes never beheld; and surely, Madam, any one inclined to be proud of human Nature, and to value themselves above others, cannot go to a Place that will more effectually convince them of their Folly. For there we see Man destitute of every Mark of Reason and Wisdom, and levell'd to the Brute Creation, if not beneath it, and all the Remains of good Sense or Education serve only to make the unhappy Person appear more deplorable!

I had the Shock of seeing the late polite and ingenious Mr.------in one of these woful Chambers. We had heard, you know, of his being somewhat disordered; but I did not expect to find him here. No sooner did I put my Face to the Grate, but he leap'd from his Bed, and called me, with frightful Fervency, to come into his Room. The Surprize affected me pretty much; and my Confusion being observed by a Croud of Strangers, I heard it presently whisper'd, That I was his Sweetheart, and the Cause of his Misfortune. My Cousin assured me such Fancies were frequent upon these Occasions. But this Accident drew so many Eyes upon me, as obliged me soon to quit the Place.

I was much at a Loss to account for the Behaviour of the Generality of People, who were looking at these melancholy Objects. Instead of the Concern I think unavoidable at such a Sight, a sort of Mirth appeared on their Countenances; and the diftemper'd Fancies of the miferable Patients moft unaccountably provoked Mirth, and loud Laughter, in the unthinking Auditors; and the many hideous Roarings, and wild Motions of others, feemed equally entertaining to them. Nay, fo fhamefully inhuman were fome, among whom (I am forry to fay it!) were feveral of my own Sex, as to endeavour to provoke the Patients into Rage, to make them Sport.

I have been told, this dreadful Place is often ufed for the Refort of lewd Perfons to meet and make Affignments. But that I cannot credit; fince the Heart muft be abandon'd indeed, that could be vicious amidft fo many Examples of Mifery, and of fuch Mifery, as, being wholly involuntary, may overtake the moft fecure.

I am no great Admirer of publick Charities, as they are too often managed; but if we confider the Impoffibility of poor Peoples bearing this Misfortune, or providing fuitably for the Diftempered at their own Beings, no Praife can, furely, be too great for the Founders and Supporters of an Hofpital, which none can vifit, without receiving the moft melancholy *Proof* of its being needful. I am, with Refpects where due, honoured Madam,

Your moft dutiful Niece.

LETTER CLIV.
From the fame.
VI. *Diverfions of* Vaux-hall *defcribed.*

Honoured Madam,

I WENT on *Monday* laft to *Vaux-hall* Gardens, whither every-body muft go, or appear a fort of Monfter in polite Company. For the Convenience of Waterage, as well as of Converfation, we were a pretty large Company, and the Evening proved ferene and clear.

The Paffage from *Somerfet* Stairs, where we took Water, was pleafant enough; the *Thames* at High-water being a moft beautiful River, efpecially above *Weftminfter*, where the green Banks, and the open Country, afford a very agreeable Profpect. The Place we landed at was crouded with Boats, and from the Water-fide to the Gardens we walk'd thro' a double Line of gaping Watermen, Footmen, old Beggar-women, and Children. As foon as we entered the Walks, I was pleafed with a fort of Stage, or Scaffold, raifed at the Entrance, for the Servants of the Company to fit out of their Mafters way, and yet within Call of the Waiters.

The Mufick-gallery and Organ look perfectly polite, and their being raifed one Story from the Ground, has a good Effect upon the Mufick. The Walks are well enough, but inviron'd with paltry wooden Boards, where I expected at leaft a good Brick-wall One Part of the Whole is thrown into Walks only, the other is on the Sides filled with Seats or Arbours, with painted Backs, on each of which is reprefented fome Scene of our moft common Plays, or the youthful Reprefentation of the Infant Games, *&c.* I happened to have at my Back honeft *Hob*, come dripping wet out of the Well; and the young Fellows, under colour of fhewing their Tafte in obferving the Beauties of the Piece, were fo perpetually ftaring in our Faces, that Coufin *Bet* and I had little Pleafure in our Supper. Perhaps you will wonder at our Supping in fo open a Place; but I affure you, Madam, no Lady is too tender for fo fafhionable a Repaft. My Uncle treated us very chearfully, but I could not help grudging the Expence he was at;

for when the Reckoning was paid, it amounted to no less than Ten Shillings a Head, which I think too dear, as the Entrance money must be sufficient to defray the House and Musick. But as the Whole is devoted to Pleasure, the Expence seems rather to create Satisfaction, than Distaste, as it gives an Opportunity to gallant People to oblige those they love, or pretend to love, in order, most of them, to pay themselves again with large Interest.

The Figure of Mr. *Handel*, a great Master of Musick, stands on one Side the Gardens, and looks pretty enough. The Musick plays from Five to Ten, about three Tunes (I believe I should have said Pieces) in an Hour. They are all reported to be the best Performers who assist here. But my rough Ears cannot distinguish.

About Ten o'Clock, many People think of Home: But the Votaries of *Cupid*, I am told, about that Time, visit the remotest Walks, and sigh out the soft Passion in Accents that may possibly be improved by the melting Sweetness of the Musick ----I would not have you from hence conclude any Rudeness can be offered; for at the Termination of every Walk, thro' the whole Garden, is placed a Man, to protect the Company from all manner of Insult. But when the Place grows thin of Company, the Lovers have a better Chance to escape being laugh'd at, on the Appearance of any amorous Symptom.

Soon after Ten, we returned to our Boat; and I found the Passage extremely cold, notwithstanding a Covering over us: I must own, I wish'd to be at home, long before I reached it; for I was taken with such a Shivering, as did not leave me for two Days.

Thus,

Thus, Madam, have I been at *Vaux-hall*, with the Croud of Fashion-hunters. But if nobody had a greater Inclination than I have to go thither again, that Amusement would soon be given up----For I see more and more, that, do what I will, Nature never designed me to be polite; and I can sincerely declare, that I take more Satisfaction in an Evening-walk with you up the *West-grove*, where I am so often benefited by your good Instructions, than in the inchanting Shades of the so-much celebrated *Vaux-hall*. I am, honoured Madam,

Your most dutiful Niece.

LETTER CLV.

From the same.

VII. *An Account of* Westminster-Abbey.

Honoured Madam,

I HAVE this Afternoon been at *Westminster-Abbey*, and not a little pleased with what I have seen there. If there can be Majesty in the Grave, here we see it: And such was the solemn Effect the sacred Repository had upon me, that I never found an awful Reverence equal to what I felt on that Occasion. Whatever be the Intention of erecting these costly Monuments, they seem to me very capable of being made an excellent Sermon to succeeding Generations; for here the most sumptuous Piles serve only to shew, that every one of us must submit to the same Fate, that has overtaken those whom Empire itself could not save. And how humble ought the Person to be, who surveys the Royal Ruins of Mortality, preserved (as if in a vain

De-

Defiance of Time) to shew nothing more than the Certainty of our Dissolution!

These, Madam, were my general Sentiments on this Occasion; but as I know you expect more particular Descriptions from me, I will tell you what most struck my Notice among the many remarkable Curiosities to be here met with.

Among the Royal Monuments, those of antient Date pleased me best, because they look agreeable to what I read of the plain Royalty of our former Sovereigns. I lamented the Loss of *Henry* the Fifth's Head, which being Silver, as they say, was stolen during the Civil War. I much wonder it has never yet been supply'd from some of his Busto's. He wanted not a *Head*, to speak in the metaphorical Style, while living, and *France* can testify, that his *Heart* deserved all Things of *English* Men: For he was the Terror of the one, and the Glory of the other.

Henry the Seventh's Chapel, in every Part of it, is surprisingly magnificent and beautiful, and, as far as I can judge of such Things, far surpasses all I have seen, either of antient or modern Date.

In this Chapel is the Chair in which our Kings, for many Ages, have been crown'd. 'Tis very plain, and looks as if it were not worth more than the Forfeit paid for sitting in it.

The Body of Queen *Catharine*, Consort to *Henry* the Fifth, was shewn us in an open Coffin; and what remains of Skin, looks like black discoloured Parchment. She is said to have been very beautiful, and, surely, to view her now, is a most effectual Antidote against the Vanity rising from that dangerous Accomplishment.

Two Embassadors Coffins are kept here, said to be detained for want of having their Debts discharged. This, indeed, does little Credit to the
Crown

Crown they ferved; but I can fcarce think it the Difhonour defign'd them, to be repofited among the Remains of our Kings, tho' indeed feveral of *them* have their Debts unpaid too, as I am told.

Several Effigies are preferved in Wax; particularly thofe of King *William*, and his excellent Queen *Mary*; as alfo, very lately, the truly Royal Queen *Anne* To be fure, this is no bad way, for a few Years, to preferve their Likenefs, but I know not whether fuch gay Reprefentations fuit the Solemnity of a Sepulchre. And yet fome that ftand here, feem not to have deferved that Diftinction, if it be deemed one, in Favour of their Memories. A Duchefs of *Richmond*, who walked at King *Charles* the Second's Coronation, never was remarkable for any thing, as I can hear, but that.

General *Monk*, in a Habit mourning the Power of Time, ftands in a Pofture fo very fierce, as to feem rather intended to fcare Children, than for any other Purpofe.

I had almoft forgot his Royal Mafter, King *Charles* the Second, who ftands in his Garter-Robes, and has long been admired by all Comers, it feems, for reftoring Monarchy; for I can remember no worthy Actions in his Hiftory, nor were we told any more, by the Perfon who expofed his Image to our View.

A very coftly Effigy of the late Duke of *Buckinghamfhire* is in this Place, who was fomewhat remarkable in his Time, but chiefly for doing what pleafed himfelf, whether any body elfe was pleafed or bettered by it, or not. And, what is odd enough, his furviving Duchefs ftands by him. Her Son too, the laft Duke, who died juft before he came of Age, is diftinguifhed with an Oftentation fuperior to all the reft, though all I can learn of him is, that he was a hopeful young Nobleman, and the Darling of his Mother.

Many Reasons make it necessary for the Wills of deceased Persons to be literally observed, tho' some Instances of this kind do little Honour to the Deceased; as a Monument erected to the Consort of a noble Lord, for whom a Vacancy being left on his Tomb, as for his second Wife, she, because she could not take the Right-hand of his first Lady, left strict Order to be bury'd where her Bones now lie, and thereby has transmitted her Pride and Folly to succeeding Ages.

Near this Tomb, is the Figure of a Lady bleeding to Death by pricking her Finger: She was Maid of Honour to Queen *Elizabeth*, and, I think, of the *Russel* Family. It seems she got her fatal Wound at her Needle; and such has been the Care of the Ladies who have succeeded her, that not one has fallen under the like Misfortune ever since.

If I shall not quite tire you, I will proceed with this Subject in my next.----And am, mean time, honoured Madam,

Your most dutiful Niece.

LETTER CLVI.

From the same.

VIII. *Account of* Westminster-Abbey *continued.*

Honoured Madam,

I NOW trouble you with an Account of what most struck my Attention in the outward Ayles of *Westminster-Abbey.*

At

At entering the North Gate, a Monument of prodigious Size, and great Expence, stood on my Left-hand. It is that of *John Holles* late Duke of *Newcastle*, and all that is left him, out of upwards of 50000*l.* a Year, as they tell me he had accumulated, and the two Heirs not much the richer for their Shares of it neither. I hope, as we say in our Country Phrase, *it was honestly got.*

Next to this, is one consecrated to the Memory of the Duke that preceded him, the last of his Name of the *Cavendish* Family, as the other was of the *Holles*; with the celebrated Lady, his Duchess *Margaret*, a great Writer, and a great Chymist (you know we have her Olio), both lying Side by Side, on a Tomb made great by their Names, and distinguished by their Adventures; but as to outward Grandeur, wholly eclipsed by the former. Behind these is a large Room, or little Chapel, separated from the publick Places, in which are reposited the *Holles* Family. One of these Gentlemen has at his Feet the Representation of a wild Boar, in Token of his having killed one of those Animals, when he was on a Croisade. Another has a large black Patch over his Right Eye, having lost an Eye on the like Expedition.

Not far from hence, a fine Monument stands, to the Memory of Dr. *Chamberlen*, a Man-midwife, of no great Fame when living, but who happened to have the Esteem of the late Duchess of *Buckingham*, who erected this to his Memory.

A magnificent Monument stands near this, of a Lady, whose Name is *Carteret*, and some Reports assign an odd Cause for her Death; viz. the late *French* King's saying, *A Lady one of his Nobles compared to her, was the handsomer of the two.*

A fine Monument of Lord *Courcey* stands near this, on which, we are told, one of his Ancestors had a Privilege granted, of wearing his Hat before the King----Here are several Monuments of Gentlemen who fell in the late Wars; Col. *Bringfield*, in particular, who had his Head shot off by a Cannon-Ball, as he was mounting the Duke of *Marlborough*, who had a Horse shot under him. Those of others, who were famous for different Talents, as my Favourite *Purcell*, and Dr. *Croft*, for Musick, decorate the North Isle; at the Head of which stands Sir *Godfrey Kneller*, Painter to his late Majesty, with a Copy of Verses on it, that have Mr. *Pope*'s Name affixed to them. In a Corner, that answers to it, on the South-side of the West Gate, stands a curious Resemblance of *James Craggs*, Esq; Secretary of State in 1720. erected by a certain Duchess, for what Reason is not said. Mr *Pope* has bestow'd great Praises on this Gentleman in a fine Epitaph on his Monument; and 'tis generally allow'd, whatever other Faults he had, he was a companionable Man, and easy of Access----A small Distance from this, is a Monument erected by another Duchess, Sister of the former, to the Memory of Mr. *Congreve*, from the great Esteem she bore him. So here are three Monuments erected to three Favourites, by three Duchesses. What a generous Sex is ours, who carry their Esteem for the Merit of those they favour, beyond the Grave! On the same Side of the Church is a very slight Monument of the great Earl of *Godolphin*, who was Lord High Treasurer during the prosperous Part of Queen *Anne*'s Reign, and the mean Appearance this makes, when compared with those of Mr. *Craggs*, Mr. *Congreve*, Dr. *Chamberlen*, &c. makes a Spectator sensible, that a Judgment of the Deceaseds Merits must not be formed from their Monuments; nor, as is to be hoped, the Gratitude and Affection of their Descendents

scendents either. Sir *Cloudesly Shovel* has great Honour done him, his Monument being erected at the Expence of his Royal Mistress. But I thought he was a rough *honest Tar*; yet his Effigies makes him a *great Beau*, with a fine flowing full-bottom'd Periwig; such an one, but much finer, and more in Buckle, than that we have seen our Lawyer Mr. *Kettleby* wear at our Assizes.

Mr. *Thynne*'s Murder is prettily represented on his Tomb----But before I step into what is call'd the *Poets Row*, I must return to the Door of the Choir, on the North-side of which is placed a noble Monument of the great Sir *Isaac Newton*, which I humbly apprehend to be needless; for has he not built for himself a much finer Monument, and a much more durable one, than Marble? And will it not out-last this we see here, and the Abbey which contains it? He lies in a contemplative Posture, leaning on the Volumes that have made his Name immortal. Opposite to him, at the South Entrance of the same Door, is a very grand Pile, to the Memory of the late Earl *Stanhope*, a brave Soldier, tho' unfortunate in one Battle; and a Man of great Probity.

On one Side of the Poets are Dr. *South* and Dr *Busby*; the one an humourous and witty Divine, the other as remarkable a Schoolmaster, being famous for his Discipline and Severity. *Geoffry Chaucer* has reach'd us *Spencer* is near him; *Philips* not far from *Spencer*. *Ben Johnson* is written on a poor Bust. And *Butler* (put up by a Printer, to make his own Name famous) bears him Company. I would fain not name *Matt. Prior*, but his Monument is so beautiful and large, and his Busto so admirable, being a Present to the Poet by the *French* King *Lewis* XIV. that I must not pass it over, tho', poor Man! it serves

only

only to proclaim his Vanity, being erected at his own Desire and Expence: A sad Instance of Pride beyond the Grave! Behind him stands Mr. *Gay*, in a Place consecrated to Mortality, declaring *Life is a Jest*, &c. *Dryden* has only his Name on his Bust. *Milton* has lately been put up by a Gentleman, who, after the Printer's Example abovementioned, has a mind to engraft his own Fame on the other's Stock; but, in this, out-does Mr. *Barber*: For, after dedicating Six single *Letters* to the Poet's Name, *M, I, L, T, O, N*, he bestows many Words upon his own; not being content to name the little Honours he, the Erector, now enjoys, but the lesser ones which he possessed in the former Reign; and from this Example, the Architect (who, no doubt, was *paid* for his Labour) has Seven Words to his Fame, declaring, That *Rysbrack was the Statuary who cut it.* Here's fine ingrafting Work for you! However, *Milton*'s Memory is a Tree that will do Honour to the weakest Scyon that shall sprout from it, or even to a Dung-hill, were such a thing to lie at its Root. But of all the Monuments in the Abbey, the modern ones especially, none comes up to that of *Shakespeare* lately erected; where the Poet is represented in Marble almost as much to the Life, as he is in his Works. I am, Madam,

Your most obedient Niece.

LETTER CLVII.
From the same.

[IX. *On a Concert or Musical Entertainment.*

Honoured Madam,

I WENT last Night to see, or rather to hear, a new Entertainment of Musick And must confess, I was much disappointed of the Pleasure I

promised

promised myself. I can't say but I liked two or three of the Songs well enough, and the Musick, that was playing all the while, I did not disapprove. But pray, Madam, can you tell me (for I have already ask'd twenty, not one of whom will answer me), What is the Reason of having every Word spoken, squeaked to----I cannot say a Tune, but to such a *Hum* as makes me quite sick? If it be the Musick that is valuable, why must the Words torture it? And if the Words be sought after, wherefore should they be broken to Pieces by Notes that drown the Sound, and quite lose their Sense? What I mean is, I believe, call'd, Speaking in Recitative: But whence was this Mode of Speech taken? In what Country is it natural? And if it be natural no-where, of what is it an Imitation? What are the Marks of its Excellencies? and how shall we judge of its Merit? Whence can arise any Pleasure from hearing it? And shall we find Cause for excusing the Time lost in such an unnatural Amusement? For myself, I must own 'twas far from delighting me, for as it was neither Singing nor Speaking, I could not tell what to make of it, for it was more like to make me cry than laugh, I was so provok'd, when the Twang of the Harpsichord rob'd me of the Word the whole preceding Line depended upon!----I must confess myself for downright Speaking or Singing: I hate Mongrels; unless my Judgment be convinced by such Reasons as I can't, for my Life, hit upon at present. Yet, after all, I begin to think, I am betraying my Ignorance all this time; and so I'll conclude myself, Madam,

Your most dutiful Niece.

LETTER CLVIII.
From the same.
X. *On the Diverſions of the Playhouſe.*

Honoured Madam,

NOW I have, by your Indulgence, tarry'd in Town till the Approach of Winter, you will expect, that I ſhould give you a little Account of the Diverſions of the Stage. To begin then. My Couſin *William* and his two Siſters conducted me laſt Night to the Playhouſe, and we took Places in the Pit.

You may believe I was agreeably ſurpriſed at the Magnificence of the Stage, and its elegant Ornaments, and I was mightily pleaſed to ſee ſuch a prodigious Number of People ſeated with Eaſe, and conveniently placed to hear the natural Pitch of a common Voice. I did not expect to find the Muſick ſo near the Audience, but believe *that* the moſt proper Situation to convey the Sound over the whole Theatre.

The Play I ſaw was a Comedy, in which the Parts acted by Women had ſeveral Speeches that I thought not quite conſiſtent with the Modeſty of the Sex. And the Freedom of their Voice and Geſtures, tho', perhaps, ſuitable enough to the Characters they repreſented, were not ſo pleaſing to a Mind bent upon innocent Amuſement (if not wholly upon Inſtruction), as Speeches that put us not to the Expence of a Bluſh. What Hardſhip muſt it be to the Minds of theſe Women, to enter firſt upon this Employment! How muſt their Virtue (and ſure no Woman is without Virtue at her Entrance into the World) be ſhock'd to offer themſelves for the Entertainment of Six hundred Men,

and

most Important Occasions.

and to utter Words which convey Ideas too gross for a modest Ear, and such as would be difficult to hear in private Company without Confusion! How hard, then, must the Utterance of them be to a numerous and gay Assembly! And yet, I am assured, several Women who get their Bread upon the Stage, are strictly virtuous. If such there are, how great must be their Merit, when compared with that of the wicked ones of our Sex, who are liable to none of their certain and numerous Temptations! But yet, where it can be avoided, why should Women expose themselves to certain Dangers, if there is a Possibility of obtaining a tolerable Subsistence without it? And those who can live by Performance upon the Stage, certainly possess Qualifications more than sufficient to subsist in safer and less dependent Stations.

The Behaviour of the Men I did not so much wonder at; for a becoming Assurance in them is rather pleasing than disobliging Nor did I perceive, that so many Expressions, which are oftener miscalled *arch*, than more truly named *obscene*, were put into the Mouths of the Men as of the Women; though the Reason the Poets have for this I cannot guess.

The Conduct of the Company I thought, to the highest Degree, commendable: The utmost Decency was observed, and I saw nothing disagreeable to the strictest Politeness, or good Manners; the Awe given by so great an Audience of Persons of Taste, being too much to admit any thing but what is decent and obliging Not that I think it adviseable for Women to go alone to the Playhouse; for the *Complaisance*, so fashionable at present, affords a sort of *Occasion* for laying them under such seeming Obligations as cannot be returned, and ought therefore not to be accepted.

These

These, dear Madam, are the rough Thoughts, on this Occasion, of

Your dutiful Niece.

LETTER CLIX.

From the same.

XI. *The Play, and the low Scenes of Harlequinery after it, described and exposed.*

Honoured Madam,

HAving, as I told you in my last, seen a Comedy, I was next carry'd by my Cousin *William*, and his kind Sisters, to a Tragedy, which was that of *Hamlet*. And I was greatly moved with the Play, and pleased with the Action. But the low Scenes of *Harlequinery* that were exhibited afterwards, fill'd me with high Disgust, insomuch that I could, for their sake, have wish'd I had not seen the other. I will give you an Account of this dismal Piece of farcical dumb Shew.

We were, then, presented with the most extraordinary Gentleman I ever beheld, who, with the ugliest Face, and most apish Behaviour I ever saw, had the most amazing Success in his Amours, with Ladies whose Appearance deserv'd a more amiable Gallant.

My Cousin *William* told me the Name of this Hero was MR. HARLEQUIN; but as you know *Billy* has no great Capacity, you will be the less surprised to hear he answer'd not one Question I ask'd him to my Satisfaction.

Whom does that Character represent, Cousin?
Harlequin.
Pray, of what Nation is the Gentleman?
France.

What

What is his Business on the Stage?
To be admired by every Woman who sets Eyes on him.

Why seem they so fond of him?
Because he is Harlequin.

Why is his Face black?
Harlequin's was never of any other Colour.

Who is the Lady with whom he appears to be in the strictest Engagement?
Colombine.

Who is she?
Colombine.

Whence came she, pray, Cousin?
From France.

Is she married, or single?
Mostly married; and at Harlequin's Service, in spight of her Husband's Teeth.

Why so?
Because Colombine is to be at his Beck on every Occasion.

For what Reason?
Because they never appear without one another.

Is this Nature?
It is Fashion, and that's as good.

Why don't these worthy Persons favour us with a Song?
They never speak.

How must I understand them?
By the Motion of their Heads, Hands, and Heels.

Have they no Tongues?
They must not use them.

Why does he wear a wooden Sword?
'Tis his Symbol, to which whatever obstructs his Wishes, must give way.

Why?
That he may come at Colombine against all Obstruction.

Why muſt they needs be together?
That the People may laugh.
Wherefore ſhould we laugh?
Becauſe they are together.
Why does Mr. HARLEQUIN delight ſo much in jumping?
To pleaſe his Miſtreſs.
Why does ſhe admire him for that?
Becauſe he can reach her over other Mens Shoulders.
Is that Wit?
We laugh at it.
So you may; but it is more like to ſet me a crying.
You're a Country Laſs, Couſin.
You, Couſin, are a Town Gentleman.

By this, Madam, you may gueſs at my Entertainment. We had juſt ſeen *Hamlet*, as I have ſaid: My Heart was full of *Ophelia*'s Diſtreſs, and the Prince's Fate had ſhaken my Soul: In this State of Mind, to ſit two Hours to ſee People run after one another as if they were bewitched, only to cuckold a poor ſimple-looking Huſband, put me ſo much out of Patience, that I ſhall not bear the Sight of the Stage for ſome time. And indeed, having now run thro' the Diverſions of the Town, I begin to be deſirous of caſting myſelf at your Feet, as becomes

Your dutiful Niece.

LETTER CLX.

From a Country Gentleman in Town, to his Brother in the Country, describing a publick Execution in London.

Dear Brother,

I HAVE this Day been satisfying a Curiosity I believe natural to most People, by seeing an Execution at *Tyburn*: The Sight has had an extraordinary Effect upon me, which is more owing to the unexpected Oddness of the Scene, than the affecting Concern which is unavoidable in a thinking Person, at a Spectacle so awful, and so interesting, to all who consider themselves of the same Species with the unhappy Sufferer.

That I might the better view the Prisoners, and escape the Pressure of the Mob, which is prodigious, nay, almost incredible, if we consider the Frequency of these Executions in *London*, which is once a Month; I mounted my Horse, and accompanied the melancholy Cavalcade from *Newgate* to the fatal Tree. The Criminals were Five in Number. I was much disappointed at the Unconcern and Carelessness that appeared in the Faces of Three of the unhappy Wretches The Countenances of the other Two were spread with that Horror and Despair which is not to be wonder'd at in Men whose Period of Life is so near, with the terrible Aggravation of its being hasten'd by their own voluntary Indiscretion and Misdeeds. The Exhortation spoken by the Bell-man, from the Wall of *St. Sepulchre's* Church-yard, is well intended; but the Noise of the Officers, and the Mob, was so great, and the silly Curiosity of People climbing

into

into the Cart to take Leave of the Criminals, made such a confused Noise, that I could not hear the Words of the Exhortation when spoken; tho' they are as follow:

"All good People, pray heartily to GOD for these poor Sinners, who now are going to their Deaths; for whom this great Bell doth toll.

"You that are condemn'd to die, repent with lamentable Tears. Ask Mercy of the Lord for the Salvation of your own Souls, thro' the Merits, Death, and Passion, of Jesus Christ, who now sits at the Right-hand of God, to make Intercession for as many of you as penitently return unto him.

"*Lord have Mercy upon you! Christ have Mercy upon you!*"----Which last Words the Bell-man repeats three times.

All the way up *Holborn* the Croud was so great, as, at every twenty or thirty Yards, to obstruct the Passage; and Wine, notwithstanding a late good Order against that Practice, was brought the Malefactors, who drank greedily of it, which I thought did not suit well with their deplorable Circumstances. After this, the Three thoughtless young Men, who at *first* seemed not enough concerned, grew most shamefully daring and wanton; behaveing themselves in a manner that would have been ridiculous in Men in any Circumstance whatever. They swore, laugh'd, and talk'd obscenely, and wish'd their wicked Companions good Luck, with as much Assurance as if their Employment had been the most lawful.

At the Place of Execution, the Scene grew still more shocking; and the Clergyman who attended was more the Subject of Ridicule, than of their serious Attention. The Psalm was sung amidst the Curses and Quarreling of Hundreds of the most abandon'd and profligate of Mankind· Upon whom (so stupid are they to any Sense of Decency) all the Preparation of the unhappy Wretches seems to serve only for the Subject of a barbarous kind of Mirth, altogether inconsistent with Humanity. And as soon as the poor Creatures were half dead, I was much surprised, before such a Number of Peace-Officers, to see the Populace fall to haling and pulling the Carcases with so much Earnestness, as to occasion several warm Rencounters, and broken Heads. These, I was told, were the Friends of the Persons executed, or such as, for the sake of Tumult, chose to appear so, and some Persons sent by private Surgeons to obtain Bodies for Dissection. The Contests between these were fierce and bloody, and frightful to look at. So that I made the best of my Way out of the Croud, and, with some Difficulty, rode back among a large Number of People, who had been upon the same Errand with myself. The Face of every one spoke a kind of Mirth, as if the Spectacle they had beheld had afforded Pleasure instead of Pain, which I am wholly unable to account for

In other Nations, common Criminal Executions are said to be little attended by any beside the necessary Officers, and the mournful Friends, but here, all was Hurry and Confusion, Racket and Noise, Praying and Oaths, Swearing and Singing Psalms. I am unwilling to impute this Difference in our own from the Practice of other Nations, to the Cruelty of our Natures, to which, Foreigners, however, to our Dishonour, ascribe it. In most Instances, let them say what they will, we are humane beyond what other Nations can boast, but in this, the Behaviour of my Countrymen is past my accounting for; every Street and Lane I passed through, bearing rather the Face of a Holiday, than of that Sorrow which I expected to see, for the untimely Deaths of five Members of the Community.

One of their Bodies was carried to the Lodging of his Wife, who not being in the way to receive it, they immediately hawked it about to every Surgeon they could think of, and when none would buy it, they rubb'd Tar all over it, and left it in a Field hardly cover'd with Earth.

This is the best Description I can give you of a Scene that was no way entertaining to me, and which I shall not again take so much Pains to see. I am, dear Brother,

Yours affectionately.

Advice of an Aunt to a Niece, in relation to her Conduct in the Addresses made her by Two Gentlemen; one a gay, fluttering Military Coxcomb, the other a Man of Sense and Honour. In Five Letters.

LETTER CLXI.

I. *The Aunt to the Niece, desiring her own Opinion of her Two Lovers.*

Dear Lydia,

I AM given to understand, that you have two new Admirers, of very different Tempers and Professions, the one Capt. *Tomkins* of the Guards, the other Mr. *Rushford.* As I know Mr. *Rushford*

ford to be a sensible, sedate, worthy Gentleman; I am a little uneasy, lest he should be discouraged for the other. And yet, as I know not the Merits or Qualifications of the Captain, I would not censure you, or condemn him, right or wrong. This makes me desire your Sentiments of both, and that you'll acquaint me to which you most incline. I have a very high Opinion of your Prudence, and can have no View in this Request, but your Good. Only, I must assure you, that I have such an Esteem for Mr. *Rushford*'s Character, that the other Gentleman ought to be something more extraordinary than is to be generally met with in his Profession, to be prefer'd to him. I hope you'll think so too; but be this as it will, the frank Declaration of your Mind will be very obliging to

Your truly affectionate Aunt.

LETTER CLXII.

II. *The Niece's Answer: Describing the Behaviour of the sensible Lover.*

Honoured Aunt,

I HAVE, on so many Occasions, as well of this, as other Kinds, been obliged to your kind Concern for me, that I should be very ingrateful, if I conceal'd from you the least Byas of my Mind on so important an Occasion. I think truly, with you, that Mr. *Rushford* is a very valuable Gentleman; yet he is over-nice, sometimes, as to the Company I see, and would take upon him a little too much, if I did not keep him at a Distance, and, particularly, is so uneasy about the Captain, that he wants me to forbear seeing him on any Occasion. Now, I think, this is a little too prescribing, for the Time of our Acquaintance, and the small Progress I have hitherto permitted to the Intimacy between us. For what is this but surrendering to him upon his own Terms? and that, too, before I am summon'd in Form? Nothing but a *betrothed* Lover, or a *Husband*, has, surely, a Right to expect this Observance; and if I were to oblige him, it is absolutely putting myself in his Power, before he convinces me how he will use it. O my dear Aunt, these Men, I see, even the worthiest of them, are incroaching Creatures!---And a Woman that would not be despis'd, must not make her Will too cheap an Offering to that of her Admirer. Then, my dear Aunt, I know not how it was with *you* formerly; but there is a Pleasure in being admired, that affects one very sensibly; and I know not whether even Mr. *Rushford* would say half the fine Things he does, if he had not a Competitor that says nothing else. And I think it a kind of Robbery that a Woman commits upon her Pleasures, if she *too soon* confines herself to one. For she can be but once courted; unless such an Event happens, that she must have a very bad Heart, that can wish for it. And why should a Woman absolutely bind herself to the Terms of *For Better or For Worse*, before she goes to Church?---I hope, when the Ceremony has passed, I shall make a very good Wife· But why should I buckle to *Honour* and *Obey*, when it is all the Time I shall have to be *honoured* and *obeyed* myself?---Indeed, Aunt, I think, there is a great deal in this. And Mr *Rushford* gives himself wonderful *grave Airs* already As I'll give you an Instance.-----But here the Captain is come, and I will give you an Account of it in my next. For I will lay before you faithfully all my Proceedings with both Gentlemen, and their Behaviour; and you will be enabled

abled to judge from my Account, *which* I prefer, were I not to declare myself as plainly as I am sure I ought to do, in every Particular demanded of me by so good an Aunt. I am, Madam,

Your truly dutiful and affectionate Kinswoman.

LETTER CLXIII.

From the same.

III. *Containing the Description of the Behaviour of the same Gentleman; which occasions a Love-quarrel.*

Honoured Aunt,

I HOPE, the Suspense I gave you by my abrupt breaking off in my last, will be forgiven. I was going to give you an Instance of Mr. *Rushford*'s grave Airs. He comes last *Thursday* with great Formality, and calls himself *my humble Servant*; and I saw he was pleased to be displeased at something, and so look'd as grave as he, only bowing my Head, and following my Work; for I was hemming a Handkerchief. *You are very busy, Madam*----Yes, Sir----*Perhaps I break in upon you*----Not much, Sir.----*I am sorry if I do at all, Madam.*----You see I am pursuing my Work, as I was before you came.----*I do, Madam!*----very gravely, said he.----*But I have known it otherwise, when Somebody else has been here.*----Very likely, Sir!----But then I did as I pleased---so I do now---and who shall controul me?------*I beg Pardon, Madam; but 'tis my Value for you*----That makes you troublesome, said I, interrupting him.----*I am sorry for it, Madam!----Your humble Servant.*----Yours, Sir.----So away he went.----Well, thought I, if thou art to be lost for this, and must put me into bodily Fear, every time thou haſt a Mind to be grave, Adieu to thee!

In the Evening he comes again----*Mrs.* Betty, *Is your Lady diſengaged? Could I be admitted to ſay one Word to her?* I believe ſo, Sir. Madam, Mr. *Ruſhford* begs to be admitted to ſay one Word to you. He was at the Door, and heard me, as I know. Do you *introduce* him, ſaid I (with as much Form as he), to my Preſence. He enter'd. I roſe up, with my Hands before me----*I ſee you are angry with me, Madam.*----I am ſorry for it, Sir, ſaid I. *Sorry for your Anger, I hope, Madam.*---I ſhould be ſorry, Sir, ſaid I, if any body ſhould ſee me angry for nothing----*I am ſorry, Madam, that you ſet as nothing one that has ſo much Value for you.* Mr. *Ruſhford*, ſaid I, we have ſo many *Sorry's* between us, that I ſhould be pleas'd with a few *Glad's!*---*Why*, ſaid he, *with this ſtiff, ſet Air, do you delight to vex thus an Heart that you can make ſorry or glad at your Pleaſure?*----Why am I, Sir, to be treated capriciouſly, and to have my Conduct upbraided, when you think proper to be out of Humour?-----*I out of Humour, Madam!-----*I thought ſo----Was it in high good Humour that you inſulted me, with that *Somebody elſe?*--*I own, Madam, I cannot bear to ſee you ſo gay, ſo pleaſed, and lively, when that painted Butterfly is here, and ſo grave, ſo laconick, ſo reſerv'd, when I pay my Reſpects to you.* Pr'ythee, pr'ythee, Mr *Ruſhford*, none of theſe preſcribing Airs!-----What Right have I given you to uſe me thus?----*Madam, I hoped my Addreſs was not quite unwelcome*---Whatever your Addreſs is, your Preſcriptions are---*I cannot, where I ſo much love, bear ſuch a Difference as I always ſee in your Temper, when that Flutterer is here, to what I experience*--The Difference perhaps may be in the *Men*, not in the *Woman*. *As how, Madam?*

Madam? As how! Why, said I, he makes me laugh, and if I was to give way to't, your grave Airs would make me cry!----*Thank you, Madam, said he! What's Sport to you, is Death to me!*----And so he sigh'd, and took a Turn or two about the Room ----I was standing all this time.

He came, and took my Hand, and look'd so silly upon me, I half pity'd him *I hope, Madam, I don't keep you standing!*----Yes, you do, Sir!----*I beg, Madam, you'll not torture me with this contemptuous Formality!*----I think I am the most complaisant Creature breathing!---*To ME, Madam, do you mean!*---Yes, Sir.---*You always mean something in your Paradoxes, Madam May I ask your Meaning now?*---When I last sat and pursued my Work, you were displeased. I now stand, and have nothing to do but to be entertain'd in such an agreeable manner as you shall think properest for me-----yet you are not pleased.

Madam, said he, *you put me quite beside my Purposes!*----*If I thought you would have it so, I would sooner die than be so troublesome to you, as I now have Reason to think myself* ----If you have Reason to think so, I hope you are Master of your own Actions, said I ----*Do you forbid me your Presence for ever, Madam?*-----I do, if you ask it, Sir. (Was not this, Madam, daring me to answer even worse?)----I ask it, Madam! *Heaven is my Witness, it would be the heaviest thing that could befal me.*----You would not thus brave it from me, if you thought so, said I, quite nettled

In this manner we went on, till we had vex'd one another to some Purpose, and then he was so *good* as to give me Leave to sit down, and I was so *gracious* as to permit him to sit by me; and we parted with no Displeasure on either Side. Thus much for Mr. *Rushford*, and his *grave Airs*. My next

next shall let you into the Qualifications of his Competitor. Till when, I am, honour'd Madam,

Your dutiful Kinswoman.

LETTER CLXIV.

IV. *From the same · Describing her fluttering Pretender.*

Honoured Madam,

I NOW give you some Account of the Captain. He is a handsome Person of a Man, of a good Family. Heir to a good Estate: Dresses well, sings well, dances well---So much for his *good* Qualities As for his others, he is insufferably vain; talkative; is always laughing, especially at what he *says himself*, and, sometimes, at the Conceit of what he is *going to say,* before he *speaks*: He has such an undaunted Assurance, that there is no such thing as putting him out of Countenance. One Instance I'll give you----He is always admiring himself in the Glass; insomuch that while he is in the Room, I cannot peep into one without staring him in the Face, and one Day rallying him on this, I asked him how the Glasses were fixed in a Camp? He reply'd, without Hesitation, O Madam! the Care our Generals take to pitch our Tents by the Banks of some transparent Stream, serves very well for that Purpose. And then he laugh'd most egregiously for five or six Minutes together.

You may believe, Madam, from what I have said, that I give no great Encouragement to his Visits. Yet is there no such thing as getting rid of him; for by all his Conduct, I plainly see, he has swallow'd the ridiculous Opinion, that the more
averse

averse a Woman appears to a Man's Addresses, the more Ground he has to expect Success; and he seems so assured of winning me, that I begin to be apprehensive, every time he puts his Hand in his Pocket, that he will pull out a Licence and a Ring.----If I admit him into my Company, I know not how to get rid of him. If I cause myself to be deny'd, he plants himself directly against my Window, that the whole Neighbourhood may know his Business. Thus, with or without my Consent, he will be either thought my reigning Admirer, or he will, Don *Quixote* like, have me for his *Dulcinea*, in spite of my Teeth.

He has three or four times *shew'd away* before Mr. *Rushford*, and, as I cannot forbear heartily laughing at the Airs he gives himself, tho' for very different Reasons from those by which *his* risible Muscles are moved, he thinks me pleased with him, and, what is more vexatious, Mr. *Rushford* thinks so too, and grows serious and sullen, as I instanc'd in my former.

Now, Madam, what can I do? I heartily despise my Soldier, I greatly regard Mr. *Rushford*'s good Sense, good Breeding, and other good Qualities: But to forbid this Fop, is what I am sure will have no Weight with him, for I have as good as done it several times, and he tells me, he will visit me whether I will or not, as long as I am unmarried. And to do it professedly in Complaisance to Mr. *Rushford*, unless Matters had gone further between us, is putting myself absolutely in his Power, and declaring myself *his*, before he asks me the Question. So, may I not laugh on a little at the one, and teize the other's causeless Jealousy, do you think, till I bring Mr. *Rushford* to speak out so explicitly, that a Woman of some Niceness, as I pretend to be, may be in no Danger of mistaking him? Besides, I think Mr. *Rushford* a little too capricious, and should be glad to break him of it, lest, if it ever should be our Lot to come together, that Temper should improve upon him, and be more troublesome from an Husband, than it is from an humble Servant. I should be glad my Conduct might merit the Approbation of so good a Judge: But if it do not, I will endeavour to conform myself to your Advice: For I am, and ever will be, honoured Madam,

Your most dutiful Niece.

LETTER CLXV.

V. *From the Aunt, containing solid Advice and Caution on this Occasion.*

Dear Lydia,

YOUR last Letter pleased me much better than your two former. For your first held me in great Suspense; your second gave me Concern for your rigorous Treatment of poor Mr *Rushford*, who, 'tis plain, loves you much; but your third confirms me in the Opinion I always entertain'd of your Prudence, in preferring a Man of Sense to a Coxcomb.

I must tell you, that nothing could give me greater Pleasure, than to see you Mr. *Rushford's* Bride. His Fortune is good, his Person manly and agreeable, and his Behaviour polite. But in my Opinion, you have need of all your Prudence and Caution, to avoid giving him a lasting Disgust; for I would have you always remember, my Dear, that nothing can give such Dislike to a Man of Wisdom and Discernment, as to make him imagine a Fool is prefer'd to him.

If

If Mr. *Rushford* did not love you, he would not be jealous of such a Fop as you describe, and it is enough to keep his Passions awake, when he sees you so grave, and so severe, as I may say, to him, and so facetious and chearful with the other. For many a Woman of Sense, in other respects, has been caught by some of those ridiculous Airs that such empty Laughers give themselves; and if you should carry your Jest too far, it might make him despise a Levity, as he would be apt to construe it, which he would think unworthy of his Addresses.

I know it is but too natural to our Sex to love to be admired, but this Humour, when not properly bounded and guarded, has many times cost us dear, even the Happiness of all our Lives. Don't be afraid of obliging Mr. *Rushford*, in a Point so material to his Tranquillity, and your own Reputation, as the forbidding the Visits of your *Man of Scarlet*: For, as you *intend* not to encourage him, and he has so undaunted an Assurance, founded on so much Folly, I think, if you had no *other* humble Servant, it would not be reputable to receive *this*; much less when you have one of so different a Cast, that Light and Darkness are not more opposite. And a Person must have a very indifferent Regard to a Man of Merit, who would not give up such an one to his Request, for the very Thought of a Competition with such a Rival, in so tender and nice a Point, must be disgusting to a Man of Sense.

And besides, you know not, my Dear, but Mr. *Rushford* may be deter'd from a formal putting the Question to you, by the Apprehension, that you see his Rival with too much Approbation: For can a Man of his Sense think of giving himself up absolutely to a Person who seems to waver in her Judgment, which to prefer of two such

Competitors? Must not the Mind that can hesitate one Moment on such a Decision, appear unworthy of the Character of his Wife?

And then, as to teizing him for his Jealousy, and breaking him of it *aforehand*, I doubt this savours a little too much of the ungenerous Tempers of some of our Sex, who love to tyrannize, when they can. Prudence in a Lady is the best Cure of Jealousy in a Gentleman. And is the Method you propose of laughing on with the Captain, and teizing a worthy Man, who undoubtedly loves you, a Mark of that Prudence?——Indeed, I fear, if you go on thus, you will either lose Mr. *Rushford*, or will be oblig'd to keep him at the Expence of a Submission (after you have provok'd him) proportionable to the Insult he will receive, and this, my dear Kinswoman, will be but little agreeable to the Pride of *our* Sex, and a particular Mortification to your *own*.

One Rule let me give you That the more obliging you are in the Time of *your Power*, the more it will move a generous Mind to indulge you, in *his*; and the Time you may reckon yours, may not be Three Months in Proportion to Thirty Years of his, or the whole Life. And pray, my Dear, remember, that young Ladies assume a Task they are very little qualify'd for, when they set up *to break Tempers*, and *manage Husbands*, before they are *married*.

Your Prudence will suggest to you a very proper Conduct, I am sure, to secure a worthy Husband, without my writing a Word more Especially as I know it will teach you to overcome the little low Pleasure, which some of our Sex take, at your Years, in being admir'd and flatter'd, and to conquer the little teizing Pride of perplexing and torturing the Heart of a worthy Admirer,

mirer, when we think we have it in our Power. And so hoping soon to hear, that you have banish'd the Captain, and are in the way to change the Name of *Fenton* for that of *Rushford*, I remain, my dear Niece,

Your affectionate Aunt.

LETTER CLXVI.

From a Lady to her false Lover, who, after having brav'd all his Friends Expostulations, at last is persuaded to abandon her for another of larger Fortune.

SIR,

'TIS a poor, a very poor Pretence, that you make, after what has passed between us, that you must, in Compliance with the Commands of your *Friends*, break off Acquaintance with me! How often have I advised you to this formerly! How often have you vow'd the Impossibility of your doing it! How have you, in pursuance of this Avowal, brav'd your Friends, and defy'd their Resentments, in such a manner, that gave them no Hope of succeeding with you! tho' I always blam'd your disobliging way of doing it, in regard to them, as *your* Relations. But just as you had brought them to expect you would not be prevail'd upon, and they had so far acquiesced in your Choice, that I had received and returned Visits from the Principals of your Family, for you poorly to plead their *Menaces*, is such a Jest, as is not to be received without Contempt and Indignation.

Well,

Well, I can *guess* at your Motives!----tho' you are too mean-spirited to *acknowlege* them, and that they are too mean *to be* acknowleged. Miss *Holles* can explain them all, by the Help of a larger Fortune than I have! I have heard of your Uncle's Proposal, and your Visit there.----Go on, Sir, and welcome! I have Spirit enough to despise the Man that *could* deceive me ----But could you not, for your *own* sake, act this perfidious Part in a more *manly*, and more *worthy* manner? Could you not find a *better* Reason than one you had always rejected, when it was more your *Duty* to observe it? But must you, when your *Vows* to me had made it your *Duty* to *dispense* with it, then shew your Levity in *adhering* to it? Yet why do I expostulate with a Person so little *deserving* Expostulation? You may think me angry, because of my Disappointment. 'Tis true, *it is* a Disappointment, and I had a better Opinion of you than this Conduct shews you deserved, or Things should never have proceeded so far as they did. But 'tis a Disappointment, I hope (tho' no Thanks to any Part of your *Conduct*, but your *Meanness*), I shall soon get over. And tho' I wish you no Harm, let us see, if, Seven Years hence, you will be so many hundred Pounds the richer, as makes the Difference to you, between Miss *Holles* and Her you have treated so unworthily. And if that will make you happier, I truly wish you may be so! For I am not your Enemy, tho' you deserve not that I should style myself

Your Friend.

LET-

LETTER CLXVII.

From a Gentleman to his Lady, whose Overniceness in her House, and uneasy Temper with her Servants, make their Lives uncomfortable.

My Dear,

YOUR kind Concern for my Absence is very obliging. 'Tis true, I have already out-stay'd my Intention by a Week; and I find the Place I am in so very engaging, and Mr. *Terry* and his Sister so agreeable, that, but to come to *you*, I could willingly stay a Month longer with *them*. In short, my Dear, Mr. *Terry* lives just as *I* would wish to live, and his Sister, who is his House-keeper, is just what I would wish *you* to be, in many Particulars; tho' no one, in my Opinion, can equal you in others.

You must know, then, that Mr. *Terry* and I are quite happy in one another, and when he has no Visitors, are indulged in a very pretty Parlour, which neither Pail nor Mop is permitted to enter for two or three Days together. And when we have Company, the Dining-room is at our Service, and the kind Lady lets us smoke there without remarking upon the beastly Fumes that we give the Furniture. Not only so, but if, by a sudden Turn of the Pipe, any one of us chances to bestrew the Floor with burnt Tobacco, we are not broken in upon either by Maid or Broom. And yet no Room can be cleaner than we find that, when we return to it from a Walk in the Gardens.

And indeed, I must acquaint you, that I never saw a Lady more prudently nice than Mrs. *Terry*.
Her

Her Person, Furniture, and House, are even Patterns of Neatness and good Œconomy. I never any-where saw the one or the other out-done. Yet how can this be, I marvel!----For I have seen her pass over the Mark of a dirty Shoe-heel, upon a Floor as white as a Curd, and never once rank the Aggressor among the worst of Slovens. Nay, more than that, I have seen her Brother drop a few Crums of Bread and Butter under his Feet, without so much as one corrective Frown· Is not this strange, my Dear? Have Batchelors, from a Sister, more Privileges, than a marry'd Man from his Wife?

More than this (it is true, upon my Honour! incredible as it may seem to you), t'other Day he happen'd to spill a Glass of Claret upon a fine Damask Table-cloth, and broke the Glass; yet met with no other Reproof than an agreeable Laugh at his Aukwardness, and, *It was well it was he that did it, who might do as he pleased with his own!* Oh, what a happy Man, thought I, is this good old Batchelor!

But, my Dear, prepare for more strange Things still: Yesterday, at Dinner, he was cutting up a good fat Goose, and, by an unfortunate Splash, most grievously bespatter'd a rich Gown his Sister had on. My Heart ached upon this, for, truly, I thought, for a Moment, I was at home. But good Mrs. *Terry* convinced me of the contrary. Oh, Brother, said she, with a Smile, what a Slip was that!----But, Misfortunes will happen!----And out she pulled her Pocket Handkerchief, to wipe her Gown. I am sorry for it, Sister, said he. It can't be help'd, return'd she, with a Smile; but I had a good Mind to put you to some Expence for this. This was all she said, and she kept her Seat, and eat her Dinner in perfect good Temper, nay, and *look'd* as easy and as pleasant as she spoke.

I must

I must still further observe, that, tho' all Things here are conducted with the greatest Decorum, and every Servant in the House knows their Duty, and does it distinguishingly well, yet I have never heard one high or angry Word pass between Mrs. *Terry* and the Maids. Is not this surprising, my Dear? What can it be owing to? I thought, for my Share, so much have I been used to a *contrary* Management, that no Servant could do their Duty, unless the Mistress of the Family put herself out of Humour with all the House. Either she is more fortunate than you, in lighting of good Servants, or, perhaps, as Persecution makes Schismaticks in the Church, so finding Faults creates them in a Family. There may be something in this, my Dear; for I have seen your Maid *Jane* blunder, out of *Fear*; and blunder a second time, to find she *had* blunder'd; and a third, because she was put quite out, and could not help it.----Then how has my poor Deary been discomposed! How have her charming Features been even distorted with Passion! Not a Bit of the Lily in her Face; for the crimson Rose had swallowed it all up, and an Eye darting Flames of Indignation and Woe mixed together! And then, breaking Silence, Nobody ever had such Torments of Servants as I have! Alas! poor Deary! How hard is thy Hap!----How much happier this good Family! For, secure of an Excuse, rather than Blame, if a small Fault should be committed, in comes each Servant, as their Duty requires, all serene, pleased, chearful, as their Mistress. Their Eye is fixed upon her Eye, with a becoming Confidence of pleasing, and a Nod, or a Beck, does more with them, than an hundred Words.

How can I, my Dear, think of leaving such a delightful House and Family as this?----Yet I long to see my beloved Spouse; and I will set out on *Monday* next for that Purpose, with as great Delight as ever I knew, since I had the Happiness to call you mine. But pray, my dear Love, let what I have said, without the least Design to offend or concern you, a little impress you, however. Let me have the Satisfaction, for *both* our sakes, of seeing you get over some of those Foibles, that make us effectually unhappy, at times, as if we had substantial Evils to encounter with. In short, my Dear, let us think the House made for *our* Use, and not we for *that*. And let us shew our Servants, that while we would have them *less faulty* than they are, we will, ourselves, try to be *more perfect* than we have hitherto been; and not, while we condemn their Failings, be guilty of much greater.

Justice, Prudence, Ease, Pleasure, Interest, Reputation, all require this of us: And could I hope what I have written will be attended to, as I wish and mean it, you cannot conceive the Delight that will double upon me on my Return to my Dearest; for it is my Pride, that I can style myself

Yours ever, most affectionately.

LETTER CLXVIII.

From a Gentleman who in a small Fortune experiences the Slights of his Friends, but being suddenly reputed to be rich, is oppressed with the fawning Caresses and Adulation of those who had before neglected him.

Dear Sir,

I MUST, for once, postpone every thing I would say to you, in order to make room for an Account you little expect. What

What will you say, when I tell you, that a current Report of my being *immensely rich* is the greatest *Misfortune* I at present labour under? Nor do I find it so supportable as you may be apt to imagine. The Occasion was owing to the frequent Slights I had received from the Gentlewoman with whom I lodge, and from others of my Friends, who, believing that I lived up to my scanty Fortune, as in Truth I do (tho' I take care to be beholden to nobody, and pay ready Money for every thing), could not treat me negligently enough. I complain'd of this to that arch Wag *Tony Richards*, who told me he would change every one's Behaviour to me in a few Days. And he has done it effectually. For what does he do, but, as a kind of Secret, acquaints my Landlady, that beside my poor little Estate (which you know to be my All) he had lately discovered, that I had Twenty thousand Pounds Stock in one of our great Companies!

Such was the Force of his whimsical Delusion, that, the very next Morning, I had a clean Towel hung over my Water-bottle, tho' I never before had more than one a Week during the Twenty Years I have lodged here.

About a Week after this, my Cousin *Tom*, who, for the two Years he has been in the *Temple*, has let me see him but three times, came, in a most complaisant manner, plainer dressed than ever I had before seen him, and begg'd, if the Length of the Evening was in any Degree burdensome, I would permit him to wait upon me with such Pieces of Wit, Humour, or Entertainment, as the Town afforded, the reading of which under my Ear, he was sure, would be a great Advantage to *him*, and assured me, that, for a Beginning, he had presumed to bring the last new Tragedy in his Pocket. I thank'd my young Spark. Upon which
he

he is so much in earnest in his Observances, that three Nights in a Week he thus entertains me: Which will, at least, be of so much Service, as to keep him out of more expensive Company. And you cannot think what Pains the Rogue takes to read with the Cadence he knows I admire, and sits till his Teeth chatter before he offers to look towards the Fire.

What you will still more wonder at, Sir *John Hookhim* called upon me before *Christmas*; and tho' I have not had a Visit from him these Five Years, was so obliging, as to run away with me in his Chariot into *Hertfordshire*, to keep the Holidays in his Family; where his Lady treated me with the utmost Respect, and her Daughters paid me their Morning Devoirs, with the same Deference as if I had been their Grand Papa. No Dinner was concluded upon, without consulting my Palate; and the young Gentlemen, his Sons, are as ambitious of my hearing their Exercises, as if their Fortunes depended upon my Approbation.

Sir *John* acquainted me with every Improvement he had made in his Estate; and assured me, that his second Son *Will.* my Namesake, has a Genius singularly turned for managing Country Business, had he not had the Misfortune of having a Brother born before him; and gave me several Reasons to believe, that a fine Estate, which lay in the Neighbourhood, and was then to be sold, would be a great Penyworth. I took the Hint, but said, I had no Inclination to purchase. He shook his Head at my Thousands, and told me, that, in his Opinion, a Land Estate was preferable to the best Stock in the Kingdom.

When I came to Town the 4th of *January*, I was no sooner out of Sir *John*'s Chariot, but my Landlady, in Person, informed me, that since I had

had been abſent, I had ſo many Preſents ſent me, that ſhe had been in an hundred Fears for their ſpoiling. I aſked her the Particulars, and found Five Turkeys, Three Chines, Three Hampers of *Madeira* for the Gout, Two Collars of Brawn, Geeſe, Chickens, Hares, and Wild-fowl, to a large Amount.

At Night I was welcom'd to Town by all my *old* Acquaintance, and about Twenty almoſt new ones: I was a little tired with my Journey; and had a ſlight Cold beſides, which being obſerved, one was running for a Phyſician, another for a Surgeon, to bleed me: One thought an Emetick not improper: Another recommended a gentle Sweat, or compoſing Draught; and, amidſt the general Officiouſneſs, I could hear it whiſper'd, that, if my Will was not made, Delays might prove dangerous. And, in the Morning, five Meſſengers after my Welfare arrived before Day.

Thus, Sir, you ſee my Peace is gone; my Tongue is of no Uſe; for no one believes me, when I declare my real Circumſtances. And, under the Happineſs of a very ſmall Fortune, I ſuffer all the Afflictions attending a Man immoderately rich, and if *you* keep not your uſual Behaviour, I ſhall not know myſelf, nor any Man elſe; ſince all my Companions are become Flatterers, and all around me are ſo obſequious, that it is impoſſible for me to know when I do right or wrong. I am, dear Sir, tho' thus whimſically ſituated,

Your real Friend.

LETTER CLXIX.

From one Brother to another, on the rash Marriage of a beloved Daughter of one of them, to a profligate young Fellow.

My dear Brother,

I AM exceedingly concerned for the rash Step your Daughter *Thomasin* has made. I know how it must affect you, and I am myself not a little troubled at it. But we see how unfit we are to chuse for ourselves! And, oh! how often are we punished by the Enjoyment of our own Wishes!--- You say, you would rather have follow'd her Corpse to the Grave, than that she should have thus thrown herself away on a Rake, a Prodigal, a Sot, and a Fool, as I, as well as you, know to be the Character of the Person she has chosen. I would not afflict you, my dear Brother, instead of pouring Balm on the Wounds of your Mind. But you will remember, that it is scarce two Years ago, when you were no less anxiously disturbed on Occasion of the violent Fever which then endangered her Life. What Vows did you not put up for her Recovery! What Tumults of Grief then agitated your afflicted Mind! And how do you know, that then she was only restor'd at your incessant and importunate Prayers, but that otherwise, God Almighty, knowing what was best for you both, would have taken her away from this heavy Evil? This should teach us Resignation to the Divine Will, and that we are most unfit to chuse for ourselves. And even this Affliction, heavy as it is, may be sent, in order to wean you from a Delight that you had too much set your Heart upon.

Mean

Mean time, you muſt not, by too violent a Reſentment and Reprobation of her, which I find you are reſolv'd upon, add to the Miſeries ſhe has choſen. The poor Creature, will, I fear, too ſoon find her Puniſhment in her Choice; and already, I underſtand, ſhe is driven to great Diſtreſs. You know ſhe has ſtrong Paſſions, and your too great Severity may precipitate her on her everlaſting Ruin, when ſhe becomes thoroughly ſenſible of the Condition ſhe has brought herſelf to, from as happy Proſpects as any young Lady could promiſe herſelf.

Let this prevail upon you to allow her Neceſſaries, for, oh! 'tis a ſad thing for meagre Want to ſtare in the Face a young Creature uſed to the fulleſt Plenty! eſpecially when 'tis aggravated by the Reflection, that it is all owing to her own Raſhneſs. And as it may not ſuit with your Liking, to appear yourſelf to allow her any thing, at leaſt till you ſee what Uſe will be made of your Favours, I will undertake, as from myſelf, and on my own Head, to furniſh, if you pleaſe, what is immediately neceſſary; and from time to time give you a faithful Account of the Diſpoſition in which ſhe receives it, and how her wretched Deluder is affected by it.

This is a Taſk I ſhould not be fond of, but to prevent worſe Conſequences, and I muſt intreat you, Brother, to weigh ſeriouſly the Matter, and as you *abound*, let not the unhappy Wretch, who, after all, is your Daughter, want thoſe *Neceſſaries of Life*, which all your *Servants* have in ſuch Plenty.

I could not bear to be a Witneſs of the great Grief which muſt tear aſunder your Heart, ſtruggling between paternal Affection, and juſt Indignation; which makes me chuſe to write to you, and

and shall wait your Resolution on this Subject. I am, dear Brother,

Yours most affectionately.

LETTER CLXX.

The afflicted Father, in Answer to the preceding.

Dear Brother,

YOU are very kind in your Intention, yet very affecting in your just Reproofs of my misplac'd Fondness for a Creature so unworthy. Resignation to the Divine Will, a noble, a needful Lesson! is the Doctrine you raise from it. God give it me, as I ought to have it! Time and His Grace, I hope, will effect it. But at present----Oh! Brother! you know not how I set my Heart on this Wretch. That was my *Crime*, you'll say: And 'tis but just it should be my *Punishment*. Do you as you please, in what you propose. I desire not the ingrateful Creature should want; yet let her too be pinch'd. Nothing else will make her sensible of her great Offence.----But don't let her be precipitated on any worse Fate, if a worse can be possible, as it *may* with regard to another Life. Yet let not her Seducer be the better for the Assistance. He shall never riot in my Substance. Let me know what you have done three Months hence, that I may retrench, or add to what you shall advance, as I shall see her Behaviour. I say in three Months, for another Reason, because I may by that time, I hope, get more Strength of Mind and Patience than at present possesses the Heart of

Your ever-affectionate Brother.

LETTER CLXXI.
To a Father on the Loss of his Son, who died under Age.

My dear Friend,

YOUR Lot, I confess, is hard, exceeding hard, to lose so promising and so hopeful a Child as that dear Boy was, who so much ingrossed the Affections of yourself and Spouse. And a suitable Grief on so trying an Occasion ought to be indulged; but yet not so, as if you were bereft of *all* Comfort, and insensible to those *other* great Mercies, which God has bestowed upon you. This, my dear Friend, would be a sinful Rejection of those Blessings which remain to you, as if, like *froward* Children, you would have *nothing*, because you could not have *every thing* you wish'd.

Look upon all the great Families of the Earth, upon all your Neighbours round you, and see if they have not almost every one shed Tears on this very Occasion, and then judge of the Unreasonableness of *too great* a Grief, and what Pretension you have to be exempted from those Accidents, to which *Royalty* itself is liable. I will not, to alleviate your Grief, remind you of a Topick, which is, however, no less important than too frequently the Case, that he *might not always* have been so hopeful, but might, as he *grew up*, many ways have administered Bitterness to you. But I think it surpasses all other Comforts, even those you hoped for from him, that he is taken away at an Age, at which God's Mercy renders his eternal Happiness unquestionably certain, and you and your mourning Spouse have the Pleasure to reflect, that ye have been the happy Means of adding *one* to the Number of the Blest above, and that he is gone before you, but a little while, to that Place, where all Tears shall be wiped away, and whither, thro' the same infinite Mercy, you will, in time, follow him, and enjoy him for ever.

You have this Comfort, that he dy'd a *natural* Death, that the Work was God Almighty's, who *gave* him to you, and has but *taken* back what he *lent* you: That you saw every thing done for his Recovery, that *could* be done; and that it pleased God *not* to grant him to your Prayers; and why should you repine at the *Dispensation*, when you know the *Dispenser?* Let it therefore be your Duty, on this trying Occasion, to shew an intire Acquiescence to the Divine Will, such an Acquiescence as may be exemplary to your good Spouse, whose *weaker* Sex and Mind want all the Consolation your *stronger* Reason can give her. And, at the same time, it behoves you to shew a thankful Spirit for the Mercies *yet continued* to you (Mercies that Thousands have not to rejoice in!), lest God Almighty should, as a Punishment, deprive you of those you have still left.

I beg you will take in good Part these few Lines, which my Affection for you has drawn from my Pen; and that you'll believe me to be, dear Sir,

Your truly sympathizing Friend,
and humble Servant.

LETTER CLXXII.
To a Father, on the Loss of a hopeful Son, who died at Man's Estate.

SIR,

I AM truly sorry for your Loss. So hopeful a Son, just arrived at Man's Estate, and who was so great a Comfort and Assistance to you, to be snatched

away,

away, is what must administer to you the greatest Grief of any thing that could possibly befal you.

But, alas! yours is no *new* Case. The greatest Families have been thus afflicted, and with the Aggravation to some of them, that perhaps they have been deprived of their *Heirs*, and have not a *Son left* to continue their Name and Honours. The late Queen *Anne*, when Princess of *Denmark*, lost her beloved Duke of *Gloucester*, not only *her* Hopes, but the Hopes of the *Nation*, and the Crown, to which he seem'd not only *born*, but *fashioned*, was obliged to be settled, on that Occasion, upon a distant Branch of the Royal Line.

The great Duke of MARLBOROUGH, who by his Merit, and his Victories, had raised a princely Estate, as well as Titles, had but one Son, the Marquis of *Blandford*, on whom he and his Duchess built all their Hopes, for the perpetuating of those new Honours in their Family, and he was snatch'd away by Death, when he was at the University, training up to become the Dignities to which he was intitled.

Still more recent was the unhappy Fate of a Lady of the first Quality in *England* Her Lord had a Son lent to his advanced Years This Son was the last of that noble Family, and on his Life depended all his Father's and his Mother's Hopes; and on his living till of Age, a valuable Part of the Estate itself, which otherwise was to fall to an illegitimate Offspring. What Care was not used to preserve the noble Youth! An eminent Physician was taken into the Family, to be made a constant Watchman, as it were, over his Health and Exercises The young Nobleman himself was hopeful, dutiful, and as distinguished in the Graces of his Mind, as by his Birth. He travelled; his indulgent Mother travelled with him. He made a Campaign

paign under his Uncle, the greatest General then surviving in an Age of Generals. He again travel'd to restore and confirm his Health, and all the noble Mother's Hopes and Views were employ'd on the finding for her beloved Son, on his Return, a Wife suitable to his Quality, and who might be a Means to preserve one of the first Families in the Kingdom from utter Extinction.

What was the Event of all her Cares, her Hopes, her Vows, her Prospects?---Why, just as the young Nobleman had (within a few Months) arrived at Age, and could have made those Family Settlements which were most desirable should be made, and the want of which involv'd his noble Mother in perplexing Law-suits, which, too, turn'd against her, it pleased God to deprive her of him, and he dy'd in a foreign Land, far distant from his fond Mother, who (still more grievous, if true!), for Reasons of State, as was said, had been deny'd to accompany and attend him And so ended all her Hopes of above twenty Years standing, and in him his Family likewise

A still more recent Calamity to a great Family, I might mention, in the Death of two hopeful Children, the only Sons of their Father, and the only Heirs Male of one of the first Families in the Kingdom, both snatch'd away, in the Space of a few Hours of one another, from healthy Constitutions, and no Ailments previous to the sudden one that carry'd them off, which was only believ'd to be a sore Throat. In vain were the Consultations of the most eminent Physicians and Surgeons, who gave Attendance all Night, minutely to watch every Change of the Distemper, in vain prov'd the Assurance of the Skilful to the fond Parents, that there was no Danger. Death mocked all their Hopes; and when the first dy'd, in vain was he open'd, in order to find out, if possible, the Cause of
the

the fatal Malady, in order to administer, with greater Hopes of Success, Remedies against it, to preserve the other. That other hopeful Youth followed h s Brother, and their Fate deeply wounded the Hearts of half a dozen noble Families, whose intimate Relationship gave them a very near Interest in the awful Event.

Like Instances of the Loss of hopeful Sons, and of the only Male Heirs, might be produced in other Families of prime Distinction in the List of the *British* Nobility; but I need not enumerate more to a Mind considerate as yours, which will reflect, that Death is a common Lot, from which no Rank or Degree is exempted. And I hope these Reflections, and such as you will be able to add to them by your own Reason and Piety, will serve to rebuke the Overflowings of your Grief, and confine it to the natural Chanels, into which both God and Nature will *indulge* it to flow.

I mention not to your inlightened Mind, you see, the Motives, that, nevertheless, might be insisted on with great Propriety, on so grievous an Occasion; such as, The Uncertainty of Life: The Gratitude you ought to shew for having had your Son *so long* continu'd to you, as he was The great Probability of his being happy in God's Mercies, by reason of his Hopefulness and Duty The *early* Release he has met with from the Troubles and Chances of a changeable and transitory Life· His Escape from the Danger of the Temptations which his Virtue might have been tried with, had he lived to *maturer* Years· That this your Deprivation is God's Work That he dy'd not in a distant Land, and by an untimely Death But that you had the Satisfaction of knowing, that every thing was done for him that could be done That his Morals were still untainted, and he was not cut off in the Pursuit of some capital Sin, as has too often

often been the Case with bold and daring Spirits in the Heat of their youthful Passions. And that he escap'd the Snares usually laid for young Men by idle Companions, and vicious Women, which too often intangle and catch the unthinking Mind. These will be all suggested to you from your own better Reason; and to that *secondarily*, as to a due Resignation to the Divine Will *primarily*, let me refer you, on this trying Occasion. Who am, with a sympathizing Affection, dear Sir,

Your sincere Friend, and humble Servant.

LETTER CLXXIII.
To a * *Widow, on the Death of her Husband.*

Good Madam,

ALLOW me the Liberty of condoling with you on the truly great and heavy Loss you have sustain'd of an excellent Husband. All we, who had the Pleasure of his Friendship, mourn, with you, the irretrievable Misfortune to *us*, as well as to *you*. But as there is no recalling it, and as it is God's Doing, we must not repine at the Dispensation, but acquiesce in it. And yet to say, that neither you nor we ought to grieve for it, would be absurd and unnatural. Sinful Grief, however, we are commanded to shun. And we ought to bless God, that he was graciously pleased to continue him with us *so long*, instead of mourning too heavily, that we had not *longer* the Pleasure of his agreeable Conversation. We were not *born* together, and some of us *must* have *gone first*, and I have sometimes

---

* With small Variations, the same Arguments may be used to a Husband on the Death of his Wife, and on other melancholy Occasions of the like Nature.

been

been ready to think (besides the Life of Glory, which, thro' God's Mercies, awaits the Good), that he is far happier than those he leaves behind him, in this Point, That he is saved from the Regret (which fills the wounded Hearts of his surviving Friends) of seeing them go *before him*, as they have seen him go *before them*. Had he not dy'd now, a few Years would have determin'd his useful Life; for the longest Life is but a Span, and *then* the Matter, had he gone before us, would have been as it is *now*.

We may make our own Lives miserable in bewailing *his Loss*; but we cannot do *him Good*, nor (were *he* to *know* it) *Pleasure*. You, in particular, Madam, who are now call'd upon to be both *Father* and *Mother* to the dear Pledges of your mutual Affection, ought to take double Care, how you suffer immoderate Grief to incapacitate you from this new, and more arduous and necessary Task. For by this means you would not only do yourself Hurt, but double the Loss which his dear Children have already sustain'd in that of their Father. And would you, Madam, make them *motherless* as well as *fatherless?*----God forbid! Consider, tho' this is a *heavy* Case, yet it is a *common* Case. And we must not repine, that God Almighty thought him *ripe* for Heaven, and put an End to his *probatory* State.

With melancholy Pleasure have I often, on the Loss of Friends, contemplated the excellent Advice of the Son of *Sirach*, who tells us how we ought to *mourn* on these Occasions, and how we ought to govern our Mourning, and reminds us most excellently, that while we are grieving for our departed Friends, *our own Lives* pass away, and we *are not*. You will permit me to transcribe his own excellent Words, as most suitable to the Subject before us

" My

"My Son, says he, let Tears fall down over the Dead, and begin to lament; and then cover his Body according to the Custom, and neglect not his Burial. Weep bitterly, and make great Moan, and use Lamentation as he is *worthy*---- And then comfort thyself for thy Heaviness, for of Heaviness cometh *Death*, and the Heaviness of the *Heart* breaketh *Strength*. In Affliction also Sorrow remaineth; and the Life of the Poor [or Miserable, or of those who make themselves so by Mourning] is the *Curse of the Heart* Take [therefore] no Heaviness to Heart Drive it away, and remember [*thy own*] last End. Forget it not, for there is *no turning again* Thou shalt not do *him* Good, but hurt *thyself*. Remember MY Judgment [saith the wise Man, speaking as if in the Person of our late dear Friend], for THINE also shall be so. Yesterday for ME, and To-day for THEE. When the Dead is at Rest, let his *Remembrance* rest, and be *comforted* for him, when his Spirit is departed from him"

To add any thing to this excellent Advice, would be, in some measure, to depreciate it I will therefore conclude with my Prayers, that God will enable you to bear as you *ought*, and as all your Friends *wish* and *expect* from you, this truly heavy Dispensation, and that most particularly for the sake of your dear Children by him, and with assuring you of my Service, to the utmost of my Ability For I am, Madam, as well for *theirs* and *your own* sake, as for his *Memory's* sake,

Your faithful Friend, and humble Servant,

FINIS.